Courtships, Marriage Customs, and Shakespeare's Comedies

COURTSHIPS, MARRIAGE CUSTOMS, AND SHAKESPEARE'S COMEDIES

Loreen L. Giese

palgrave
macmillan

COURTSHIPS, MARRIAGE CUSTOMS, AND SHAKESPEARE'S COMEDIES
© Loreen L. Giese, 2006

First published in 2006 by
PALGRAVE MACMILLAN™
175 Fifth Avenue, New York, N.Y. 10010 and
Houndmills, Basingstoke, Hampshire, England RG21 6XS
Companies and representatives throughout the world.

PALGRAVE MACMILLAN is the global academic imprint of the Palgrave Macmillan division of St. Martin's Press, LLC and of Palgrave Macmillan Ltd. Macmillan® is a registered trademark in the United States, United Kingdom and other countries. Palgrave is a registered trademark in the European Union and other countries.

ISBN-13: 978–0–312–16604–5
ISBN-10: 0–312–16604–4

Library of Congress Cataloging-in-Publication Data

Giese, Loreen L.
    Courtships, marriage customs, and Shakespeare's comedies / Loreen L. Giese.
        p. cm.
    Includes bibliographical references and index.
    ISBN 0–312–16604–4 (alk. paper)
        1. Marriage law—England—History—Sources. 2. Antenuptial contracts—England—History—Sources. 3. Church of England. Diocese of London. Consistory Court—History—Sources. 4. Depositions—England—History—Sources. 5. Courtship—England—History—Sources. 6. Shakespeare, William, 1564–1616. Twelfth night—Criticism, Textual. 7. Shakespeare, William, 1564–1616. Two gentlemen of Verona—Criticism, Textual. I. Title.

KD 753.G54 2006
346.4201'6—dc22   2006041559

A catalogue record for this book is available from the British Library.

Design by Newgen Imaging Systems (P) Ltd., Chennai, India.

First edition: November 2006

10 9 8 7 6 5 4 3 2 1

Printed in the United States of America.

For CL, GG, and DD

Contents

LIST OF FIGURES

ACKNOWLEDGMENTS

In the process of completing this book, I have incurred many debts. I am very appreciative of the assistance I received from the staffs at the Bodleian Library, British Library, and the London Metropolitan Archives—my home away from home. I am particularly thankful to Geoff Pick, Nicola Avery, Sally Bevan, Elliott Gosling, Elizabeth Scudder, and David Tennant of the London Metropolitan Archives, and Julie Cochrane of the Museum of London. I am especially grateful to Deborah Jenkins, Head Archivist, London Metropolitan Archives, who gave me permission to read DL/C/215 and DL/C/216 immediately after they were conserved. The completion of the research for this study was made possible by generous suppor from the National Endowment for the Humanities (summer stipend), the Baker Research Committee at Ohio University, the College of Arts and Sciences at Ohio University, and the Ohio University Research Council, with special thanks to Barbara Reeves. I would also like to thank Alden Waitt, Kim Bowman, and Lars Lutton for their help with this project.

I am grateful to many friends and colleagues for their support and encouragement. I wish especially to acknowledge David Burton, Dolora Cunningham, Lodge Davies, Toni Dorfman, Janet Giese, Edward J. Holland, Leslie Johnson, Rhys Griffith Jones, Betsy Knies, Earl Knies, June Kurtz, Hwa-Lei Lee, Morag McCullum, Kasia Marciniak, Barb Pfeiffer, Gary Pfeiffer, Diane Stromp, and Umamahesh Yellamraju. I also wish to express my gratitude to the Right Reverend and Right Honourable Richard Chartres, Bishop of London, for his interest in and encouragement of this study.

For rich and provocative questions, stimulating discussions, and valuable advice, I am deeply indebted to Marsha Dutton, Hazel R. Forsyth, Thelma Greenfield, Richard Helmholz, Sharon Huge, Martin Ingram, Anne Lancashire, Naomi Liebler, Lena Cowen Orlin, Nigel Ramsay, and Linda Woodbridge. My greatest debt is to

Susan P. Cerasano and Vanessa Harding for their sound critical expertise, unstinting patience, and friendship. Professor Cerasano, Dr. Dutton, Professor Greenfield, Dr. Harding, Professor Knies, and Professor Liebler generously read chapters of this book, and their insightful criticisms and advice have greatly improved it.

CONVENTIONS

I have marked an omission in manuscript transcriptions with an ellipsis. Square brackets in the transcriptions indicate my insertions. In many instances, the depositions contain multiple references to the speaker, such as "this respondent" or "this deponent," in addition to the appropriate pronouns. For ease of reading, I have not transcribed these multiple references and supplied an ellipsis to indicate their omissions, and, where needed, I have substituted the appropriate name or pronoun and indicated such additions with square brackets. Punctuation and spelling in the quotations have not been modernized, except for u/v. I have replaced abbreviations for "and" with the word itself. I use italics to expand abbreviations. In passages from the manuscripts, I have transcribed the names of deponents, places, and occupations as they appear. In my discussions of the manuscripts, I spelt the surnames by their first usage in the heading in the deposition and use Christian names supplied in the first usage in the heading in the depositions. If it does not appear in a heading, I use the first reference in the first surviving deposition for the case. I have anglicized from the Latin and rendered according to modern usage occupations, place names, and Christian names. ff has been transcribed as F. Some depositions contain an "als" (*alias*) both for surnames and place names. I have included both when given. I have taken the beginning of the year to be 1 January, and I have shown both the old and new dates from 1 January to 24 March. Since DL/C/215 and DL/C/216 do not contain folio numbers, all foliation is my own. These manuscripts have been subsequently filmed. I have not included the frame numbers from the tapes when referring to these two deposition books because the frame numbers do not match the actual page numbers and several of the depositions on the tape of DL/C/216 were filmed out of chronological order.

INTRODUCTION

CONSENTING ADULTS:
"IN THE WAY OF MARRIAGE"

In a personal response repeated on 21 May 1590 from a suit in the London Consistory Court, Edmund Billwyn explained why he was not married to Margaret Luke. He followed his assertions that "he did never contracte anie matrimonie with her" and "neither hath he had anie comunication or talke with her . . . of or for marriage" with a comprehensive denial of any actions that might have been understood as supporting her claim: "neither hath he at anie tyme gyven unto . . . margarett Luke anie guifte or token in respecte of anie contracte," "neither hath he confessed at anie tyme before anie person or persons whatsoever to his knowledge or remembrance" that he and she "were betrothed or assured togithers in matrimonie," "neither hath he at anie tyme saied . . . that he wold shortelye marrie the said margarett," and "neither doth he beleeve that there is anie publique voyce or fame" that he and she "were or are leafullie contracted or betrothed one unto an other" (DL/C/213/647). Billwyn's deposition is similar to many from this court in its identification of different kinds of courting and marrying behaviors—to use a phrase that appears repeatedly in the depositions—"in the way of marriage." This study focuses on these behaviors as identified in "matrimonial enforcement" suits in the London Consistory Court between 1586 to 1611 and in two Shakespearean comedies, *The Two Gentlemen of Verona* and *Twelfth Night*.[1] Detailed readings of these behaviors in these legal and literary texts examine the roles available to women and men within courtship and marriage and probe the ways in which they perceived and contested their behaviors within these processes.

The issues relating to marriage are fundamental and far-reaching because marriage is the essential process transforming subjects into couples, thereby creating the economic and political units basic to society: the household and the family. As John R. Gillis points out,

"Because the household was the central unit of both production and reproduction, its formation was a major public event, subject to the politics of both family and community" (13). Because early modern England viewed the household as a microcosm of the society, the process leading to a commitment between two persons is vital to understanding a culture's structure and definitions of gender. In the societies dramatized in Shakespeare's works, marriage plays an equally important role. As Ann Jennalie Cook explains, "The significance of matrimony to social institutions like the family, the community, the church, and the government is assumed throughout Shakespeare's plays" (*Making* 240). The importance of marriage in contemporary ideology and social practice (as the above quotation by Gillis suggests) may cause one to expect that "the way of marriage" would be clearly defined. That is, one might expect mandated steps, gestures, and procedures to marry. However, as I discuss in more detail in chapter 4, marriage in early modern England came under canon law, and the letter of that law did not mandate behaviors. Instead, it stipulated that the basis of marriage was the present consent of the marrying parties, as long as they did not violate any of the Church's requirements.[2] As Martin Ingram notes, "The lack of a single, plain, obligatory formula inevitably allowed scope for uncertainty and dispute" ("Spousals" 45). In early modern England, then, "marriage" was a much less clear cut term than it is today. It included a variety of agreements, many of these unfamiliar to modern readers. A valid marriage in "matrimonial enforcement suits" in the London Consistory Court depositions could include: a verbal contract without solemnization (which according to canon law was legally binding), a verbal contract with solemnization, a verbal contract witnessed by a clergyman away from church, a ceremony from the Book of Common Prayer conducted by a clergyman in church, and a ceremony from the Book of Common Prayer conducted by a clergyman away from church. In some cases, the specific form of the marriage is unclear. Because of the variety of forms a valid marriage could take, ecclesiastical courts heard many suits for "matrimonial enforcement," seeking a ruling on the validity of an alleged marriage, and such cases often turned on the issue of consent and intent.[3] Depositions in matrimonial enforcement cases heard by the London Consistory Court in the period 1586 to 1611 demonstrate that deponents had an understanding of the letter of marriage law. The kinds of evidence that deponents pointed to when assessing individual consent indicate that litigants and witnesses in the early modern diocese of London accepted this definition of marriage and carried it out in practice.[4]

The London Consistory Court depositions from matrimonial enforcement cases indicate that "the way of marriage" included wide-ranging behaviors operating concurrently over several stages in a variety of circumstances. While the words exchanged during a marriage were substantial proof of consent, these depositions document other kinds of evidence that also became important in assessing individual consent. They also reveal that proofs related to establishing consent were open to interpretation. Further, these depositions expose the difficulties of deciphering intent and commitment in not well-specified behaviors. For example, as I clarify in chapters 3 and 4, material objects exchanged during courtship and even during the marriage itself had meanings as fluid as the processes themselves. One might think that the giving and receiving of a certain gift would serve as a material means of discerning the intentions of the parties, since it could possibly be measured and quantified. For instance, one might expect a ring to have intrinsic meaning, especially given its role in the marriage ceremony from the Book of Common Prayer. Yet individuals gave rings before marriages as signs of goodwill as well as during and after marriages as signs of confirmation. Meaning, then, did not usually lie in certain words, gestures, or objects alone but in the intentions behind them and in those reading the intentions. Since marriage was an important metaphor of and for social and political paradigms, it is surprising "the way of marriage" was not more clearly mapped out with an obligatory formula of behaviors. As the following chapters explain, "the way of marriage" in the early modern diocese of London for many couples was more like a maze than a way.

Although women and men took divergent paths in the depositions and in the two Shakespearean comedies in their courting and marrying behaviors, the basis of whether two people were married was the same—individual consent (rather than the consent of a person's family friends, and kin) was the basis of marriage. In this respect, these depositions and dramas reaffirm the letter of canon law in early modern England in defining the basis of marriage. This definition does not automatically exclude the influence, consultation, or use of family and friends. The fact that litigants needed others to testify on their behalf and that they filed suits to contest the credibility of some witnesses suggests that others played an important role in the marriage process for parties in this court. In some cases, as that of Joan Carewe against Ralph Yardley cited in chapter 3, the influence of others could be extensive. However, the testimonies indicate that the consent of the individual rather than of family or friends determined the validity of a marriage. One could argue that such a pattern results from deponents skewing their testimonies to appeal to a court that enforced a law based on individual consent. However, the number of deponents who stressed the intentions of the individual parties and the amount of detail of the behaviors they provided suggest a common understanding of the letter of marriage law. This emphasis on individual consent in these records may result from the geographical area they represent. As Richard Adair comments, "It cannot be stressed too often that in many ways the capital was a law unto itself" (202). The migration to and mobility within London may influence the importance of individual consent in the depositions, because many women and men were either on their own or prevented by distances from consulting family and friends. Vivien Brodsky Elliott's calculations that in London "as many as 47 per cent of daughters had lost their fathers by age 20" and "some 64 per cent of all women migrants . . . had in fact lost their fathers" may explain some of the freedoms evident in these marriage litigations ("Single" 90).[5]

Most of the extant matrimonial depositions from the Bishop of London's court are from matrimonial enforcement suits. These suits usually involved determining whether someone consented to a marriage to establish a marriage contract, restitution, and jactitation (a plaintiff sues a party to stop her or him from reporting that a marriage occurred). Some suits may be fictive or collusive. That is, one person may have been trying to establish a claim of marriage not to enforce a contract with one person but to prove she or he was not married to another. In this set of depositions, most of the suits are instance cases (party *v.* party).[6] Due to the richness of these records, I focus on the specific courting and marrying behaviors identified within them rather than examining other aspects of marriage (such as festivities and customs surrounding a wedding or the roles of wives and husbands within marriage) or ecclesiastical law (jurisdictional issues or the effectiveness of ecclesiastical courts) which have been the subject of excellent studies by others. The wide jurisdiction of the diocese of London during this period (the City of London, the counties of Middlesex and Essex, and parts of Hertfordshire and Buckinghamshire) prohibits a parish-by-parish comparison of behaviors in these records. That the records provide more information about the residence of the witnesses rather than the litigants complicates such a study further. These records are nonetheless extremely informative about courting and marrying behaviors in London, since over one-half of the witnesses in the surviving depositions came from metropolitan parishes. I am aware that the courting and marrying behaviors of early modern Londoners included in these depositions were neither the only experiences deponents had nor can we determine if they were typical. While it is, of course, impossible to discern how representative these behaviors in the depositions were for the diocese of early modern London that did not end up in this court, these records nonetheless provide us with a unique glimpse into the experiences of many individuals.

Although I have examined the merits and structures of these records elsewhere,[7] I survey briefly their usefulness here. Ecclesiastical court records overall are a very valuable source of information for marriage. These courts in early modern England had wide jurisdiction concerning matrimonial matters: "They adjudicated," as Ingram outlines, "disputes over marriage contracts, issued marriage licences, heard petitions for separation and annulment, and brought prosecutions for irregular marriage, unlawful separation and similar offences" (*Church* 3). "There was no competing secular jurisdiction in England" (R. H. Helmholz, *Marriage* 117). For unlike ecclesiastical courts, civil courts usually litigated marriage suits in terms of remuneration for economic damages; for instance, as is well known, Shakespeare testified about the dower arrangements for Mar Mountjoy in a suit heard in the Court of Requests.[8] Within the ecclesiastical court system, the Consistory Courts are particularly valuable. As Ingram points out, "the most important forum was the bishop's consistory court . . . . [I]t formed the hub of diocesan administration and justice" (*Church* 35). Within the court records, the depositions— rather than the act books, which usually set out procedure, and "marriage allegations" (applications for license to marry), which do not detail behaviors, practices, and attitudes—are an extremely rich source of information about marrying behaviors, marriage practices, and the daily life of married couples. Helmholz underscores the richness of the depositions: "they are the most informative and interesting documents which have come down to us from marriage causes" (*Marriage* 19). Within the depositions from matrimonial enforcement suits, proctors asked deponents a series of questions, the answers to which could provide evidence of courtship (verbal exchanges, physical displays of affection, gift exchanges before a marriage), verbal marriage contracts, confirmation of a marriage (hand holding, drinking, token exchange during and after a marriage), and public fame.

Among the church court records, the London Consistory Cour depositions in particular are extremely valuable for information about courting and marrying behaviors and attitudes toward marriage. While the matrimonial enforcement suits include a small percentage of the population, the detail included in the depositions, the number of depositions which have survived, and the variety of social and economic classes participating in the courts are suggestive. The majority of the litigants and witnesses were laborers, artisans, craftsmen, shop-keepers, husbandman, yeoman, small landholders, and a few of gentry or aristocratic standing. These depositions, then, are a more socially representative source than marriage allegations. As Elliott points out, marriage allegations are "biased to the higher status groups in the London diocese" ("Single" 82). Moreover, unlike those from the Archdeaconry Courts and the Court of Arches, the depositions from the Consistory Court are the most complete from London for the six-teenth and seventeenth centuries. Depositions vary case by case in number and in length—some are only a few lines, while others can be as long as ten double-sided folios.

Some believe these records are problematic sources for contempo-rary courting and marrying behaviors. One possible concern is that these records show courtships and marriages that proceeded with confusion or conflict. As Adair comments, "fully successful spousals leading smoothly to marriage leave little or no mark on the historical record" (174). Depositions were usually the last step in the litigation process before the final sentence, thus revealing cases in which litigants interpreted courting and marrying behaviors so differently that the cases could not be settled out of court. However, a disputed contract can illuminate rather than distort attitudes toward and expe-riences of courtship and marriage. Jennifer Kermode and Garthine Walker point out one insight we gain when studying such cases: "By closely examining behaviour when individuals exhausted social toler-ance or broke fundamental taboos we gain insights difficult to achieve by other means" (8). It may seem contradictory to be using records to argue the primacy of individual consent as a basis of marriage when the lack of consent could motivate a party to sue. However, the fact that individuals brought these cases indicates autonomy. Another concern is that many of these lawsuits, unfortunately, do not have rul-ings or do not spell out the sentence. Those lawsuits that have sentences yield both legal prescriptions and behaviors, while those that have not yield valuable information concerning behaviors and attitudes. Yet another concern is that we lack direct access to early modern courtships and marriages. Of course, since clerks recorded the testimonies, we cannot claim that these records represent the actual voices of the witnesses. In addition, although witnesses were asked whether they were in debt or credit to the litigants or had received anything for testifying, it is impossible to discern whether the witnesses in these suits were accurate, thought they were accurate, or manipulated the evidence to affect the outcome of the case. While we can never be sure that the accounts given by deponents represent what actually happened, the patterns in their narratives nonetheless point to a common understanding of what was considered legally plausible. The 1146 folios of testimony for 232 litigants by 456 deponents of different genders, occupations, social standings, and times of life contain vivid pictures, full of rich details of courting and marrying behaviors and attitudes in this diocese.

I focus this study on the depositions for 1586 to 1611. These twenty-five years are of special interest to social, legal, economic, and ecclesiastical historians because of sharp increases in the population of London and in the number of cases coming before the Consistor Court, together with important changes in canon law (1597 and 1604) and in the monarchy. They are also of great interest to literar scholars because of the important developments in poetry and drama and because this is the period when drama was at a high point and Shakespeare most likely was in London. Most depositions within this period refer to courtships and marriages which occurred a few weeks or months prior to the date of the deposition; however, a few contain accounts of courtships and unions prior to 1586. For example, a deposition repeated twenty-nine years after the event included that "Anthony Lambert and Adrian de la pere were married in the parishe Churche of St Botolphe above named the thirtith day of May in the yeare of our Lord 1581" (DL/C/219/34ᵛ).

I hope this study contributes further to discussions of courtship and marriage, especially supplementing the research of others based on ecclesiastical records in and out of London. Many insightful analyses have been published of courtships and marital contracts documented in Consistory Court depositions from medieval and early modern England, such as those by Adair, Eric Josef Carlson, Laura Gowing, Helmholz, Ralph Houlbrooke, Ingram, Diana O'Hara, and Peter Rushton. Yet the London Consistory Court, Commissar Court, and Court of Arches depositions for the late sixteenth and early seventeenth centuries have only partially been analyzed in print. To cite three examples, Richard M. Wunderli's *London Church Courts and Society on the Eve of the Reformation* concentrates on a pre-Reformation ecclesiastical judicial system in London; Ian W. Archer includes selected cases from this court in *The Pursuit of Stability: Social Relations in Elizabethan London*; and Gowing's *Domestic Dangers: Women, Words, and Sex in Early Modern London* uses Consistory Court depositions from defamation and marriage suits and is the first full-length study of these records for this period.

I overlap very little with Gowing, however, because she focuses mor heavily on the depositions from defamation suits, whereas I examine depositions from matrimonial enforcement suits and concentrate solely on courting and marrying behaviors. My study also differs from hers because I focus on a shorter time frame (1586 to 1611) and include material from DL/C/215 and DL/C/216, two deposition books for 1597 to 1601, that were recently made available for consultation. Due to length considerations, I have had to be much more selective than I desired in choosing examples from these rich and provocative depositions. I have selected examples from DL/C/215 or DL/C/216 where others may have sufficed from different volumes, because these volumes only became available for consultation in fall 1999 (Figure 0.1). Until that time, they were available neither in manuscript nor on microfilm (Figure 0.2).

In addition, this study differs from previous ones on courtship and marriage in Shakespearean plays. The studies devoted to Shakespeare and courtship and marriage thus far mainly focus on prescriptive texts, such as marriage manuals and courtesy books, and the like, such as the thorough and insightful one by Cook, entitled *Making a Match: Courtship in Shakespeare and His Society*. Others compare the patterns in Shakespeare's plays to other literary texts. William G. Meader in his *Courtship in Shakespeare: Its Relation to the Tradition of Courtly Love*, argues, as the title indicates, that "Consciously or not, Shakespeare has accepted the pattern of the medieval romances for his romantic plots. This pattern of Inception, Development, Betrothal, Ordeal, and Union Shakespeare occasionally uses simply by assigning one aspect to each of his five acts" (231). The studies that focus on Shakespeare and the law mainly focus on biographical issues, common law, civil law, or criminal law, such as Frances E. Dolan's study, *Dangerous Familiars: Representations of Domestic Crime in England, 1550–1700*. A recent study of Shakespeare, marriage, and the law by B. J. Sokol and Mary Sokol concentrates on the letter of the law, while the one study devoted to Shakespeare and ecclesiastical records—E. R. C. Brinkworth's *Shakespeare and the Bawdy Court of Stratford*—examines act books of the Church Court of Stratford.

This study does not attempt to read Shakespeare's plays as social histories. Marianne Novy cautions against such a practice: "the plays are theatrical transformations of the social tensions that give them some of their subject matter and their appeal to a divided audience, not examples of Elizabethan social history" (6). Instead, this study presents courting and marrying behaviors in the depositions and two Shakespearean comedies. A detailed reading of these behaviors in the London Consistory Court depositions contemporary with Shakespeare's plays demonstrates the complex ways those plays participate in and comment

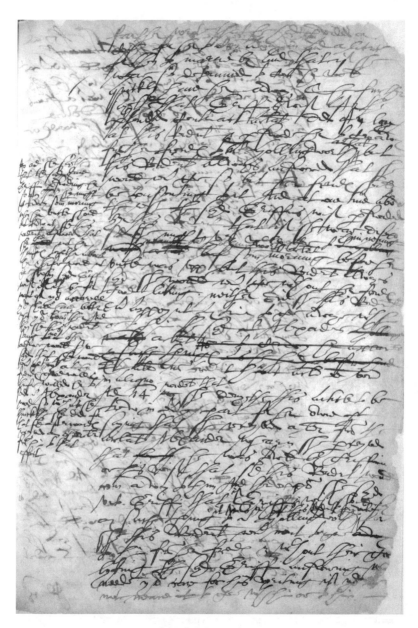

Figure 0.1 DL/C/215/116ʳ, Corporation of London, London Metropolitan Archives. Reproduced by permission.

Figure 0.2 DL/C/215 prior to conservation, Corporation of London, London Metropolitan Archives. Reproduced by permission.

upon their culture, rather than stand apart from it. Cook argues for the necessity of just this kind of comparison: "In short, Shakespeare's plays profit by a comparison with the social reality they reflect, regardless of whether that reflection is accurate or distorted" ("Wooing" 83). In considering the courting and marrying behaviors in these legal and literary texts, I am aware of their differences—besides the obvious differences in format, presentation, and purpose, the testimonies of the deponents, for example, could deeply affect the lives of people living in Tudor and Stuart England since these cases could redefine a person's marital, legal, economic, and social status. In addition, the Italian and Illyrian settings do not prohibit these plays from dramatizing London behaviors. Meader points to the connection between Shakespeare's plays and local behaviors: "London was of course the setting for most of the plays as far as laws and customs were concerned" (55).[9]

Owing to length considerations, a comparison of Shakespeare's plays with those of other contemporary dramatists such as Jonson and Middleton or a survey of all Shakespearean plays or even those in a certain genre is unworkable. Such comparisons might reveal very different courting and marrying behaviors and conclusions than those I present here. Rather than discuss different plays, I examine the same two Shakespearean comedies in each chapter. By comparing two plays of the same genre by the same dramatist, their sameness highlights their differences more clearly. In addition, by focusing on the same plays by one dramatist throughout the study, we gain a clearer understanding of the courting and marrying behaviors in these plays of this dramatist, and our discussion is more consistent with the depositions since we examine several aspects of these behaviors for each couple. I selected *The Two Gentlemen of Verona* and *Twelfth Night* due to their place in Shakespeare's canon and their content.[10] In terms of their place in the canon, while *The Two Gentlemen of Verona* is an early comedy, *Twelfth Night* is a mature one and is possibly, as Joseph H. Summers argues, "the climax of Shakespeare's early achievement in comedy." As Summers argues, this play looks forward and backward in terms of Shakespeare's artistic development: "The effects and values of the earlier comedies are here subtly embodied in the most complex structure which Shakespeare had yet created. But the play looks forward: the pressure to dissolve the comedy, to realize and finally abandon the burden of laughter, is an intrinsic part of its 'perfection' " (143).[11] In terms of content, courting behaviors saturate both these plays, and the latter contains what Carol Thomas Neely labels as a "decorously conventional" yet "the most irregular nuptial of all" (37). In addition, *The Two Gentlemen of Verona* has special importance as a possible source for *Twelfth Night* (Harold Jenkins 74). Concentrating on these two plays in particular allows us to see more clearly similarities and differences in the courting and marrying behaviors between these two comedies and between the comedies and the depositions.

The organization of this book reflects the narrative order present in many depositions. The testimonies often include accounts first of the courtships and then of the contracts and church ceremonies. Deponents talked more about the courtships and marriages than about how or on what basis couples chose each other. Nonetheless, I thought it appropriate to include chapters on choice and suitability, since they provide a further context for the courting and marrying behaviors in the early modern diocese of London. Thus, the first two chapters of this study focus on choice and suitability, and the following two chapters echo the order of testimony often followed in the depositions: chapter 3 examines courting behaviors; chapter 4 concentrates on the different kinds of behaviors occurring during or immediately after a marriage that deponents pointed to in order to determine consent to a marriage; and the postscript discusses another category of evidence of consent occurring after a marriage that deponents sometimes included. The use of "contract" in this study includes marital contracts without solemnization and marital contracts with solemnization. With this order, I discuss the roles of go-betweens as they relate to the specific experiences and gifts suitors gave prior to marriage in chapter 3 and during or after marriage in chapter 4. This organization means that I must omit a few gifts from my calculations in chapters 3 and 4 because deponents in those cases did not specify when the litigants gave the gifts.[12] For example, in a tantalizing case Henry Hall reported that he saw "a silke and silver poynt with silver togges tyed about the sayd ffrancis Normans arme which he wore as a bracelett, and he . . . heard . . . Alice [Webster] confesse that she tied it about . . . his wrest" (DL/C/219/250ʳ). Unfortunately he neither said whether Alice gave Francis the item nor explained the circumstances in which it was given. In each chapter, I examine the common courting and marrying behaviors arranging them from most common to least common. While this arrangement does not enable us to enjoy the nuances and variations in each separate suit, it presents the behaviors in a more succinct form to highlight the patterns within them. The discussion of the relevant situations in Shakespeare's two comedies follows the discussion of the behaviors in the depositions. Such a division is not to privilege one kind of text over another but to clarify the behaviors in each.

I hope that this book appeals to a wide audience of readers interested in social, legal, and literary history and that readers interested in gender studies find it useful, especially in terms of supplying a context in which to read the agency women in dramas and in depositions enjoyed in late-Tudor and early-Stuart London. Evidence found in the legal and literary texts under consideration here undermines and complicates a monolithic, stable ideal of female conduct in regard to courtship and marriage. While social historians note the increased autonomy of women during courtship,[13] these records expose the autonomy in the courtship and marriage process many women from different social standings enjoyed in the early modern diocese of London. Some women were allowed an active role in choosing their husbands. Women in these depositions did not often subscribe to Helena's belief in *A Midsummer Night's Dream* that women "cannot fight for love, as men may do; / We should be woo'd, and were not made to woo" (2.1.241–42).[14] Overall, what the evidence indicates here is that the men were often the initiators in "the way of marriage," and they, rather than the women, were almost always labeled the suitors. Statements such as "Thomas Wye did resorte unto her and was a sewter unto her in the waye of marraidge" (DL/C/213/805) are common in the records. However, deponents also identified a few women who took the initiative. That only a few women took the initiative in courtship does not mean that on the whole they were passive participants. Whether in the courtroom or on the stage, these texts show that women often enjoyed autonomous roles within those processes: they were both suitors and objects of suits, givers as well as receivers of gifts; they could either accept or deny a suit, set the conditions of acceptance and refusal, and negotiate the terms of the exchanges. Thus, both the court records and the plays themselves present women as agents capable of challenging the roles traditionally assigned to them in courtship and marriage, so that rather than gender being wholly determinative, the evidence shows that it also allowed space for agency. These records provide evidence of women and men manipulating the courtship process to their advantage, by such measures as using the need to consult friends as a stall tactic and claiming parents would never accept a specific suitor. These records contribute further to this discussion by showing the extent to which individuals employed these measures. The depositions from the London Consistory Court concerning courtship and marriage, then, show negotiations of gender relations in daily life in the early modern diocese of London.

A detailed reading of the courting and marrying behaviors in these depositions provides a context by which to understand better the behaviors in early modern English dramas. Rather than presenting societies within the plays as the only place where women such as Maria, Olivia, and Sylvia could hope to gain greater autonomy for themselves, Shakespeare's portrayal of Maria, Olivia, and Sylvia, for instance, represents a dramatized version of what the records of the London Consistory Court document was at work in contemporary London. Particularly as they participate in courtship and marriage, they struggle against a distribution of power imposed by their society, and just such struggles were going on in the society outside the play, struggles documented and illuminated by the court records of the time.[15] Olivia's case, however, is different than Sylvia's—no other Shakespearean female character has such financial and personal autonomy.[16] She is wealthy, titled, head of a household, and has never been married. Within the play's society, she neither can be defined in terms of a man nor is under the control of a dominant male figure: she is not a wife, and, in a sense, not even a daughter or sister, since neither a father nor a brother actively dictates her behavior or choice of a spouse or meddles with her inheritance. Portia's father in *The Merchant of Venice*, for example, influences her "choice" even from the grave: "O me the word 'choose'! I may neither choose who I would, nor refuse who I dislike, so is the will of a living daughter curb'd by the will of a dead father" (1.2.22–25). Olivia's inheritance, however, is contingent neither upon a male relative's approval nor a devised "lott'ry" (*Merchant of Venice* 1.2.28). Unlike Juliet in *Measure for Measure*, Olivia is not a ward either. Instead, Olivia possesses self-authorization, resulting from her position as head of a household and sole property owner. Yet her situation echoes the court depositions, since she, as the women documented in the cases, has some autonomy in courtship and marriage. In his study of *Twelfth Night*, John W. Draper points to the need to study Olivia's suitors in light of contemporary behaviors and concludes that "The wooing of Olivia constitutes indeed the 'organic unity' of *Twelfth Night*: three of the four suits begin in the first act; and all four of them continue to the last. This wooing, granted the initial situation of an eligible heiress, progresses reasonably according to Elizabethan customs and ideals, without either the 'absurdity' or 'extravagance', or indeed much of the romance that critics have imputed to it" ("Wooing" 45). But what exactly these customs were in regard to the progress of Olivia's courtship compared with those for individuals living in the early modern diocese of London need further exploring, and thus I begin.

1

Choosing a Spouse

she had made her Choyce of him and him she would have.
(DL/C/216/355ᵛ)

my father would enforce me marry
Vain Thurio, whom my very soul abhorr'd.
(*The Two Gentlemen of Verona* 4.3.16–17)

In a deposition repeated on 18 June 1591, William Smithe reported the comments of Joan Mortimer regarding her freedom to choose her husband: "neither her ffather nor mother should chuse for her, she was of herselfe able enoughe" (DL/C/214/34). Many London Consistory Court depositions for 1586 to 1611 contain similar statements in which men and women self-consciously emphasized such autonomy. These statements support the conclusions of social historians such as Richard Adair, Eric Josef Carlson, Laura Gowing, Ralph Houlbrooke, Martin Ingram, Alan Macfarlane, and Keith Wrightson concerning the autonomy the non-elite experienced when choosing a partner in late sixteenth- and early seventeenth-century England.[1] For instance, Adair comments that "among the middling sort and even more the propertyless, individual choice of partner seems to have been commonplace" (134).[2]

While, as these historians argue, individuals made their own choices within these social statuses, they sometimes sought the guidance or approval of others. The extent to which the agreement and advice of family, friends, neighbors, and others influenced the choices of prospective partners; at what point such consent was sought; who was asked for their consent; and what those relationships meant are questions that still inform discussions of a choice of spouse in early modern marriages. Ingram notes the preference in theory for consent to a union from those outside the union: "Plainly the ideal was not parental dictation but the *multilateral* consent of the various interests involved in marriage formation, within the framework of respectful attention to parental guidance" (*Church* 136). Several social historians comment on the way in which this ideal was put into practice. For example, Wrightson points out: "It seems reasonable to conclude that among the greater part of the common people marriage partners were freely chosen, subject to the advice of friends and a sense of obligation to consult or subsequently inform parents if they were alive and within reach" (*English* 78). Yet Adair comments on the need to examine further how regional variations influence "the degree of direct community control" and "parental control of marriage" (137–38).

This chapter explores the extent to which choice of partner was subject to the counsel and consent of family and friends in practice in the matrimonial enforcement suits studied here for mainly the middling to lower orders and in Shakespeare's *The Two Gentlemen of Verona* and *Twelfth Night* for mainly the middling to upper orders and contributes, I hope, to this discussion on patterns of choice in early modern London. The narratives in the depositions support, contradict, and manipulate the expectation that women were more circumscribed than men in choosing a mate, patterns which are also apparent in Shakespeare's two comedies. The differing patterns of choice in these depositions suggest more varied experiences than in the dramas. Despite the differences in the patterns in the texts and the differences in the social statuses of the deponents and dramatic figures, both these literary and legal texts illustrate the importance of individual consent in choosing a partner.

London Consistory Court Depositions

In the surviving matrimonial enforcement cases, some depositions include information regarding choice. I only note those depositions that include testimony on choosing a partner and have not interpreted the silences as suggesting any pattern in particular. For the purposes of discussion, I divide the patterns of choice into four categories. The prominent pattern is women and men choosing a prospective partner without acknowledging the need for or seeking the approval of another. In some of these cases, individuals made these choices, according to deponents, acknowledging that parents and friends would not approve their choice and in some cases knowing that disapproval would result in a loss of material or emotional support. This prominent pattern of choice in the depositions supplements the research of historians who argue that men and women of the middling to lower orders in particular had a self-determining choice in a prospective spouse. The second most frequent pattern that occurs in slightly fewer cases is of individuals who acknowledged that their choices were contingent on the approval of another. More women pointed to their choices being contingent on another. In addition, a few women self-consciously pointed to using this contingency as a stall tactic, although it is impossible to assess exactly how many other references were stall tactics as well. These two patterns in the depositions regarding choice suggest a more varied experience in practice, at least normatively, for the middling to lower orders in the diocese of London than is sometimes acknowledged. The third category of choice is of individuals who sought guidance and approval of prospective partners from others after the partners agreed between themselves. One could consider this category as part of the first or second: it could be part of the first category since couples chose each other first on their own without acknowledging guidance; and it could fit in the second category since couples sought or acknowledged the need for outside approval. However, I separate it into its own category in an effort to identify more clearly the patterns in the depositions. The fourth and least frequent pattern of choice is of individuals who had choice thrust upon them, who had no choice, or who momentarily consented out of fear of physical, emotional, or material harm.

Many factors contributed to individuals choosing for themselves and these factors can be seen in the depositions as playing a crucial role. Diana O'Hara identifies features that can influence the extent of parental consent: "it is to be expected that the degree of parental control found within a society is allied to certain structural features such as social groups, inheritance systems, mobility, age of marriage, and mortality" (" 'Ruled' " 14). Such features contributed in varying degrees to the contexts in which suitors made choices and partly account for the amount of self-determination in the middle and lower orders.[3] In terms of age at marriage and employment patterns, John R. Gillis points out: "The recession of the arranged marriage was perhaps inevitable in a society where first marriage occurred in the mid- to late twenties, and wher women as well as men left home in the early teenage years to begin a period of service or apprenticeship which encouraged a certain degree of independence" (21–22). In terms of gender, Ingram identifies the degrees to which a woman's behavior could be circumscribed. While "it was evidently common at all social levels from the lesser gentr downwards for men to take the initiative in finding a wife," he argues that "for women the situation was more variable":

> Females (especially younger ones) of more substantial families were often
> very dependent on parental guidance and suggestion—though even so

their preferences were usually consulted and they were rarely subjected to blatantly "arranged" marriages. But some women of middling rank, and the majority of females of poorer classes, evidently enjoyed a good deal of freedom to seek out a potential mate. ("Reform" 135)

Mortality rates also influenced choice, as Vivien Brodsky Elliott's calculations cited in the introduction suggest. In addition, migration could also influence the practices of choosing one's own spouse. Based on marriage allegations, Elliott argues that "migrant women in general enjoyed greater freedom in the choice of a spouse," while "the extremely high percentage [of 'London-born daughters'] living with their families at the time of marriage suggests that most London daughters' marriages were arranged" ("Single" 97). Because these depositions seldom include the residential history of the litigants, it is impossible to calculate the number of London-born brides and grooms compared to those who migrated to London who appear in these cases. Yet the number of women acting independently of their parents challenges Elliott's argument.

Before looking at the patterns in the depositions, the kind of records themselves should be examined as a possible influence on the patterns. Since cases seldom contain all the pertinent information for each suit concerning employment, age, status, and the like, the patterns I discuss in this chapter represent an impression of the information provided. In discussing the need for more information about age and social status in court records, Houlbrooke notes that "some young people were ready, at least initially, to resist parental pressure. The full significance of their resistance cannot be evaluated without more precise indications of age and social status than the court books themselves provide . . . . Yet it is possible that in other cases informal pressure of which no evidence survives in the court books was brought to bear on parties to conform with their parents' wishes" (*Church* 63). In the London Consistory Court depositions, deponents seldom noted if the lack of approval to a match by parents and friends motivated a suit. In response to such observations by Houlbrooke, Peter Rushton, in his study of the impact of family networks on choice in Durham ecclesiastical records, concluded that we are then left with what he labeled an "uncritical victims'-eye view" ("Property" 208). More information would certainly aid in a fuller understanding of the patterns; however, the patterns that exist in the narratives of the surviving London depositions are nonetheless suggestive.

The sources of the statements regarding choice in the depositions should also be examined as a possible influence on the patterns. Many statements that pointed to individual choice without acknowledging the need for approval from others outside the match may appear biased since the deponents who provided them were mainly either plaintiffs suing to enforce a union or witnesses for those plaintiffs. In addition to bias, the lack of details concerning outside influence could, of course, be an oversight on the part of the deponents. However, the numbers of deponents who did not mention outside influences suggest more than a few oversights. Moreover, the stress on the autonomy of the individual in making a choice, and, in some cases, the recounting of explicit dramatic and defiant declarations of self-determination by individuals, who also acknowledged the possibility of adverse circumstances or consequences, suggests more.

The specific kind of records may account for the prominent pattern of choice in the depositions—individuals who chose a spouse without acknowledging that they sought or needed the approval of someone outside the match—since this pattern can be seen as appealing to a canon law court. The extent of parental influence on consent in practice is of particular interest, since the letter of canon marriage laws in England did not require it. David Cressy comments that "Parental approval was advisable and negotiable, but individual consent was the *sine qua non*" (*Birth* 256).[4] Yet, as Ann Jennalie Cook points out, the church tried to make parental consent necessary rather than advisory:

> In many ways, civil and canon law reinforced parental power in nuptial affairs. The Church of England forbade a priest to marry any minor unless the father or guardian "shall either personally, or by sufficient testimony, signifie to him their consents giuen to the said Marriage." As early as 1559, the Articles of Inquiry sought to discover weddings performed without parents' approval, and subsequent articles in 1584, 1597, and 1604 prescribed suspension for any minister violating these rules. (*Making* 75)

To consider one of these articles in more detail, in the revised canons of 1604 the church forbade children under the age of twenty-one to marr without consent of their guardians or parents, and marriage by license required proof of parental consent regardless of the age of the prospective partners. Canon 100 states: "No children under the age of one and twenty years complete shall contract themselves, or marry, without the consent of their parents, or of their guardians and governors, if their parents be deceased" (Edward Cardwell, *Synodalia* 304–05). Despite these canons, only one case in these depositions—as far as I could find—directly referred to a law regarding marriageable age.

The 1600 case of *Katherine Holmeden v. John Sherman* indicates an awareness of a statute that had been put through Parliament in regard to marrying age and parental consent. Thomas Pyborne reported that John was not concerned about Katherine's age. Although he told John that Katherine "was no fitt matche for him in respect she was a Child," John admitted that he "knew her age before . . . [he] went about it" (DL/C/215/436ʳ). While Thomas expressed concern over Katherine's age, other deponents showed concern over John's marrying Katherine without her parent's consent. William Morrell, a rector of St. Margaret Pattens, deposed that he told John that "he thought ther was a strayt statute made the last parliament against suche as should marrie with mens dawghters without Consent of their parentes." Yet John's response indicates that the statute did not worry him: "why I am not married yet." To Morrell's point that if John "be . . . Contracted to her, who ellse can have her," John answered "Saye that she is contracted to me, and I not to her" (DL/C/215/436ʳ-436ᵛ). John's attempt to sidestep the law by claiming Katherine was contracted to him and he not to her may suggest that he at least was aware of the legal ramifications, since he appears to be trying to protect himself. In another account, Pyborne reported Morrell's words to John concerning the statute, an account indicating John's boldfaceness in going against it: Morrell said to John "how dare yow John marrie . . . your selfe unto any mans Child without the Consent of her parentes Considering the statute that was made the last parliament" (DL/C/215/438ʳ). The comments of these deponents about this statute are all the more intriguing since the exact statute to which they pointed is vague. The bill that went through Parliament in 1597 focused on "taking away of Women against their wills unlawfully." The testimony does not suggest that John took Katherine away against her will. The deponents here apparently remembered this law in terms of the need for parental consent.[5] While no sentence survived for this case, ecclesiastical courts in practice did not always consider marriages which did not adhere to these stipulations as invalid. Thus, to point to a person making the choice himself or herself emphasizes the mutual agreement of the individuals themselves, a point that could possibly explain why so many of these statements came from deponents called to testify in support of the union.

This prominent pattern of choice suggests an attitude of flexibility in behavior for men and women in the way of marriage. Even when choice was made without acknowledging outside influences, patterns of choice varied between women and men. In most suits contained in the London depositions for this period, men were the initiators of the

matches; however, the few rare instances in which women were initiators
are worthy of note. Robert Scarre reported that "in the monethes of
October and November 1607," he, being a widower, hired Helen
Tinckham to "make his bed washe his cloathes and to do suche other
busynes as by reason of his keping of howse he had to do." Helen,
"having contynually at tymes . . . good resort to his howse," grew
"into some familiarity with him" and asked him "yf he would marr
her." He answered her proposal, saying "marry? . . . yf . . . I marry an
I will marry thee" (DL/C/218/303). In another deposition, which
was inexplicably crossed through, another woman set her cap to a man.
Edward Corbett reported how he and Ann Jaques, "dwelling together
in one howse," had "muche familiaritie togither they both
being . . . free from other contractes of matrimonie." Ann "moved"
him "to take her to wife" and said, "if he would promise her marriage
she would stay seaven yeares for him." However, Edward testified that
he "had no suche intent nor used any comunicacion with her to that
ende" (DL/C/219/78ᵛ). In addition, even if an individual sent a
go-between to introduce a suit directly to a prospective partner, the
initiative almost always came from the man. Alexander Hollinworth
"had spoken" to John Griffith "to be a meanes unto . . . Mistris Ann
Hide before that time that he might speake with her and be a suter
unto her in the way of marriage" (DL/C/215/120ʳ). In another case,
Henry Bowles "did first acquaint . . . [him] that he had an intent to
become a suter in ye way of marriage to the sayd Susan and required
him to . . . move the matter to her and . . . [he] promised so to do and
to do what he could to further his suite therein" (DL/C/219/315ʳ).
The latter go-between had more self-interest in the match than helping
Henry, since Henry offered to "content him for all his paines" if he
"did speede in this busines" (DL/C/219/315ʳ).

While more men in the depositions usually initiated courtships and
made offers of marriage than women, women usually made choices
by accepting or refusing a partner. In a deposition repeated on [. . .]
4 June 1587, George Nicholls' testimony includes his recollection of
Elizabeth Cage's words concerning her choice, words that indicate
that acceptance was choice: "she was contente to yeald her selfe to the
said John Nicholls and make choyce of hym for her husbande"
(DL/C/213/176). Many deponents carefully recounted the language women used in their acceptances or refusals. Gowing comments on the importance of this language: "Whatever kind of
proposals men made, in the customs of marriage and at the cour
the exact words of women's answers were critical" (152). In regard
to refusals, many women denied their suitors directly. To cite one of

many examples, Margery Cuthauck testified that Henry Caplin "had treatie and Conference" with her "for a marriage to be had and solemnized betwene him and her." However, she "utterl[y] mislyked and refused to Conferr with him to any s[aid] end or purpose" (DL/C/214/651). In another case, Margaret Callowell refused to proceed in a match. At first, she had agreed to letting her brothers choose for her, saying that "she wolde be contente to performe that which her saide brethren shold doo" (DL/C/213/452). Yet she refused their choice of John le Sage. She defended herself by saying that since her brothers "never signified her that they were absolutelie concluded abowte the said marriage," she "consequentlie never made thereof absolute resolucion with her selfe neither will she in anie wise in this respecte more referr her selfe unto them althoughe they now wolde thereupon conclude" (DL/C/213/454).

In rejecting their suitors, some women sent friends to reinforce their message. Alice Oliver testified how she "always denied . . . [Anthony Tristram's] request" and, particularly about last Christmas, Anthony asked her "whither she woud lik of him or no" to whom she answered that "she was not minded to match hir self with any but requested him to for bear to move hir any more in that matter." She also "caused divers of hir friendes to talk with him" and "to diswade him from moving that matter . . . any more to hir" (DL/C/214/179). When her direct refusals did not dissuade him, she sent her brother to discourage him, instructing him "to desire the said Anthony Tristram to forbear to coom any more to hir howse, or to desier hir in marriage, and withall to tell him that shee had no manner of minde to bee married to him" (DL/C/214/215). Rather than through a brother, Agnes Bushey sent her refusal to her suitor via his laundress who he was using as a go-between. After the laundress told Agnes "how farr the said Thomas Wye was in love with her," she responded that "she was sory for itt and wished her to persuade hym from itt for that she could neither like nor love hym" (DL/C/213/805–06). Men also made such refusals. The difference in how they often refused an offer—the woman usually telling the man she was not interested and the man usually denying the offer ever occurred—underscores that men were almost always the initiators in suits. To cite one example of the latter, John Lowen alias Cockhall "dyd never in anie of the yeeres or monethes articulate conceave anie good lykinge to the said Margarett in the way of marriage nor did sollycitt or woe her in the way of marriage nor did . . . at anie tyme . . . obteyne the good lykinge or consente of the said Margarett to marry" him (DL/C/213/597).

Many examples exist of women accepting suits without acknowledging the need or practice of seeking outside influence or guidance. A widow reportedly went against her son and Lady Wroth in her choice of husband. Although Susan Jason alias Jackson "knewe . . . [her son] would by very muche against" her union with Henry Bowles "never the lesse sayd she I am at my own disposing and will not be ruled by him in that matter" (DL/C/219/313ᵛ). Henry was also worried about another party who might change Susan's mind. A witness overheard the concerned Henry advise Susan to be wary of Lady Wroth. As Susan was about to join Lady Wroth for dinner, Henry took "her by the hand," saying, "I desyre you to be constant and faithfull to me according to your former promise for you are going to my Lady Wrothe and I knowe she will urge you to marrie some other." Susan then assured him that "she would be constant unto him and not make any promise to any other" (DL/C/219/314ʳ). While the necessity of the consent of Frances Edmondes' father in her alleged two contracts to John Stubbes and William Busshopp varied between the cases, in the case with John Stubbes the witnesses more often recounted Frances' belief in her right to choose her partner herself. Although Prudence Joyce testified that after the contract Frances "desyre[d]" John "to Com to her ffather as he had sayd sayd before he would to ask his good will" (DL/C/216/315ᵛ), Grisill Mills deposed that the consent of Frances' father was a concern for the groom and not for the bride. After the contract when Frances said to John "to com fetche her awaye to marrie her," John then pointed to the necessity of the consent of her father to solemnize the union: "he would so doe so soone as he Could but he would first aske her fathers goodwill." Frances, however, did not concern herself with her father's consent: "I care not wheather I have my ffathers goodwill or not it must com as it will come" (DL/C/216/312ᵛ). According to Grisill, John apparently later shared the same opinion as Frances on the matter after her father "denyed him his goodwill with his dawghter." After this denial, John told her father that "ffraunces was his wief and he would have her" (DL/C/216/313ᵛ).

The extant depositions also contain several examples of people, including both widows and single women, making their choices fully aware of the potential consequences and disapproval. The disapproval arose not over the right of the individual to choose for oneself but over the lack of parity with the specific suitor. As in *The Two Gentlemen of Verona*, *A Midsummer Night's Dream*, and *Romeo and Juliet*, such choices are often striking since many deponents noted that individuals made choices that they knew opposed the wishes of parents, relatives, and friends. Jane Browne confirmed her choice of husband on the way from Cliffe to Rochester in saying to Richard Sheperd that "she was contracted to Henry Jackson and that he was her husband and she would nev*er* forsake him so longe as she lyved what truble soev*er* she did endure" (DL/C/215/12ᵛ). In another case, a deponent testified that Ann Hyde declared if "her uncle should refuse to give his Consent" to her union with Alexander Hollinworth then "she would take him the sayd Alexander by the hand and take him for her husband before her uncles face" (DL/C/215/123ᵛ).

The testimony here is often more dramatic since witnesses reminded individuals of the severe economic and personal consequences that their choices will cause. In considering the consequences of her choice of a husband, Deborah Woodhall's responses varied, according to several deponents, from resignation to acceptance of the economic provisions of her husband to confidence that her father will accept the match. After Deborah announced that she and William Sadler were "sewer togithers in marriadge," Roger Sadler alias Sariante told her "that she had made a badd choyce for her selfe, because her ffather and mother would nott be contented w*i*th itt." However, according to Roger, such discontent was not as important as Deborah's choice. After being warned again that she "shall never have . . . [her] ffather and . . . [her] mothers good will to marry hym and then . . . [she] shall lyve to . . . [her] owne greife," Deborah said that "she knewe her ffather loved her nott so yll, butt that he would healpe her to lyvinge . . . althoughe he frowned on her a while" (DL/C/213/817). If she could not get her father's goodwill, she would suffer the consequences: "yf she could nott obteyne so much att her ffathers hand*es* she would be contente to lyve w*i*th the p*ro*ducente in a fryse gowne, aswell as she . . . then did in all her best attyere" (DL/C/213/818). Another witness in the case, Thomas Pratt, gave a similar account of her desire to secure her father's goodwill and her awareness of the consequences if she could not. After he told her that "she had made a badd choyce for that he thought her frend*es* would nott consente unto her choyce," Deborah "answered againe she had made her choyce and [would] nott forsake hym for any other, and therfore she wa[s] contente to be maynteyned as he was able, and she dowbted nott butt she should one tyme obteyne her fathers good will" (DL/C/213/819–20). A financial sacrifice would be considerable in her case, for several witnesses in the case commented that "m*aste*r woodhall is a gent of great lyvinge" (DL/C/213/826).

The deponents in *Richard Campion v. Joan Mortimer* pointed to Joan making her own choices despite the consequences. Joan's parents sent an uncle, William Smithe, "to diswade their daughter Johan from matchinge" with Richard since "they had herde there was good likinge betwene them, and . . . [Richard] of hymselfe nott able to maynteyne her" (DL/C/214/34). When Joan came to his house, he "fell in talk with her usinge such perswasions as he coulde to the said Johan to have her to forsake" Richard and "nott sett any liking towardes hym, shewinge her whatt her ffather and mother had tould hym." Yet according to this defense witness, "nott withstandinge all hys speaches and perswasions," Joan would not yield: instead, as cited in the opening of this chapter, she "tould hym she would have" Richard

> to her husbande whatsoever became of her, all thoughe she begged with hym and that she had made hym the said Richard Campion suche a promise that she could nott with a saffe conscience forsake hym saieng further, thatt neither her ffather nor mother should chuse for her, she was of herselfe able enoughe . . . that . . . [Richard] should be her husbande yf ever she married any man and none butt he . . . for she had made choyse of hym. (DL/C/214/34)

Witnesses for both the plaintiff and defendant testified that she chose Richard herself. Roger Foxe provided a similar account. While in the King's Head in Clement Lane, he heard Joan "affirm and say that shee had chosen . . . Richard to bee her husband and that shee would have him if she went a begging with him" (DL/C/214/30). A third witness told a very different story about Joan's feelings for Richard. In this account, she was not so willing to honor her choice if it meant begging with him. Katherine Hawfeild saw Joan sitting in the kitchen "very dumpishlie and grevouslie weeping." After "demaunding of her the cause of hir sorrow and whearfore she wept," Joan answered "very . . . lamentablie that she . . . had cast hir self away contrary to all hir frends goodwill, and had doon that which she could not undoe, but said shee if hee weas a good woorkman I cared not, but now it cannot bee undoan" (DL/C/214/32). Yet Joan obviously felt it could be undone. Despite the man who "served the processe upon her did by virtue of that processe chardge . . . and Inhibite her from marrieng with any man (unlesse itt weare with the articulate Richard Champion) duringe that sewte upon payne of lawe" (DL/C/214/90), she married Thomas Goodwyn "openly in the Chappell of the tower" of London (DL/C/214/91). Despite the different accounts of what Joan said, the testimony of all four witnesses points to Joan choosing her partner herself, even if she later regretted it.

Male suitors also made choices that they said went against the wishes of their families. In the case of *Susan Powell v. Edward Brookes*, Edward, when asking Susan's mistress for permission to court her maid, explained that he was financially assured of having his choice: "a kinsman of his had geven hym a hundred mark*es* yerlye" in case his father "should dislike of his choyce." He added that "his fath*er* was a Gentleman and should nott rule hym in his love for he was to Chuse his owne wyfe hymselfe" (DL/C/213/748). In another case, Richard Marsh defiantly chose a spouse without the consent of his father. William Isen testified that Richard "sayd expressly that he would marrie . . . Suzan Wilson w*i*thout his fathers consent," explicitly declaring that "Suzan*ne* was his wief and he her husband and he nev*er* ment to for sake her but he would marrie her whatsoev*er* his father sayd" (DL/C/215/292ᵛ).

Although several of these deponents mentioned the possible material, physical, and emotional consequences of their choices, only a few identified the results. In one case, George Leake testified that "Eliz*abeth* Wilson was shutt out of her sayd brothers dores by reason of the love betwene James Harrison and her." Despite Elizabeth being shut out, George recounted that James told her brother Jeffrey that "she was his contracted wief and he would have her thoughe he nev*er* had grote w*i*th her" (DL/C/215/385ʳ). In another example, Susan Fidgett testified that her choice of Thomas Baines resulted in physical abuse: Susan's father "did beat . . . [her] bycawse he suspected that thear was love beetween" her and Thomas and "once threatned hir to putt hir owt of dores" (DL/C/214/171 and 173).

In these examples representing the prominent pattern of choice, deponents pointed to people choosing for themselves, sometimes even defiantly going against the wishes of family and friends or not caring about the approval of others. However, the second and third most frequent patterns—individuals making their choices contingent on others and individuals seeking the consent of family and friends in regard to their choice of partner after the couple had agreed between themselves—involve the influence of others beyond the couple. Ingram identifies the hierarchy of influences based on the specific relationship:

> Parents, step-parents and occassionally masters and mistresses acting *in loco parentis* were predictably most prominent. Uncles and occasionally aunts played a role either when they intended to bequeath property to their nephew or niece or if they were acting as "tutors" or guardians of youngsters who had lost one or both parents. Siblings were occasionally

involved, usually when brothers had been directed by their father's will to hold the portion and oversee the marriage of younger sisters. In some cases respected "friends" from outside the family (including god-parents on occasion) were also in evidence, either to reinforce parental advice or, again, when they had been designated to act as tutors or guardians. (*Church* 200)[6]

A study of the dynamics of the different groups of influence from which couples sought approval or guidance is beyond the scope of this chapter. However, we should note that the influences deponents cited in these London records generally follow the pattern Ingram identifies. In regard to friends, many deponents in the London records did not specify exactly who they were. To seek approval or advice from family and friends could be more than a courtesy, since transfers of property and household goods, familial harmony, and emotional support could depend on it.

Deponents commented on the need for such approval. The fathers of a couple in one case complained that their children did not seek their approval. Sir Robert Stapleton testified that the fathers of the bride and groom "hathe protested unto him . . . that they knew not of the Contract betwene their . . . sayd Children before suche time as it was reported that it was don*e*." Stapleton felt that a contract "wi*th*out their parent*es* Consent" is "neither god[l]y nor La[wf]ull" (DL/C/215/512ᵛ). In another suit, John Bacheler, himself a father and witness in the suit of *William Busshopp v. Frances Edmondes and John Stubbes*, also expressed his belief in the necessity of parental consent to a match, a belief that governed his actions with the daughter of another. When Thomas Bisshopp, junior, the brother of the groom, asked John to give Frances away at her marriage to William, John "denyed to doe saying he knew not wheather she had her ffathers good will or not and it would greeve him . . . him selfe . . . to have an other give his dawghter fro*m* him" (DL/C/216/354ᵛ). The testimony of other witnesses in this suit indicates a similar concern regarding whether Frances had the approval of her father to the match. Unlike the witnesses in the suit between John Stubbes and Frances Edmondes that I cited earlier, the witnesses in the suit between William Busshopp and the same Frances offered several statements indicating that she sought her father's advice and guidance. The testimony of Thomas Bisshopp represents statements made by others: "her ffather had willed her to marrie wi*th* any man except John Stubbes" (DL/C/216/356ʳ). Katherine Warner reported that even after the marriage, Frances perhaps ironically identified the match as a fulfillment of her father's will: "now . . . I have fulfild my fathers will for he willed me to marrie with any man whom I would so I did not marrie with Stubbes" (DL/C/216/360ᵛ). The comparison that Frances allegedly used included in this same witness' testimony between a "hangman" and the lack of her father's consent suggests the consequences of not having it: Frances "tooke old Bisshopps wief by the arme and sayed be of good Chere mother the hangman is deade that should doe my . . . husband and me harme, I towld yow my ffathers goodwill would soone come" (DL/C/216/361ʳ). The testimonies of Thomas and William Warner include a slightly different account of the role her father's approval played in this union: Thomas testified that Frances "earnestly desyred of him . . . that she might goe to some place wheare she might be married spedily . . . before her father should finde her for she towld him . . . that it had bynn towld her that her ffather had bynn ther at his . . . ffathers howse to seeke for her before she Came" (DL/C/216/356ʳ). While the accounts regarding the approval of her father to the match differ, they nonetheless point to the need for such approval. In the suit I cited earlier of *Deborah Woodhall v. William Sadler*, the uncle of the groom acted to stop a union that lacked the consent of the bride's family, even though the match would be advantageous for the groom's family:

> soe sone as he was acquaynted with this matter and could possiblye geve leysure namely upon the tewsday followinge he made . . . Debora Woodhalls graundfather acquaynted therwith and tould hym that yf the said Debora weare nott loked unto she should be carried away, and married . . . the nexte day after to the said William Sadler and soe muche he coould have tould Master William Woodhall hymselfe yf he hadd nott bynn att Debden . . . And he saieth he did open this matter of mere goodwill he bore unto . . . Master William Woodhall and was the onlye man that prevented the marriadge. (DL/C/213/818)

In a later case, Ellen Pulley alias Pullen testified to the adverse consequences that would occur if Grace Cooper's friends would not approve Grace's choice of Thomas Harrison to be her husband: "sundry times" Grace told Ellen "that she loved him well and so well as if . . . she might not be suffred by her frendes to have him she knew she should never doe well" (DL/C/215/242ᵛ).

To look more specifically at cases within the second most frequent category of choice—individuals making their choices contingent on that of another—in the records (rather than choosing for themselves without acknowledging outside influences, as in the first pattern, or choosing for themselves, then asking for the approval of someone else, as in the third pattern) gender again influences patterns of choice, since in the depositions more women than men identified that their choices were contingent upon the approval of another. Gowing comments on the pattern of dependency she sees in the London Consistory Court depositions:

> When women were unwilling to make a final marriage decision, the invocation of such authority was a particularly useful strategy; suggesting the proposal was being taken seriously, it also provided them with a legal way out of it. Whether women actually used conditional responses like these, or whether they found in them a useful story with which to defend themselves at court, the formulas that invoked the advice and goodwill of friends in marital decision-making were clearly well-established ones. (154)

It is, of course, often impossible to tell whether women were self-consciously using the consent of others as a means to put off a suitor However, a few women called attention to how they used the expectation that they would need approval from another as a stall tactic, a topic to which we will return shortly.

The women who made their consent contingent on someone else often made their approval contingent on a father or a father figure.[7] In one deposition, Alice Hawkyn twice mentioned the contingency of her acceptance being based on that of her father, one of those being: "she did allwayes answeare" to William Wrennall "in satisfienge his demaunde for marriadge with her, that she could well like of hym and be contented to chewse hym above all other . . . so that he could obteyne her ffathers good will consente and likinge thereunto: otherwise she beleveth nott . . . this article to be true for she saieth withowt her fathers good will she still answered . . . yt she would doe nothing" (DL/C/213/601). In another case, Margery Dickers alias Thornewerke pointed to the approval of her uncle as necessary befor making a match, a point that she raised with both her suitors. While Humfrey Greene "wold have had her contracted her selfe unto him," she "refused so to doe unles he cold first get her uncles good wi[ll] sayinge that yf he cold obtenie her uncles good will she wold then give a Resolute answere" (DL/C/215/227^r). When Uncle Grey separately asked her and another suitor, Thomas Thorneworke, what was between them, they both separately answered "ther was nothing betwene them without . . . her unckles good will and likeing" and "ther is nothing betwene us without your good will" (DL/C/215/324^v). The necessity of his approval in the latter case was more complicated, since, as William Greene recounted, Margery's Aunt Grey had married her to Thomas before this conversation. Within that context, the approval seems unnecessary; however, it did seem to have material consequences, since, despite their pleas that "nothing" was between them, Master Grey responded that "if ther be any thing betwene yow, on god*es* name take her to yow but she shall have no land of myne neither will I medle w*i*th her." Thomas, in response, "did utterly disclaime her" (DL/C/215/324ᵛ).

In addition, deponents pointed to the necessity of the approval of a mother. As Gowing and Sara Mendelson and Patricia Crawford explore, mothers played a major role in the courtship process.[8] While George Nicholls testified that Elizabeth Cage chose John Nicholls for herself, he had the couple repeat a contract due to concern over her mother's influence. Although George claimed that "he had nott distruste att all in the saide Elizabethe whoe was then under her mother and to be ruled by her," he decided to have another contract in front of more witnesses because Elizabeth's mother and "other [of] her ffrend*es* (once knowinge of the matter) would be greatlye againste the same" (DL/C/213/177).

A few women manipulated an expectation that they would turn to another for final approval to put off a suitor. In one instance, Elizabeth Jackson self-consciously pointed to her technique of using her father's approval as a stall tactic. When Thomas Thorpe visited Elizabeth, although "she did not send for him," he took her "by the hand and asked her yf she would be contented to be his wife." She responded that "she was contented if he could get her fathers goodwill w*hi*ch she knewe he could not or els she would not have sayd so" (DL/C/219/24ᵛ). In another case, Alice Danson referred to the need for the approval of her friends to block the suit of John Botheroyd. While at her mother's house "at the signe of the white hart in the strand," she "being held betwene M*aste*r Rutland and M*aste*r Kays,"

was abruptly and upon a sodayne demanded by M*aste*r Rutland whether she cold be Content to take the sayd Botheroyd to her husband (he sayeng that the sayd Botheroyd was a fit mach for her and able to mantayne her yf she wold marry w*i*th him) whereunto she not having at all any entent to Contracte m*at*rymony at that pres*en*te did withowt any deliberacion answer I yf her frend*es* good will might first be thereunto obtaned and otherwise not upon w*hi*ch her answer the said Botherod willed . . . [her] to give unto him her hand w*hi*ch she did and in a shorte tyme after dep*ar*ted. (DL/C/213/348)

In a different suit, Ann Hyde also referred to the need of her friends' approval as a way to deter Alexander Hollinworth. He wrote a letter to Ann telling her that "he had provided a Coche for her to Com away in and a licence for them to marrie by and that if she wear so deter mined to Come he wold quickly have her away" (DL/C/215/116ʳ). Despite Alexander's entries and those of "Griffins wief" who "did often . . . perswade her to Come away from her frendes to Maste Hollingworth," Ann "alwayes answered that she would never goe so but her frendes should be consenting to it." She pointed to the necessity as she saw it, to use this tactic: she "seeing no other answere would serve sayd that she would never goe so without her frendes goodwill" (DL/C/215/116ʳ).

In an apparent effort to ensure goodwill for a match for all involved parties, a few deponents pointed to mutual contingency of approval: a couple made their consent to a match contingent on the goodwill of parents, family, and friends; and parents, family, and friends made their goodwill contingent on the couple. After John Bawcocke "mooved" Henry Hawke "for his good will to come as a sueter unto his daughter Agnes Hawke," Henry replied, "John my daughter is yett but a childe and over yownge for marriage. But when she is of more yeeres and knowledge If yow then come unto me and that I see her to fancie and lyke of yow truelie for the good lykinge that I have of yow I will give yow my good will" (DL/C/213/487–88). When John renewed his suit to Henry for his daughter, he received a similar response: "he shold have" Henry's "good will" if Agnes "cold lyke and fancye him" (DL/C/213/488). Agnes' mother told a similar story. When John requested her goodwill to proceed in his suit to marry her daughter she reported that she told him: "If yow can gett the good will of my daughter meaninge . . . in this cause so as yow may come togithers in the feare of god I am well contente" (DL/C/213/488). Agnes also pointed out how her goodwill was contingent on both her and her parents approving (DL/C/213/470). In a later case, a woman made her goodwill contingent on her mother, who made her choice contingent on that of her daughter. While John Fitzwilliams told Susan Peele, "yow are the woman that I have made Choyce . . . of to be my wife afore all the women in the world," she answered that "she for her par was contented . . . to love him above all others if he Could gett her mothers good will." When he asked "her mother then present what she sayd to the matter," Susan's mother answered that "if he had her dawghters goodwill he should have hers . . . withall her hart" (DL/C/216/332ᵛ–333ʳ). In this case, the mother's goodwill played an even more significant role. Both the daughter and mother explained the circumstances and context informing the display of goodwill more as a common courtesy than as approval of a match. Susan testified that when John arrived at their house in West Ham, Essex, "her mother in kindnes as to all other men that come to her howse as straungers did . . . bidd him welcom and likwise his frend that came with him" (DL/C/216/299ʳ). The mother stated that the reason for her kindness was due to the weather: "it being a very rayney daye and they wett she . . . caused . . . fier to be made to drye them and she Caused one of her dawghters . . . to dry their bandes and so used them kindly as straungers yet she sayeth it was more for the diers sake then for John ffitzwilliams sake that she did soe" (DL/C/216/346ᵛ). In her personal response, Susan also noted that her father expressed his lack of consent to this match even as he lay dying: "when he laye uppon his deathe bed" her father "sayd expresly that he never graunted his good will to John ffitzewilliams to marrie with her . . . at any time" (DL/C/216/299ᵛ).

Although some deponents did not stress mutual consent, it was carried out. For even when parents, family, and friends initiated a match, individuals usually were consulted on whether they could consent to it. In regard to who initiates a match, Wrightson comments: "What mattered was less the identity of the initiating party than the securing of the consent or 'goodwill' of all those concerned" (*English* 72). William Reignoldes provocatively reported that "the Scottish Ambassadour did once perswade" him to marry Agnes Swinborn alias Swayten (DL/C/214/166). In another case, "while they weare at plowghe in the field together," two men discussed a match between their relatives. While William Adams and John Stondon were ploughing, William "made a motion to him," saying "he had a kinsman . . . that would be a good husband . . . for his . . . kinswoman . . . meaning and naming George Adams and Alice Stondon." John responded that if George "wear an honest man he . . . for his part would be contented," and so they "appoynted a time that they should meet togither at his . . . howse" during which "they did and ther had talke and Confer[ence] together" (DL/C/215/188ʳ). When the groom met the prospective bride, he was not pleased, since "he did percyv[e] her and fynde her somwhat softely as he sayd . . . meaning therby for so he seemed in other of his speeche to utter that she was somwhat foolishe and againe he for awhile misliked her substan[ce] and . . . portion" (DL/C/215/189ʳ–189ᵛ). At the request of George, William and Thomas Adams "talked with her" and found her in "their talke to be bothe wise sensable and discreet . . . and willing to marrie with him the same George" (DL/C/215/189ᵛ). After William told George "that it then rested only in him that the marriage should goe foreward or no," George again talked with Alice in this witness' parlor, both parties promising "I will be as good as my word and promis." In addition to the visits of George and Alice in order to see if they consented to the match, the consent of her uncle and her brother "with whom she dwelt" was also needed (DL/C/215/189ᵛ and 190ʳ).

The third most frequent pattern of choice in the depositions is of couples who first made decisions for themselves and then sought the approval and guidance of others or those instances in which outside influence stopped a match, allowing the approval to have more control over the couple than the individuals within the couple. In terms of seeking consent, the surprise Ann Foote's parents experienced must have been one that many parents feared. The tardy return of Ann who had been sent to Lawrence Grimshawe's house to return "his lynnen" concerned her stepfather, Edmund Hawes, who "intended to go looke for her." Dramatically, just as he "had put on his cloake ready to goe out," Lawrence and Ann "knocked at this Jurates . . . dore and were let in." Lawrence told Edmund that

> your daughter hath given me her faith and her troathe in the waye of marriag and promised to be my wife and I have done the lyke I have given her my faithe and troathe and have vowed and promised to her to be her husband and therefore I pray you let me intreate your favour and goodwill and furtherance of our marriage and yt you will . . . no longer accompte of her as yours but as my wife for so she is and I am her husband and we must not parte till God by death shall parte us.

When asking Ann for confirmation of Lawrence's account, Edmund's questions suggest his shock: "mayd have you done this? have you contracted your selfe without my consent?" (DL/C/219/135ʳ–135ᵛ). Ann confirmed Lawrence's account, and her parents, upon considering the situation and his occupation, "at the last" gave their approval (DL/C/219/136ʳ).

The depositions sometimes contain details concerning what could result if mutual agreement or approval by all parties was not secure. In one case, John Swinsted testified that, despite the consent of Elizabeth Brode alias Ibotson to accept his suit, the lack of consent from her mother stopped the match: Elizabeth told John that "in case he could gett the goodwill of her mother she for her part would be content to love him and take him for her husband but not otherwise." John then "moved the same Elizabethes mother for her goodwill that he . . . might marrie her dawghter who as he sayethe denying him . . . her goodwil[1] he sayethe he did nev*er* speake or move any speche of marriage w*i*th the same Elizabethe Brode after" (DL/C/215/92ʳ). However, whether Elizabeth's mother actually granted her consent was at issue. Richard Done reported that John told him that when he asked her mother for her goodwill to marry her daughter, she told John "that it weare good that he stayd fro*m* marriage 2 or 3 . . . yeares but did not absolutely deny her good will unto him the same Swinsted neither did graunt him her good will" (DL/C/215/93ʳ). William King, another witness in this case, identified the lack of goodwill as not coming from Elizabeth's mother but from John's friends: "synce this sute began John Swinsted towld him . . . that he would not marrie w*i*th the said Eliz*a*beth Brode but would deny her in the Court for all his frend*es* wear aganst it that he should marrie w*i*th her . . . and he hathe likwise heard M*is*tris Hurtly say . . . to him the said Swinsted that he should Chuse wheather he wold have her or no" (DL/C/215/98ʳ). Although we can never know what actually transpired between Elizabeth's mother and John, the case nonetheless indicates the importance of consent from a third party in some cases, since the testimony of many witnesses hinged on the presence or absence of the mother's consent as evidence for the presence or absence of the couple's intentions to marry.

In another case, Alice More's mother prevented the solemnization between her daughter and Richard Thomas. Two witnesses testified on behalf of Richard concerning the dislike of Alice's mother to the match: "her mother hath often showed dislyke and he never heard say yt ever she consented yt Richard Thomas should be maryed to the sayd Alice More" (DL/C/219/8ᵛ). Thomas Clemence testified that Alice herself was worried that her mother knew of her contract with Richard. Alice told Richard that

> yow . . . cannot kepe yo*ur* owne Counsell but yow have revealed it to my mother w*hi*ch he denying she sayed yes for I coming by yow a while a goe and did not speake to yow as I was wont to doe yow strayt waye thincking that I was angry w*i*th yow and so yow sayd and therupp*on* towld my mothers men what love and affection was between us and that I was becom unkynde unto yow in that I did not speake w*hi*ch my mothers men have acquainted my mother w*i*th all and I know not now how to doe. (DL/C/218/540)

According to this witness, Richard allegedly told her mother because, as Alice interpreted his behavior, he felt slighted by her. Richard's actions here suggest a misunderstanding of the extent of the influence of

Alice's mother, an influence Alice well understood—"I know not now how to doe." Her mother, who disapproved of the union, "knew what to doe." Thomas Morley deposed that "before this suite began there was a common report in theyr parishe . . . that . . . Richard Thomas and Alice More should have bin married togither yf her mother had not hindered it" (DL/C/219/7ᵛ). He did not explain how this union was hindered, but Robert Scott suggested one obstacle: "ther being meanes made to end this matter of controvrsie about this Contract he . . . was sent for to goe to Mistris Mores howse and then he going did see Alice More at that time locked upp into the howse of Sir Robert Bannister knight by pudlewharf for he sayethe he sawe her goe in and sawe the dore lockt againe by the howse keper after her" (DL/C/218/552).

The lack of consent of Ralph Yardley's friends to his possible match with Joan Carewe stopped his suit. When some of Ralph's friends "had heard of his . . . conversing with . . . Joane Carewe and of the . . . affection that he . . . had to her," they told him that "if he did any wayes contract him selfe to her or to any suche as . . . they heard she was reported to be, none of them would doe any thing for him" and they told him that "he would utterly undoe him selfe" (DL/C/218/252). Due to the disapproval of his friends, Ralph did not go further with the match. He

> Confessed that he had loved her, but quothe he seng I percyve it is not pleasing to my frendes and I now considering better of it I will never contract my selfe unto her in marriage nor goe any forewarder in that busines and yet . . . this deponent . . . pressing him with it and telling . . . him that . . . that . . . this deponent did hardly belev him, to satisfe him . . . Raphe tooke a booke that was by him and voluntarily swore by that booke he would never com in her Company any more meaning the Company of her the same Joane Carewe. (DL/C/218/286)

However, the woman's mother told a different story in which he sought her goodwill to the union after having obtained that of her daughter. Ralph went to Joan's mother's "howse at tower hill" and told her "that he had byn a suter to her dawghter for marriage but quothe he all this while I have byn but an usurper of her I praye yow now give her unto me whearuppon she . . . tooke her sayd dawghter Joane by the hand and Layd her hand in his the same Raphes hand and so ioyning ther handes together she . . . sayd I praye god blesse yow" (DL/C/218/289). Yet, according to the mother, lacking the approval of Master Erbie, brother-in-law to Ralph, and Master

Hutton, Ralph's master, Ralph "hathe forborne and refrayned the Company of her the same Joane Carewe" (DL/C/218/290). As in many of the above cases, Ralph chose for himself and then sought the approval of her mother and his own friends, although, in this case, he refused to proceed without the latter.

The least common pattern of choice in these depositions is complete control of the choice of partner. Perhaps few historians today would accept the positions put forward by Christina Hole and Lawrence Stone in regard to the extent that arranged marriages occurred in early modern England,[9] although some literary critics still hold similar assumptions. Other historians have argued that the lack of choice of partner was rare in matches regardless of class.[10] Wrightson argues,

> Having reviewed the evidence relating to the selection of marriage part-ners at different social levels, it would appear that interpretations based upon the conventional dichotomies of arranged as against free matches, and parental choice as against self-determination by the child, do less than justice to the complexities of reality. There is little evidence of cold-bloodedly "arranged" matches outside the very highest ranks of society. The likelihood of parents initiating or proposing a match was not uniform even at the highest social levels, while even when they did so, children usually seem to have enjoyed a right of refusal. Below the level of the aristocracy, upper gentry and urban plutocracy, the actual initiative usually seems to have lain with young people, subject to the advice and consent of parents, friends and even principal neighbours. (*English* 78–79)[11]

Only a few examples exist in the depositions when another controlled a choice of partner and took no account of the feelings of the prospec-tive bride or groom. While deponents rarely identified the motivations of the people taking control, they more often identified the individu-als making these choices for others: fathers, judges, brothers acting as fathers, friends of the bride, and caretakers. The fact that these cases appear here indicates that the agreement for these individuals, who apparently went along willingly or complied out of fear for their lives or of punishment, was not permanent. While unfortunately we cannot know how many parties permanently lacked the power to challenge marriage at law, we see in these court records several individuals who took legal steps to change their marital status or restore their ability to choose a partner. As R. H. Helmholz points out, from medieval times the ecclesiastical courts defined duress in choice of partner in terms of "force and fear": "The standard adopted by the canon law was this: if the threat of force were such as to have moved a 'constant man' or a 'constant woman' the marriage could be invalidated. If it were less, no divorce was available" (*Marriage* 91). While the judicial process could take away one's control of choice, it also could restore that choice.

The age of the prospective partners played a major role in some of these cases in the initial agreement of an individual to comply with the union. In one such case, one witness explained that "the matche for matrimony betwene Peerce Price and Mary Wyn was concluded uppon . . . betwene the frend*es* of the sayd p*art*i*es* before the p*art*i*es* them selves knew therof" (DL/C/216/302ᵛ). Another witness detailed how the decision came about: "John Price moved her . . . for a marriage to be had betwene his son Peerce Price . . . and Marie Wyn who then was Com*m*itted to the governement of her . . . whearunto she . . . answerd that . . . her ffather was com*e* ovr againe into England and was then in London and if he Could gett . . . his Consent ther in she . . . would be very willing and further it in what she Could." After writing a letter detailing John Price's "offer of his sonn in marriag" and "what . . . John Price had offered w*i*th his son in marriag" to Mary's father, he

> was very willing w*i*th the matche and referred the same wholley unto her . . . and then she . . . and . . . John Price aforesayd talking together and Concluding uppo*n* the match made Mary Wyn acquainted therw*i*th who was very willing and ioyfull therat and then it was consented that Perce Price . . . who then was in London w*i*th an uncle of his should be gon*e* for to com*e* . . . into the Cuntrie. (DL/C/216/322ᵛ)

The bride told how unsuccessful this union without choice was: she "hathe absented her selfe fro*m* the Company of . . . Peerce Price theis five yeares or ther about*es* as she belevethe w*h*ich she doeth for that as she sayethe . . . she was married to him the same Peerce Price . . . bothe against her owne good lyking and her self being ver young not above xiiii yeares as she belevethe and he the same Perce not above xii yeares of age" (DL/C/216/367ᵛ).

Some individuals who had a choice of partner thrust upon them consented to the choice out of fear. In a most unusual case, Richard Kilcup recounted how his bride's father sent men to abduct him and force him to marry. Because of the unusual circumstances surrounding this abduction, I quote extensively from the deposition. At the time of the abduction, Richard, aged "xiii or xiiii yeres or thereabowtes," was "a gramer scholler at Egebason a myle distant from Brunegha*m* in the county of Warwick." As he came "from schole abowt xi of the

Clock . . . in the midwaye twixt Egebason and Brunegham," he
encountered "two horsmen whose names wer Tho Mylward and
Walker" and as Richard "wold have passed by the *m*" Walker "lifted him
on horsback behind the said Mylward and violently tooke . . . [him]
away w*i*th them and the same night brought . . . [him] to one M*a*st*er*
Thornetons howse by the forest of Wyer twenty myles distant from
Brunegham." After two days, "Cicely the daughter of John Mylward an
inkep*er* of Brunegham was convayed thither to the foresaid M*a*st*er*
Thornetons." Thorneton "broke to him a marriage to be made
betwene" him and Cecily. Thorneton, seeing that Richard "had no liking to the said marriage," threatened that if Richard would not "con-
scent and agree to this union and mariage" he "wold cary . . . [him]
where he shold nev*er* se frend more." He then took Richard "to a pale
syde not far distant from the sayd Thorntons howse having a long bow
bent and arrowes in his hand" to Richard's "greate feare." Richard testified that he thought that if he did not marry Cecily, Thorneton "wold
have then slayne him." He then "for feare and danger of his liffe being
but a childe" did "pr*o*mise to take the said Cicely to wiffe."
Accompanied by Cecily's father and Thorneton, they "did ride to a lyt-
tell chappell a myle and half distant" where "there was a priest redy and
so" Richard and Cecily "wer willed by the Priest to come togither."
Both he and Cecily by "Compulsion and for feare" repeated after the
priest what "is sett downe in the Book of Comon praier towching
the soleminzac*i*on of mariage" (DL/C/213/280–81). After the
"pr*o*miss*es* by violence," Richard lived with John Mylward for "abowt
thre quartes of a yere" since "he knew not to whome he might open his
mynd nor cold have accesse to any." During this time, Richard, despite
the kidnapping and forced marriage, managed to consummate their
marriage, deposing that he "had the use of her body div*er*s and sondry
tymes during that . . . tyme" (DL/C/213/280–81). Such evidence
would not necessarily help Richard dissolve the marriage. As
Houlbrooke notes, "living together, kissing, and other marks of intimacy
were held to constitute signs of consent unless they could be shown to
have been compelled" (*Church* 73).

In a different case, Ann Payne alias Harris alias Bull agreed to
marry one Thomas Harrys against her will. Unlike Cecily, her fear was
not of her father, but of her mother. "Abowt xxiiii yeares synce,"
Ann's mother, "beinge desierous to marry her" to Thomas, did
"threaten and terrifie" her, "shee being*e* then younge and betweene
xii and xiii yeares of age." Ann's mother "did then force her against
her will and good likinge to come in to the Companie of . . . Thomas
Harrys." "After many threates," she "procured" Ann "against her will

to Consent to goe to the Churche to be marryed to him." Ann "standinge still in awe of her saide mother above xx yeares synce went with the saide Harris to the parishe Churche of Hyhopp in the dioces of St David and there one like a priest that Could scarce read (but was faine to be taught by a servinge man that stoode by) did reade some wordes towchinge marriage but what they were shee knoweth not." She argued that "for her parte she spake nothinge nether answered anye thinge after the preist" (DL/C/216/369ᵛ).

In a different case involving a ward, Sara Eyer's brother, Robert, testified that Sara contracted herself to Nathaniel Page "for feare and compulsion" (DL/C/217/46). In testimony from another witness, the seeming house arrest under which Sara was held indicates she may have been fearful of her custodian, Elizabeth Pert, her sister: Sara "might not goe abrode to speake with . . . [her brother] or with any other of her frendes . . . for Mistris Pert would not suffer her" (DL/C/217/89). This case, however, may be more about who has control over Sara rather than Sara not having control of her choice of a prospective partner, since the same witness testified to his desire to have the Lord Mayor take control of her. The will of Sara's father "bequeathed" her portion "to be putt into the handes of Mistris Pert." As her brother Robert explained, Elizabeth had not honored the wishes of their father:

> it was so willed unto her condicionlly which condicion on her part hathe not byn performed which is that she the same Mistris Pert should fynde her the same Sara sufficient meate drinck and apparell and fitt education which she hathe not don and therfore he thinckethe that bequest to be voyd and the Lord Mayour of London who is the ffather of all orphans in London maye dispose of her as he thinckethe fitt. (DL/C/217/54)[12]

This control by the Lord Mayor extended to consenting to Sara's choice of marriage partner: "my Lord Mayour did then presently . . . cause her the same Sara to be taken from Master denman and Committed to [her brother's] . . . keping he . . . entring into Rocognichance in five hund[red] poundes that she should not contract her selfe or marrie w[ithout] the private knowledg and Consent of the Lord Mayour of London and the benche [. . .] Aldermen" (DL/C/217/43).

Some deponents claimed that they were tricked into their unions. Along with fear of her caretaker, Sara was, according to her brother Robert, misled to believe that he agreed to the match discussed above. He testified that Sara, who "presently brust . . . a weeping and pittifully lamented saying was suche a matter which she with all her hart repented," told him that "she was made beleve that he . . . was willing and Consenting . . . ther unto" (DL/C/217/45–46). In another case that I cited earlier, despite some witnesses' claims that Frances Edmondes consented to her match with William Busshopp, Frances told a different story. Contrastingly, she reported how, while wanting to be taken to her father's house or to John Stubbes, the man she wanted to marry, she ended up marrying William in Hedsor Church in Buckinghamshire as a result of being literally misled and influenced by "sinister perswacions":

> shee thinckinge that she had bene goinge towardes her fathers howse or to . . . Stubs at length they brought her to a Churche the name whereof shee knoweth not And presentlie after lightes brought . . . [she] beinge amazed and not knowinge what she said or did as she beleveth was by the sinister perswacions of the persons there present induced to saie certeine wordes after one that was like a minister which shee beleveth . . . Bushopp and his Companie then tooke to be wordes of matrimonie and that they did import a marriadge betwene him and . . . [her] but she for her parte . . . did never soe take them. (DL/C/216/304ᵛ)

Margery Dickers alias Thornewerke was another woman who claimed to have been "drawne and constrayned" by "sinister meanes" into a marriage with Thomas Thorneworke (DL/C/215/264ʳ), although she did not identify the sinister means. William Greene, another witness from this case, recounted Margery's explanation to him of how this marriage happened. After Margery's aunt requested permission at Margery's master's house in Temple Bar that she "might have leave to goe abrode with her," her aunt "had her into the Cloysters at Christchurch and then into a Chruche about Smithfeild wheare Thornewerk was and ther came in a man with a wooddenleggwho spake certeyne wordes and she the same Margery sayd I to it" (DL/C/215/324ʳ).

In two other cases, the consent to a union was not due to youth, fear, or being tricked; instead, the two men ultimately agreed to marry the two women with whom they had sexual relations before marriage to escape being "locked in." In a personal response repeated on 16 October 1591, Thomas Perrye agreed to marry Elizabeth Newdigate in an effort to escape punishment from a judge for his sexual promiscuity. After "havinge had Carnall knowledge of the bodye of the sayd Elizabeth," Thomas was "convented before the Judge of this Courte in his Chamber in the Doctors Commons." In hope "of avoydinge punishement and publique pennance for his offence," Thomas told the judge "thoughe untrewlye" that he and Elizabeth "weare contracted together." After Thomas' "confession," the judge "moved" him "to contracte himselfe agayne to the sayd Elizabeth." Thus, "before divers witnesseis," he did "contracte matrimonye by woordes of the present tyme" with Elizabeth "in hope of releasinge his publique pennance And for no other cause." He underscored his lack of consent to this union by saying, he "never intendinge or meaninge to marrye her . . . notwithstandinge the Promisses." He stressed his lack of consent further: "all that he did at the tyme and place aforesayde was done by him for vearye ffeare" (DL/C/214/68). As social historians such as Adair, Ingram, and Peter Laslett document, many couples had sex after a contract and before a solemnization of that contract. If the solemnization did not occur, some unfortunate couples, especially women, could face charges of fornication or bastardy.[13] Here, Thomas used the expectation of sexual relations after a contract as a defense. In a lengthy 1598 case, to be discussed further in chapter 4, Alan Car agreed to marry Helen Vaughan after she locked him in his chamber According to Helen, Alan "had the Carnall use of her body divers and sundry times" and, she, as she thought, "was with Child by him." Thinking he "would goe awaie," Helen assisted in gaining his consent by locking him into his chamber ("and kept the keye hir selfe") until he agreed to marry her (DL/C/215/76ᵛ and 87ᵛ).

Of course, people did not always comply. Frank Awsten was willing to go to prison rather than comply with the judge's order to marr Joyce Awsten. Although the archbishop and high commissioners committed Frank "for causes ecclesiasticall to the Counter in Woodstreet," he "refused to performe an order" from them "towchinge marriage" with Joyce. He recounted that he "remayned there untill suche tyme as he had procured subtelie and craftelye a warrant . . . from on Captaine Dennard to employe hime as a soldier in his maiesties affaires by meanes of which warrant he was taken owt of pryson." The Masters of Bridewell called Frank before them "throughe the meanes" of Joyce's father because Frank "had promised her sayd father to marrye her by a day." Based on this witness' account, Frank's attempts not to comply were successful since he apparently was not punished: "she beleveth that the sayde ffranke receaved noe punishment ther for any suche supposed causes mencioned in this article or any other" (DL/C/213/673).

Two Shakespearean Comedies

The London Consistory Court depositions provide a localized context by which to read choosing a partner in *The Two Gentlemen of*

Verona and *Twelfth Night*. As women and men in the depositions exercised freedom of choice, so too do the dramatic figures in these two plays.[14] In regard to Shakespeare's dramatic figures, Suzanne Gossett argues that his plays support in varying degrees an individual's choosing of a partner: "Shakespeare's dramas, often treated as uniformly romantic, take careful account of the differing constraints upon young people of different classes. His plays usually convey a sense that young people should have a say in picking, or at least accepting, their own marriage partners" (59). While Cook also sees Shakespeare's plays as supporting a dramatic figure's autonomy to chose, she identifies this pattern as a "challenge" to "patriarchal authority": "Without diminishing the strength of patriarchal authority, Shakespeare nevertheless challenges it in a variety of ways. Not only do some fathers willingly accede to their offspring's wishes, but some find their power effectively challenged. And throughout a number of plays certain characters follow the dictates of their own affection without interference" (*Making* 103).[15] Even though these two plays offer very different experiences for some in regard to the presence of others who try to block a union, the dramatic figures nonetheless end up in unions in which the partners choose mutually or have both consented. As the depositions indicate, that so many of Shakespeare's figures exercise individual choice when "picking" a partner is not simply the product of a literary imagination. The freedom with which Julia, Silvia, Maria, and Olivia choose their partners was not limited to women in literature or to those in their particular circumstances.

In *The Two Gentlemen of Verona*, only those unions proceed in which the dramatic figures make choices for themselves—Silvia and Valentine and Julia and Proteus—despite initial objections of some of their fathers. Although fathers in the play dislike and even try to prevent unions based on their children's rather than their own choice of mates,[16] the choices of the children win out in the end. This play shows a daughter's choice wins out against the objections of her father, and another son's choice takes precedence over his father's. Fathers influence the choices of Silvia and Proteus more than of Valentine and Julia. J. L. Simmons comments on the lack of fatherly influence on the latter two dramatic figures: "Valentine, like Julia, is after two casual references textually disengaged from a father who never appears; unlike Proteus, he has apparently undertaken his quest to the Duke's court autonomously" ("Coming" 865). The issues surrounding choice arise more in the union of Silvia and Valentine rather than with that of Julia and Proteus.

The dramatic action supports Silvia's choice of partner by allowing her to end up with her choice rather than that of her father, thereby suggesting in the action of the play—if one approves of her union with Valentine—that mutual choice is more important than obeying parental wishes. Throughout most of the play, the Duke wants Thurio, whom he has chosen, to be Silvia's husband: " 'Tis not unknown to thee that I have sought / To match my friend Sir Thurio to my daughter" (3.1.61–62). The details the Duke provides of the measures he carried out to ensure her compliance to his choice underscore his insistence on his choice: "I nightly lodge her in an upper tower, / The key whereof myself have ever kept, / And thence she cannot be convey'd away" (3.1.35–37). The physical imprisonment here is emblematic of the mental containment he attempts to exercise over her. Even Silvia's attempt to intercede with her father for Valentine is unsuccessful: "But neither bended knees, pure hand held up, / Sad sighs, deep groans, nor silver shedding tears / Could penetrate her uncompassionate sire; / But Valentine, if he be ta'en, must die. / Besides, her intercession chaf'd him so, / When she for thy repeal was suppliant, / That to close prison he commanded her, / With many bitter threats of biding there" (3.1.229–36). The Duke himself details how she will not bend to his will but remains steadfast in her choice. Valentine, self-interestedly, asks the Duke, "Cannot your grace win her to fancy him?" (3.1.67). The Duke's answer reveals his feeling that she has disregarded her duty to him: "she i peevish, sullen, froward, / Proud, disobedient, stubborn, lacking duty, / Neither regarding that she is my child, / Nor fearing me as if I were her father"(3.1.68–71). He even tells Valentine of the consequences of her not accepting his choice of partner: he is resolved to "turn her out to who will take her in. / Then let her beauty be her wedding-dower; / For me and my possessions she esteems not" (3.1.77–79).

Despite her father's attempts to secure her consent to his choice, Silvia chooses for herself. The behaviors documented for most women in the depositions in regard to choice are seen here as well. Silvia chooses her partner through acceptance and refusal rather than initiating a suit. Her refusal of the suits of Thurio and Proteus and her acceptance of the suit of Valentine are all instances in which she chooses for herself. Silvia, while not being given the right of refusal, escapes. She bases her plea for help to Sir Eglamour on the need to love freely and comments in the process (in language reminiscent of Protestant ministers) of the miseries of an enforced marriage:

> my father would enforce me marry
> Vain Thurio, whom my very soul abhorr'd.

> Thyself hast lov'd, and I have heard thee say
> No grief did ever come so near thy heart
> As when thy lady and thy true love died,
> Upon whose grave thou vow'dst pure chastity.
> Sir Eglamour: I would to Valentine,
> To Mantua, where I hear he makes abode; . . .
> Urge not my father's anger, Eglamour,
> But think upon my grief, a lady's grief,
> And on the justice of my flying hence,
> To keep me from a most unholy match,
> Which heaven and fortune still rewards with plagues. (4.3.16–31)

Silvia ultimately prevails in her choice of partner since the dramatic action shows her father agreeing with her choice. Charles H. Frey writes of the consequences of a daughter selecting a partner other than one chosen by her father: "When the daughter chooses radically against the father's will, she effectively shuts him off from patriarchal domination of the son-in-law and consequent sonlike extension of his power and values" (66).[17] In light of this line of arguing, this play could indicate the restoration of this domination since the Duke accepts Silvia's choice and reconciles with her, thereby restoring his position of "patriarchal domination." Even if one argues along these lines, her choice is not necessarily contained by the drama, since the Duke's acceptance and approval of her choice of partner supports her right to choose for herself, a support that the end of the play under-scores. Stanley Wells' description of what happens to Silvia at the end of the play may seem to suggest a lack of choice on her part—"Sylvia says nothing at all while she is first donated by Valentine to Proteus, then rejected by him in favour of Julia, then claimed by Thurio, only in his next breath to be renounced by him, and finally handed back to Valentine by her father" (165). Yet her silence may be seen to call attention to her autonomy in choosing in that it is her father who "hands her back" to the man she chose for her husband.

While the union of Silvia and Valentine highlights choice made in light of parental disapproval, the union of Proteus and Julia under-scores the need for mutual choice and consent. Despite Proteus' con-cern over his father's disapproval of his choice of partner, which, we might note, does not bother him while he woos Silvia, ultimately his first choice of partner takes precedence. His remarks in regard to a letter from Julia suggest the need in his eyes for parental consent: "O that our fathers would applaud our loves / To seal our happiness with their consents!" (1.3.48–49). Proteus again shows worry about his father's approval: "I fear'd to show my father Julia's letter, / Lest he should take exceptions to my love, / And with the vantage of mine own excuse / Hath he excepted most against my love" (1.3.80–83). Although Proteus expresses concern about the necessity of his father's approval of his choice, he also acknowledges that the lack of approval will not, and within the play does not, prevent a union with Julia.

The course of the wooing of Proteus and Julia also stresses the need for mutual choice. Like Silvia, as the above quotations indicate, Julia chooses Proteus herself in light of the disapproval of her father. Yet, unlike Silvia, the dramatic action shows that her union is more dependent on Proteus' approval than her father's. Lori Schroeder Haslem points to the dependency of Julia in the course of the play: "As involved in the plot as Julia is throughout the rest of the play, she can in fact do little more than wait and hope to be chosen—indeed, rechosen—by Proteus in the end" (128). Haslem argues that this dependency is even more apparent at the close of the play where, despite Valentine's faithfulness to his choice through most of the play, at the end Silvia as well as Julia must be "rechosen" by their prospective partners:

> That Julia is reduced from subject to object, from being the chooser (in the private, female realm) to be the chosen (in the male realm) becomes most painfully obvious at the problematic close of the play, whereupon Valentine—wanting to demonstrate his forgiveness of Proteus's overtures toward and attempted rape of Silvia—offers up Silva, trophylike, to prove his sincerity to Proteus. At this moment, both Julia (still disguised) and Silvia are utterly powerless. It is as though they are indeed behind the scenes—with no equipment left to polish—observing the male-centered drama in which they play no active part. (129)

Despite their "powerlessness," these women end up paired with partners of their—not their fathers'—choosing.

Twelfth Night, while sharing some similar patterns of choice with *The Two Gentlemen of Verona*, also differs. *Twelfth Night* neither has parents blocking proposed unions, influencing, or advising about prospective partners nor does it contain self-conscious comments regarding autonomy in choice. Instead, the dramatic action teems with dramatic figures choosing for themselves, but Olivia is the figure whose act of choosing for herself receives the most comment. Many readers identify the source of her initiative in the play as her class standing and even as the date of the first performance.[18] While her social and economic circumstances put her in a position to initiate a match with Cesario and Sebastian, they do not explain totally her ability to choose for herself, since many figures in this play of varying status and class do so as well. The six individuals in the three couples at the end of the play—Orsino and Viola,[19] Olivia and Sebastian, Toby and Maria—all mutually select each other themselves without acknowledging the need for guidance or approval from someone else. Although at first Olivia's choice of Sebastian may not seem to be based on mutual consent since she thinks he is Cesario, Sebastian, as I argue in the following chapter, is what she was looking for all along.[20] Even where the consent and choice is not mutual, dramatic figures in this play choose for themselves without acknowledging the need for outside approval: Orsino chooses Olivia; Olivia, Cesario; Aguecheek, Olivia; and Malvolio, Olivia.

The women and men in this play as in the depositions and in *The Two Gentlemen of Verona* also choose for themselves in either accepting or refusing a suit.[21] Olivia refuses the Duke's suit, using, as do some women mentioned in the depositions, a stall tactic to dissuade him— not pointing to the need for the approval of others but to the need to mourn her brother for seven years. While she uses this tactic as the play opens, she is not successful in putting Orsino off since he sends another messenger. Through most of the play, Olivia does not employ further tactics but sends messages through Cesario clearly saying that she "cannot love" the Duke. This play also shows a "man" refusing a suit as well. Cesario refuses the suit of Olivia not by requiring, like Ralph Yardley, the approval of friends, but by pointing to the love of Orsino. This play also puts a man in the position to accept or refuse a suit, since Sebastian accepts the suit of Olivia. Viola and Maria also accept the suits of the Duke and Toby, respectively, and both women do so without acknowledging the need to seek outside approval. John W. Draper points out how independent Maria is in her choice in particular: "without apparent leave or notice, she weds her mistress' uncle—a nuptial that certainly should have had the consent, if not the benison, of Olivia as head of the house" (*Twelfth Night* 79–80).

To read *The Two Gentlemen of Verona* and *Twelfth Night* in light of contemporary behaviors of choice as documented in the London Consistory Court depositions helps us to understand better the connections between choice of partner on and off the stage. Here men and women choosing partners for themselves, even despite adverse consequences, is not simply the product of fantasy but also reflects behaviors—despite possible class differences between dramatic figures and audience members or readers—that would have been known to many viewing or reading the plays. To examine the patterns of choice in both the depositions and the dramas under discussion contributes not only to the discussion of choice in marriage in early modern

England but also to our understanding of the extent to which marriages based on individual consent, rather than relations between parents and children, were the building blocks of early modern England. It is difficult to determine the extent to which factors such as wealth, physical appearance, and age influenced choice. Yet the next chapter examines the different criteria deponents cited that women and men assessed in the process of forming these building blocks.

2

DETERMINING MARITAL SUITABILITY

she would rather see hym hange and behanged her selfe then she would matche with hym.

(DL/C/215/260ᵛ)

She'll none o' th' Count: she'll not match above her degree, neither in estate, years, nor wit; I have heard her swear't.

(*Twelfth Night* 1.3.106–08)

In addition to choosing a spouse, determining suitability was important to the making of a marriage. In 1608, William Hutton, the master of Ralph Yardley, testified that he, along with other friends and family of Ralph, "disswaded" him from a match with Joan Carewe, "she being a wief muche unfitt for him" (DL/C/218/283). While William did not detail the criteria that made Joan an "unfitt" match, many deponents in several different cases identified the specific criteria that made someone a fit or unfit match. In the surviving London Consistory Court depositions for 1586 to 1611 and in Shakespeare's *The Two Gentlemen of Verona* and *Twelfth Night*, deponents and dramatic figures cite a variety of considerations when selecting a mate, such as wealth, status, occupation, personal affection, age, and character.[1] The emphasis on individual rather than group interpretation of suitability criteria and the categories of criteria are generally the same between these dramas and depositions. However, within the topics discussed in this study, the widest divergence between the patterns in the depositions and the dramas occurs in regard to the prominence of criteria. That is, worth was the most cited criteria in the depositions, whereas it is a minor consideration in these two comedies. As such, the basis on which dramatic figures select partners in these two comedies is on the whole more romantic and unworldly compared to the depositions.

LONDON CONSISTORY COURT DEPOSITIONS

Before looking at the specific suitability criteria in the London Consistory Court depositions in detail, I would first like to comment on the use of these records as sources of criteria. Deponents did not always detail or even comment on the criteria that influenced choice in the cases. Fewer than half of the extant depositions from matrimonial enforcement cases include testimony regarding suitability. Rather than identifying and discussing the basis on which people chose each other, the depositions contain more testimony regarding the process of courtships. A study of the comments and attitudes concerning criteria is nonetheless instructive. In addition, it is difficult to determine if deponents actually *believed* the criteria they cited to be the most important. Yet even if these comments regarding criteria occasionally seem a bit incredible—as the quotation from a deposition serving as an epigraph for this chapter suggests—they were said as being legally plausible. Furthermore, we should note how deponents cited suitability criteria. They more often pointed to it as evidence of why a partner was unsuitable rather than suitable. In respect to this pattern in ecclesiastical courts, Ralph Houlbrooke points out that "Witnesses were often asked about differences in wealth between the parties in the hope that their answers might throw doubt on plaintiffs' claims" (*Church* 63). As Houlbrooke suggests, to raise an objection concerning suitability may be an effective defense in court, especially when pointing to financial resources which can be measured.

The attitudes and comments of deponents in the extant London Consistory Court depositions indicate the necessity and desirability of parity. Historians such as Richard Adair, David Cressy, Laura Gowing, Houlbrooke, Martin Ingram, and Keith Wrightson detail how parity was expressed in practice.[2] Wrightson emphasizes that parity influenced the choice of partner regardless of who made that choice: "it is evident that in the selection of marriage partners the notion of parity in a match, so much stressed by contemporary moralists, did indeed deeply influence choice, whether that choice lay entirely with the individuals concerned, or was subject to the direction or consent of others" (*English* 86). Ingram identifies the specific considerations: "the essential yardstick was *equality* or at least comparability between the couple, especially in respect of religious commitment, virtue, age, birth and breeding, and wealth and estate" (*Church* 136). While parity, as these historians note, played a central role in the selection of a partner, the combination of or emphasis on particular criteria varied from one couple to another. What seldom appears in the records is a clear distinction between what parents, or those serving as parents, such as masters and mistresses, said should be the criteria on which to select a partner.

Deponents pointed to more than one criterion as being important in deciding whether to accept or reject a suit. Ann Hyde indicated that she needed to consider the "Condic*i*ons" of Alexander Hollinworth when assessing his suitability. Before Ann spoke with Alexander, John Griffith called her into the "Church porche" where he "tooke forthe of his pockett a littell pickture no bigger then a mans hand and showed it to her and asked her how she liked the p*ar*tie whose pickture it was she answering . . . that it was a hansom pickture." After John "asked her how she . . . thought she could like the man whose pickture it was and how she could finde in her hart to love him," Ann responded that "she could not tell how to like him for that many a man . . . was well picktured whose Condic*i*ons weare not to be liked" (DL/C/215/114^r). Here, being "well picktured" is not an accurate indicator of a potential partner's "Condic*i*ons."

Ann's insistence on multiple "Condic*i*ons" seems to have been the norm. To cite one of two representative cases, according to John Bellott, Alice Oliver singled out Anthony Tristram's equivocation about his financial worth and the age difference between them as two equal reasons of his unsuitability: "thear wear many cawses but specially bycawse she and he weer unequall in years and bycawse she had found him soomwhat double in his woord*es* he having one time tolld her that his land was woorth 40^li a year and an oth*er* time that it was but xx^li a year and hir conclusion was that then she was then determined nev*er* to marry w*i*th the said Tristram" (DL/C/214/273–74). Witnesses in this case cited other reasons as well. John Norton testified that Anthony's position made him unsuitable, "bycause hir friend*es* thought that he beeing a serving man was a very unfitt match for hir" (DL/C/214/216). Yet John Harris, another witness, deposed that Alice's brother put a halt to the match not for the amount of the jointure, but supposedly due to the location of the property offered. Although Alice "lyked" Anthony's offer "to make hir a ioynture of x a year in yorkshir," her brother "misliked the same draught and was not willing that she should go into yorkeshire and that it was tolld hir that it was a barren Country" (DL/C/214/239/1–240).

In another case in which Henry Bowles sued Susan Jason alias Jackson, William Durant's recount of Henry's courtship of Susan provides many of the suitability categories that appear in these depositions. When considering a match with Henry, Susan considered their estates. After she enquired how she should "stand secured for . . . [her] estate,"

Henry suggested that "he would put her in ii sufficient sureties and named ii Aldermen of London," but Susan "would not meddle with suche great men but asked what the other mens names were whome he nominated before." Then, Henry

> nominated . . . Master Haselfoote and Master yeamans and she accepted of them and sayd if they will be bownd yt you shall not make away any of my estate during my life And yt if you dye before me you shall . . . leave me your estate except one C^{li} which you may bestowe where you please I am . . . content and do give you my hand and my hart in token of my love and consent . . . and then . . . Henry did accept thereof. (DL/C/219/314^v)

The depositions also detail Susan's concern with Henry's estate, providing different accounts of his suitability in this regard. Durant claimed, as did Robert Hayes, that she found Henry's estate to be suitable, finding "all thinges according as . . . had tolde her saving she sayd she had heard that . . . Henry Bowles was indebted to Sir Vincent Skinner with whome he had formerly dwelt and durst not looke him in the face, and this deponent satisfued her there in yt it was not so and she acknoweledged her self to be fully satisfied" (DL/C/219/313^r). Susan told a different story. According to her, "his estate" was "not as the sayd Henry had related" (DL/C/219/311^v).

In discussing the terms proposed for this match, the depositions include concerns regarding parentage, age, family, and character. After Durant "signified" to Susan that Henry "intended to become a suter to her for her goodwill in the way of marriage," she inquired about his age, "abilitie parentage and suche lyke matters" (DL/C/219/312^v). In terms of Henry's age, Hayes testified that when he asked Susan "yf she ment to have . . . Henry Bowles to her husband," she at first said she "was too younge" but afterward confessed that "she had made choice of him for her husband and that she entended to marry him and no other and that should be done shortly and secretly and desyred this deponent not to be a knowne what she sayd especially to my Lady Wrothe because she had made motion for an other" (DL/C/219/316^v). Susan, according to Durant, also detailed the kind of treatment she desired from her husband, treatment that played a part in determining suitability. Susan told Henry that she hoped he "will be an honest man and be loving and kinde to me and you shall be sure that I will be loving and kinde to you yf you will be so to me for yt . . . is all I desyre it hath byn my prayer to God to have an honest and loving man to my husband as for wealthe I desyre it not or the lyke in effect and then . . . Henry Bowles accepting of this her love sayd I pray God I may lyve no longer then I shalbe loving trythfull and kind unto you" (DL/C/219/313ᵛ). Hayes further suggested being unencumbered with children as a consideration. He reported Susan's perception that children would be a "trouble" to her suter: "at her howse she sayd you see I have here little children and . . . this deponent sayd I thinke these be your sones children and she sayd I but these shall not trouble Master Bowles for I will send these home to their father and come single to him" (DL/C/219/316ᵛ). In a marriage to her, he could possibly secure his standing by producing the only heir.

As the above cases from the extant London Consistory Court depositions exemplify, many deponents pointed to a variety of criteria; however, they mentioned certain factors more than others. For the purposes of discussion I organize this chapter by the frequency of the item deponents cited in terms of the most to least: worth (wealth, status, occupation), personal affection, age, character, marital status, and other criteria to which people pointed. While the use of the term "worth" in this period indicates that it could be described by the modern term "character," deponents used the term "worth" when pointing to prospects of wealth, class standing, and occupation. Although character or reputation can be seen as property, I have placed it in its own category here to represent more clearly the patterns in the depositions.

Deponents cited the worth of an individual more often than any other criteria. In commenting on worth in mate selection, Ingram points out the variety of considerations that were involved: "marriage thus served to reinforce and perpetuate the distinctions of the social order. Yet social worth and eligibility as a marriage partner were not assessed wholly in terms of pounds, shillings, and pence. Across a broad social spectrum, marriage candidates and their families also attached some weight to 'ancestry', 'breeding' and good reputation" (*Church* 141). In the depositions examined here, deponents similarly calculated worth in more than "pounds, shillings, and pence." Given the class standing of the litigants and witnesses in this court, deponents spoke of financial worth more in terms of currency than of land or property. Surprisingly—especially in light of the class standing of the majority of deponents—neither household goods, which could be important to a couple trying to establish a household, nor domestic or business abilities were often mentioned when assessing worth. Perhaps, when discussing the financial suitability of a match, sums of money were a more tangible way to measure worth during litigation.

To cite a representative case, the occupation, financial provision, and status of Susan Atkinson and John Payne played a significant part in their courtship. One witness pointed to the disparity between them. Although Richard Edwards did not know the "worth" or "welth" of John and Susan, he knew that "Payne is servant to George Parker waterman and is a sculler on the Thames" and "hath two yeres to serve as an apprentice," whereas Susan "hathe a plow and teme and kepeth a man and a mayde and hath two children" (DL/C/213/335). Edwards, who testified "at the request" of Payne, assessed that Susan "far passeth . . . Payne in degree and welthe" (DL/C/213/335). John himself defended the parity of a match with Susan by detailing how his present circumstances did not reflect his status and future prospects. John, who identified himself as "a waterman," "a prentise," and "an honest man," testified that "he hath taken order to be released of the sayde prentiship at such tyme or before as he shall marry." In addition, he testified that, although some consider him "a man of small accompte," he is "the second sonne of a gentilman in oxfordshier" and his brother, who "may dispend xx^{li} by yeres in freehold in the sayd County," promised to give him "xx^{li} to his marriage" in addition to his "owne stock." Because of his parentage and worth, he "beleveth this article to be onely to . . . disgrace him" (DL/C/213/388).

In other cases, deponents commented on the occupation, status, and wealth of a parent of a woman (particularly that of a father) in assessing the suitability of a match. In the case of *Deborah Woodhall v. William Sadler*, several deponents noted the wealth and status of their fathers. William's uncle, Roger Sadler alias Sariante, pointed to the disparity in the match: "his kinsman is nott able to mayntayne . . . Debora Woodhall accordinge to her callinge" (DL/C/213/818) and "he knoweth not any thinge att all that . . . [William] hath to lyve with upon or by, butt onlye his service and his fathers helpe who kepeth an Inn, butt he saieth he is sewer that . . . [William's] father hath nott a fote of lande to lyve upon" (DL/C/213/819). Thomas Pratt and Jane Burles also noted the lack of William's financial resources and prospects due to his reputation and occupation. As Jane deposed, William "hath nothing to lyve upon but only his service and that he is taken to be a man of litle credit or callinge and lesse wealth" (DL/C/213/825). In addition, deponents detailed the wealth of Deborah's father. The comments of William's uncle are representative: "Master William Woodhall is . . . a man of greate lyvinge and . . . may dispende all manner of wayes a thowsande markes a yeare and one that kepeth a greate howse and good hospitalytye and accompted for a Cheife man in those partes where he dwelleth and therby he saieth his dawghter Deborah [is] liklye to be well per*f*ered in marriadge" (DL/C/213/819). In another case, when testifying to the worth of Thomas Kighly in the case of *Jane Ponsonbie v. Thomas Kighly*, the witness included Kighly's occupation and income. He knew Thomas was a servant to Lord "Shandwis" [Chandos] and "hathe always taken him" to be "very pore and nedy and not to be worthe above xl*es* more then the bountie of his honorable Lord and Lady" (DL/C/215/513*r*). Another witness in the same case noted that she believed both Kighly and Simon Ponsonby, the father of the bride, were gentlemen; the disparity in wealth that could accompany this status is apparent. While Kighly was "a se*r*vingman," Ponsonby was "accompted a gentleman of good worthe and hable to bestowe twoe or 3 hundrethe pound*es* w*i*th his dawghter if he will" (DL/C/215/515*r*). For Joan Carewe, the wealth of her mother, Sara, played a role in determining Joan's suitability. Edward Erbie testified to the poverty of Sara: "at that time she seemed to be so needy and so pore a woman as a little payle of sudd*es* being by chance spilt she cryed out saying she was undon whearuppo*n* ther was a peny offered to have byn given her for that losse but shee seing to be distracted at it and sayd that they brought her out of her witt*es*" (DL/C/218/287–88). Sara told a different story. Identifying her occupation as "being a laundres to a gentlewoman and to other her neere neighbo*urs*" (DL/C/218/291) and her worth as "xl*s* . . . all men payd" (DL/C/218/292), she interpreted the spilling "a little payle of sudd*es*" not in terms of financial want but in terms of convenience: she was "somthing greeved and disquieted by the spilling of her water w*hi*ch was to make an end of her wasshing and by reason it was then night when she Could gett no more and for spilling the same in her howse having but one roome as afore sayd but not in respect of that needynes she had of . . . a penny or twoe pence to buy more" (DL/C/218/292).

As these cases indicate, deponents considered a variety of criteria simultaneously when they measured a person's worth. In a few cases, however, one criterion stood out much more prominently than others. Some deponents identified the transfer of land or money as determining whether a couple married.[4] As I cited in chapter 1, upon hearing Margery's uncle, Master Grey, say "she shall have no land of myne neither will I medle w*i*th her," Thomas Thorneworke "did utterly disclaime" Margery (DL/C/215/324*v*). In terms of money in the case of *Elizabeth Willson v. James Harrison*, the insufficiency of Elizabeth's portion stopped the union. Elizabeth's brother, Jeffrey offered to "give her what he was hable he would give her x*li* and afterward*es* sayd he would give her xx*tie* mark*es* And att last yelded he would make her worth xx*li*." However, "James Harrison and

Oliver White required xl^{li} and so they could not agree about the matter but so brake of and departed" (DL/C/215/385^v–386^r). Deponents in the case of *Katherine Jones v. William Tomlinson* recounted that a missed payment prevented their marriage. After greeting Katherine as his "wief before god" while sitting at dinner in his house at Pye Corner, William explained the financial arrangements of his union. John Cope deposed that William reported that he was to have "vi^{li} at the day of . . . [his] marriage" and "her frend*es* are bounde to paye . . . [him] xiiii^{li} more at a daye afterward*es*" (DL/C/216/26^r). Despite the contract, the missed payment of six pounds stopped the match in its tracks. William himself testified that if Katherine "had brought him . . . vi^{li} in money" he "should have married her." Since Katherine did not bring him the money, he "nev*er* ment to marrie w*i*th her while he lyved" (DL/C/216/83^r).

While Tomlinson's marrying was contigent on a payment, in some situations, as in the case involving Susan Jason alias Jackson, some widows insisted on financial securities regarding money and goods for their children before they would wed. Ann Breamer said that, despite the many attempts of William Payne to move her to marry him, she always answered that "for as muche as she being a widowe and having ii Children she would first have bothe her owne portion of goodes and her Childrens likewise sett downe and assured unto her before ever she would contract her selfe to any man" (DL/C/215/9^r). In another case, Joyce Griffin insisted that a bond be drawn up to protect her daughter. Going to a scrivener in Aldersgate, she told him that before marrying Ralph Grymes, who "is muche indebted," she "will have him bound." The scrivener, "according unto her instructions made a bond or obligac*i*on bearing dat the 21th of September 1608," specifying that her daughter, Fortune, was to receive "x^{li}" and "howshold stuff": "one Woolbed a woole bowlster ii feather pillowes and ii payer of good flaxen sheet*es*." A "daye or ii after" the scrivener "made the same bond," Joyce and Ralph went to his shop and "sealed" and "deliv*ered* it to the use of ffortune Griffin" (DL/C/218/447).

Although occupation alone did not usually play a major role in determining the suitability of a partner, it did in the case of *Ann Foote v. Lawrence Grimshawe*. Ann's parents cited that Lawrence's occupation was central in convincing them to grant their goodwill. Lawrence told Edmund Hawes that Ann, his stepdaughter, "is my wife and I am her husband though her frendes give her never a groate we must not p*ar*te till death do p*ar*te us or the lyke in effect and requested this Jurate to accompt of him as his sone." Edmund and his wife, Ann, "hearing all this and not knowing how to breake the matche . . . and knowing . . . [Lawrence] to be a scrivener and hoping he would take paines in his trade and be able to . . . lyve and mainteine the sayd Anne hereuppon at the last they graunted their good will that . . . [Lawrence] and Anne should be maried togither" (DL/C/219/136ʳ).

Few cases in these records contain individuals who based their choice of partner solely on blatant, economic self-interest. The basis of choice for Tide Clear was apparently in keeping with his name: very clear. In choosing his wife, Clear reportedly placed economic resources at the top of his list: "she hath xxˡⁱ and if she will by and by . . . or within these v dayes give mee xˡⁱ lett her bring her clothes and coom to me when she will and I will marry hir and mak her my wife." He reinforced such an interest by saying, "I will consent to nothing except I have the money first and lett hir bring me the money and I will be as good as my word" (DL/C/214/324). Elizabeth Spakman disagreed with his priorities: "if he like the mony better then he likes me lett him goe where he list" (DL/C/214/325). A few days later, when she met with him but did not bring the money, Tide abandoned his courtship, reportedly commenting that "I am glade of it this is the last day I am now free" (DL/C/214/325). Conversely, another witness reported that Elizabeth "had no great minde to him if she could have been ridd of him but he was earnes[t] with hir" (DL/C/214/384). While Elizabeth cited the insincerity of Tide's love for her, Anthony Mitchell assessed Tide as a suitable partner for her in terms of being able "to live well" with him and to have autonomy in the relationship: Elizabeth "beeing a good ancient maid wished that . . . she had a good husband," and Anthony "wished that she had Tide Clear" because she "may live well . . . and use him as . . . [she] list" (DL/C/214/323–24).

In addition to concerns regarding wealth, occupation, and status, deponents cited considerations of personal affection and age. In terms of the role that affection played in making a match in early modern England, Ingram notes that "personal attraction played a much mor significant role in matchmaking than contemporary moralists recommended or modern historians like Lawrence Stone have supposed" (*Church* 141).[5] Based on a detailed study of evidence from Wiltshire and Ely, he concludes that "something very close to our idea of 'romantic love', with all its heartaches and inconstancies, emerges quite strongly from the pages of depositions in matrimonial suits" ("Spousals" 50). Based on evidence from Norwich for 1450 to 1750, Houlbrooke reaches a similar conclusion: "Cases in the church courts reveal that passionate attachment was a common experience further down the social scale and suggest that the ideal of romantic love was deeply rooted in popular culture in the first half of our period" (*English* 78).

The records from the London Consistory Court provide many examples. In *Thomas Feild v. Agnes Howe*, Agnes' statement that love was necessary for marriage is similar to ones that can be found in many other depositions. Agnes' uncle Peter How testified that part of her denial that a contract existed between her and Thomas included her comment, "I would be lothe to Contract my selfe with one that I cannott love for it is not for a monethe nor a yeare but for one of . . . our lyves" (DL/C/216/51ᵛ). The Court of Arches heard this suit as well. In remaining notes from the case, Agnes' lack of love for Thomas was more explicitly stated. In addition to comments that she "never loved ffield, and could not abide his company," they include her saying, "shee would either kill her selfe or him rather then be maried to him, and be torne in pieces" (Lansdowne MS 131, 144ᵛ). In another case I cited in the previous chapter, the lack of "loving affection" was evidence that a match did not exist: "for ought that he . . . could ever see she the same Sara never had any loving affection towardes him the same Nathaniell Page" (DL/C/217/55). As the next two chapters discuss, these depositions contain a plethora of rich and provocative examples of behaviors exposing personal affection of couples before, during, and after marriage. For some, behavior was proof of the feelings: Thomas Clemence "hathe perceyved . . . for the space of this yeare and halfe Last past that ther hathe byn love and affection in the way of marriag betwene . . . Richard Thomas and Alice More by reason of very kynde familiarite betwene them" (DL/C/218/539).

Deponents citing a lack of personal affection between individuals as the basis to reject a suit further demonstrates that they believed it was a necessary component. Although Francis Norman "did divers tymes importune and sollicite" Alice Webster "to love him," she told him "that she did not nor Cold love him anie otherwise then she did other men" (DL/C/219/201ʳ). Likewise, Joan Mortimer rejected the suit of Richard Campion because she "could nott love hym" (DL/C/214/9). As I mentioned in the previous chapter, despite Katherine Freame telling Agnes Bushey "how farr the said Thomas Wye was in love with her," Agnes answered that "she was sory for itt and wished her to persuade hym from itt for that she could neither like nor love hym" (DL/C/213/805–06). Most cases that cited love as the reason for rejection most often cited the inability to love the other party; however, a few examples occur in which deponents cited insincere love as the reason the match was unsuitable. As seen earlier, Elizabeth Spakman pointed to the insincerity of Tide Clear's love for her, but the sincerity of his love for her money as a reason to reject his suit (DL/C/214/325). In a different suit, Agnes Hawke pointed to the insincerity of John

Bawcocke's affection: John "did shew some fained love to her which was not perfecte nor from his harte" (DL/C/213/470).

Deponents cited age less frequently than personal affection but more frequently than character. While parity in wealth, status, and affection were matters of choice and custom, canon law had specific rules regarding age for younger brides and grooms. The canons of 1604 mandated that children under the age of twenty-one must have the consent of parents or guardians in order to marry. As I noted in chapter 1, canon 100 stipulates, "No children under the age of one and twenty years complete shall contract themselves, or marry, without the consent of their parents, or of their guardians and governors, if their parents be deceased" (Edward Cardwell, *Synodalia* 304–05). According to the canons, marriage by license required parental consent regardless of the age of the couple.[6] While the canons attempted to strike some balance between individual and parental consent, the church courts did not always rule marriages formed without the consent outlined in the canons as invalid.

In light of these ecclesiastical mandates concerning a minimum marriage age it comes as no surprise that deponents sometimes pointed to the youth of a litigant as proof that a union was invalid. In addition to providing the physical age of a litigant, they sometimes pointed to "youth" without specifying a numerical age as a reason to reject the suit. In the case in chapter 1 of *Katherine Holmeden v. John Sherman*, William Morrell testified that Thomas Pyborne told John that Katherine "was no fitt matche for him in respect she was a Child" (DL/C/215/436ʳ). In some cases, "youth" made one unsuitable for a match due to one's inability to make well-informed choices. Susan Fidgett identified her age as the cause of her inability to understand the conversation between her suitor and her: "by reason . . . [she] was then very younge shee did not perceave . . . [Thomas Baines'] meaning towardes hir which as she afterwardes perceaved was to obtein hir goodwill in the way of marriage" (DL/C/214/171). Some references to age concerned a person's unreadiness for marriage. As I cited in chapter 1, Henry Hawke told a suitor his daughter was too young to be courted, both due to her physical and mental age (DL/C/213/487–88).

Contrastingly, canon law did not legislate a maximum age of marriage. Because the Solemnization of Matrimony and the Homily on Marriage both include that marriage was partly for procreation, one might expect the ecclesiastical mandates to stipulate a maximum age, especially in light of Keith Thomas' comment regarding popular attitudes toward the sexual relations of elderly spouses: "sexual relations between married couples too old to conceive children were regarded as harmful by doctors and of doubtful morality by some divines" (243). According to Thomas, these attitudes toward the marriages of elderly couples were more widespread than another Protestant doctrine that stated "comfortable society" was also an aim of marriage (243). However, since, as Wrightson points out, parity of age was one of several factors that "made the perfect match" (*English* 80), one might also expect that marriages between older individuals would be seen as "comely." Yet Thomas comments that "suspicion surrounded the marriage of the elderly" (243). For example, Henry Swinburne defends "the Marriage of the Aged from unlawfulness," but he could not "commend it for comliness" (50). He also comments on contemporary opinions regarding January-May marriages. Although "Marriages betwixt Youth and Age" are lawful, some people "utterly condemn" them "as a most unseemly, unequal, unpleasant, inconvenient, and perilous Match; the one Party desiring that thing most of all, which the other Party (of all things) is least able to perform." The possible consequences he details of the resulting frustrations include "continual Jars," "filthy Adulteries," and sometimes "cruel and wilful Murders" (46).

The extant London Consistory Court depositions are extremely valuable for attitudes in early modern London toward aged suitors and January-May pairings, since they offer another perspective. These deponents on the whole were neither ageist nor sexist in their assessments of the marital suitability of older individuals. While deponents did not embrace elderly suitors eagerly, pointing to their advanced years as an asset of maturity, experience, or material resources, they also did not reject suitors based solely on her or his advanced years. These records also do not contain statements in which deponents condemned marriages between elderly individuals as "uncomely." In addition, the deponents did not specify that the union of an older man with a younger woman was more or less favorable than an older woman with a younger man. Instead, deponents acknowledged that advanced age made someone an unsuitable partner only when a large disparity existed between the numerical ages of the potential partners *and* when other unequal factors were present.

Two women from the London depositions I mentioned previously in this chapter cited the disparity in age between them and their suitors as further proof of the unacceptablity of the match. Additional examples include Agnes Bushey, who pointed to her youth and the advanced age of her suitor as making him in part an unsuitable partner for her: "she did veryly thinke that *Master* wye loved her and was an honest gentleman, but he was an ould man and going owt of the

world and she younge and that his lyvinge laye att sea, which she
could nott away with, neither could she ever . . . marry with hym, nor
hate hym, but she knewe in her harte he was noe fitt matche for her"
(DL/C/213/829). While Agnes cited the advanced age of the suitor
Susan Atkinson pointed to her own advanced age: "she regarded
neyther there woordes nor the matter they went abowte being a match
unfitt that . . . [she] being an elderly woman . . . and having children
and charge of howse . . . sholde marry a boy and a prentize"
(DL/C/213/343). Both the younger woman and older woman
rejected suitors because of differences in occupations, economic
circumstances, and social positions in addition to age disparities.

Thomas Halle's concern with the disparity of age between him and
Margaret Horne suggests another category of criteria that deponents
cited in determining the suitability of a partner, "character." For
Thomas, his youth (he was aged twenty) indicated his vulnerability in
being taken advantage of by an "ould and ancient" woman—she was
"fiftie or fortie yeres" (DL/C/219/212ᵛ):

> beinge younge as aforesaid and being allured intised and drawen unto
> lewdnes by the said Margarett . . . and beinge afterwardes feared and
> terrified by her and her freindes to make his freindes and parentes
> acquainted therwith and to drawe him into question publiqely to
> shame him did Confesse that he had the use of the bodie of the said
> Margarett . . . and by reason of her and her freindes threates
> did . . . write to Oxford for to have a license to marry hir and the said
> Margarett but presently afterwardes understandinge of the badd and
> lewd liefe that the said Margarett had longe lived in and his freindes
> uttered dislikinge that he should marry with soe ould and soe lewd a
> person hath and did refuse to marry her. (DL/C/219/213ʳ)

Deponents cited character as a consideration in only a few cases,
and the specific criteria that made someone's character suitable or
unsuitable varied in terms of gender. In her examination of the
London Consistory Court depositions for a longer chronological
period than I am studying, Gowing comments on the role sexual honesty played in selecting a mate:

> More influential for some men than these concerns of status was the
> issue of the moral reputation of their prospective wives. But given the
> stress laid on sexual honesty in contemporary definitions of femininity,
> the disputes over disrupted courtships devote a surprisingly little
> amount of attention to women's sexual chastity. Those men who
> claimed the collapse of a betrothal was due to a woman's unchastity

argued that they had made chastity and virtue, as other people did
financial standing, a condition of the match. (171)

As she notes, such stress on the sexual honesty of a woman as a
requirement for a match appears in only a few cases in the depositions.
This concern regarding sexual honesty, though rare in the depositions
from matrimonial enforcement suits, appears mainly in the few
comments regarding character. As in the above case, Thomas' testimony
suggests that Margaret's sexuality was the source of her "lewdness"
and in part, of her unsuitability. Likewise, although James Flussher
"once thought well" of Margaret Hall, "he had heard so ill report of
hir that he had given her over" (DL/C/214/433). As a witness testified in his behalf, the change in the relations between the couple
resulted, according to James, from "hir unhappy tonge for thear is no
such matter beetween us, but so long as I give hir maintenance she
was quiett and now bycause I give hir nothing that is the cause, and
indeed I have heard that she is a lewd woman and hath been nought
with tenn men" (DL/C/214/432). In another suit, Oliver
Hasseldon testified to the lewd behavior of Ann Keningham alias
Terrill: "by the space of these 6 yeares last past," Ann "hath byn and is
a woman of ill report and accompted to have bene of lewd behaviour
and . . . an incontinent person of her body and namely he heard it
often reported in St Katherines parishe by the Tower where she did
and doth dwell tha[t] she hath lyved incontinently and committed
adultery [and] fornication with an other dutche man a . . . smithe
dyvers tymes and that she had a bastard borne of her bodie begotten
by the sayd smithe" (DL/C/218/5–6). In another case, William
Breeche testified that, after living with his wife, Margaret Miller, for
one year, he "lawfully seperated" from her "for notorius adulterie by
her comitted and confessed" (DL/C/215/210ᵛ). In the case of
Thomas Harrys v. Ann Payne alias Harris alias Bull cited above, Ann
was not rejected because of her reputation regarding her sexual activ-
ities; instead, she tried to preserve it. Ann testified to how she had not
lived with Thomas after the "supposed mariage," but moved in with
him later after she was impregnated by another man to protect her
reputation: "about vii viii or ten yeares after the tyme of the supposed
mariage," she "(whoe Continually had lived from the saide Harrys)
finding her selfe to be with childe by another man, to save her creditt as shee thought repayred to the said Harrys to his howse in old
Radnor and there lyved with him in his howse at bedd and at bord by
the space of three quarters of a yeare for the moste parte and noe
more but duringe all that tyme the saide Harrys never had the Carnall

knowledge of her bodye" (DL/C/216/369ᵛ). The depositions indicate that some people assessed the character of men differently than of women as it related to suitability for marriage. While explaining why Richard Houghton was an unfit match for Katherine Hawes alias Mone, Richard Jacob cited Houghton's sexual behaviors by noting that he courted "div*er*s women in the way of marriage" such as "Captayne winters mayd," "Joane Loughton," and "a widow at St Katherines," one of these courtships resulting in a child (DL/C/214/549). However, unlike the cases I cited above that relate to marriage, Jacob failed to cite Houghton's sexual behavior as evidence against the match. Nonetheless, he raised the issue.

In three other cases, deception ruled men out as suitable partners although honesty or reputation was not openly identified with sexuality as it was in the above cases. The testimony of Mary Phillips included Alan Carr's desire to protect his reputation in not marrying Helen Vaughan: "Carr was very unwilling to be maried at yᵗ time unto hir . . . yf he Could have tould how to have escaped it w*i*th his Creditt and honestie for he seemed to be verie fearfull of some impeachm*en* of his Credit by reason of speaches she the same . . . [Helen] had used unto him" (DL/C/215/88ʳ). In addition, in a case I cited earlier Agnes Howe's father determined that the "honesty" of Thomas Feild made him a suitable partner for his daughter (DL/C/216/51ʳ). Yet, as Agnes testified, in a passage I cited earlier, after their contract she discovered that Thomas "is not so honest a man as he was reported to be" (DL/C/216/48ᵛ). In this case, Agnes assessed his "honesty" in relation to deception rather than sexuality. In yet another case, while Elizabeth Willson's brother cited the occupation of James Harrison as a reason why he was an unsuitable match, she refused him because of a prior deception: "abowt the monethes of January ffebruary or March 1597," James, who was "before acquainted w*i*th the ar*ticu*lat Elizabeth Willson," came "by her as she satt on a bentch at her brothers dore had some speech and conference w*i*th her and asked her yf she Could finde in her hart to accept and like of him for her husband." She responded to his proposal saying "that he had deceived her once and she would trust him noe more" (DL/C/215/343ᵛ). (Interestingly, the words of Elizabeth are contemporary with those of Beatrice in *Much Ado About Nothing* who says of Benedick, "Indeed, my lord, he lent it me awhile, and I gave him use for it, a double hear for his single one. Marry, once before he won it of me with false dice, therefore your Grace may well say I have lost it" (2.1.261–64).)

While Gowing notes how surprising it is that the records do not contain more references to sexual honesty, it is also noteworthy that few deponents cited marital history as a criterion that made men or women more attractive. This rarity is surprising particularly because of the stereotypes in contemporary literary texts of the remarrying widow, specifically in light of the popular view that suitors sought widows because of their money or sexual appetites. Kathryn Jacobs discusses the source of this stereotype: "it was social ambition and wishful thinking, more than precedent or practice, that put the lusty widow on so many Renaissance stages, and kept poor ones off it" (134). Jennifer Panek identifies sexual empowerment rather than ambition and economics as the source of this stereotype: "men sought to empower themselves by deploying the lusty widow stereotype in ways which foregrounded not only the widow's sexual susceptibility, but their virility—their ability to arouse a woman, satisfy her, even impregnate her" (200). In her discussion of these stereotypes with regard to the marriage practices of the women of Abingdon, Berkshire, between 1540 and 1720, Barbara J. Todd points out the contradictory attitudes toward widows in early modern England. Todd notes the theoretical and practical ways in which a widow could upset social order: "The woman heading her own household contra-dicted the patriarchal theory; the ungoverned woman was a threat to the social order" and "without the support of a man's earnings she and her family were likely to become a financial burden on the com-munity." Yet, if a widow remarried, she also can be seen to upset social order: "the remarriage of any widow confronted every man with the threatening prospect of his own death and the entry of another into his place" ("Remarrying" 55). Compared to many depictions of wid-ows in contemporary literary texts, the depositions are surprisingly silent in terms of either widows self-consciously considering financial, physical, or emotional needs when accepting or rejecting a suitor or suitors self-consciously considering the attractiveness of a widow—in terms of herself, her money, or her position—when accepting or rejecting a widow as a marriage partner.[7] One case in particular seems to indicate a woman was chosen because of her status as a widow alone. Joan Johnson was one of several witnesses who testified that Richard Warren "was before a stranger to . . . [Margaret Perry alias More]. . . concerninge any intent of being a suter to her in the way of marriage" (DL/C/219/85ᵛ). Despite this unfamiliarity, Richard became interested in Margaret because of her marital status:

> Warren came in . . . while they were at supper and went at ye first to . . . Margaret More *alias* Perry where she sat at the board and asked her if she were a widowe and she sayd I where upon he sayd it was not

fit she should sit there and tooke her up to the upper end of the table and sate downe there togither and spent all this comunicaion with her, and was before a stranger to her. (DL/C/219/85ᵛ)

This "comunicaion" resulted, according to several witnesses, in a *verba de praesenti* contract. In another case I cited earlier, Elizabeth Spakman, without detailing her reasons, pointed to Mary Robinson's marital status as a widow as making her a more suitable partner for Tide Clear. After Elizabeth told Mary that Tide "had made suit unto hir . . . in the way of marrage," she noted that "yow are an widow and he is more fitt for yow then for mee." Mary's reply that Tide "was not unmeet for" Elizabeth "having . . . a howse to bring hir unto" may suggest why Elizabeth thought he was a more appropriate match for Mary. That is, Elizabeth may have identified his suitability in terms of meeting Mary's financial need due to her marital status as a widow (DL/C/214/383–84). Comments regarding widowers are even more rare than those few regarding widows (DL/C/218/293).

The evidence from the depositions demonstrates that only a few widows considered the timing of the marriage in determining the suitability of a match. Nevertheless, this concern occasionally emerged. In the case of *Robert Archer v. Bridget Iles*, three witnesses testified that social etiquette was the basis of Bridget's concern over the timing of her contract with Robert with respect to her late husband's death. However, Bridget told a different story. In her testimony, her concern over the timing of her husband's death lay not with social etiquette but with the need to straighten out her finances: "a fortnight" after the death of her husband, Robert "did move and sollicitt" her "for her good will in the waie of mariage." She responded that "she had noe minde at all of mariage" because her financial arrangements took priority: "she must first paie her husbandes debtes and provide for her Children before she wold or Cold sett her minde of mariage with any man" (DL/C/216/309ʳ).

In addition to other factors, marital history came into play in some cases regarding previous contracts or the return of a spouse who was considered deceased. In the case of previous contracts, Hase Gowldinge testified how she "Lawfully divorsed" her husband Richard Gowlding since he "was contracted to an other woman named Elizabeth before he and she . . . weare married or contracted togither" (DL/C/215/152ᵛ). In another case, Christopher Purk discovered that his new bride was not "free from all men." He testified that when he married Joan Praise "hee took . . . [her] for a widdow and to bee free from all men as shee her self then confessed." Yet, "contrarie to his knowledge," Joan "was within two dayes after the marriage all the day in companie" with Henry Procktor and "afterward she robbed" Christopher "of a great deal of linnen and other substance and went away from him." Even though Christopher and Joan "did consumate the matrimonie solempinzed . . . beetween them," he will "never hearafter accompt hir . . . for his wife" (DL/C/214/265).

With regard to a different, but related issue, several cases appear in which one party married another assuming that a prior spouse was dead. Margaret Borrowghs testified that Jane Buck alias Burton thought her husband Thomas Burton "had bene dead because he came not home" for the space of two years. Less than six weeks after Jane had been living with her new husband, Richard Buck, Margaret said that Thomas came to their house in St. Sepulchre's Parish and after Thomas "perceaved that she had gott . . . a new husband he went from her agayne" (DL/C/213/340). In another case, Ann Dixon alias Tailer alias Mills testified that while living with her then husband John Taylor for "almost a yeare," she had another living husband, Matthew Newton, "who she had heard was dead but it fell out otherwise."After discovering her mistake, she left her then husband for Matthew: she "cominge up to London mett with him and went over sea with him . . . in to Utrick wheare she sayeth he the same Mathew Newton dyed after they had continued together in Utrick about xvi yeares" (DL/C/214/647).

TWO SHAKESPEAREAN COMEDIES

When reading Shakespeare's *The Two Gentlemen of Verona* and *Twelfth Night* in light of the London Consistory Court depositions, some provocative similarities and differences emerge in terms of the kinds of criteria that deponents and dramatic figures cite, patterns which deepen our understanding of courtship in early modern London. As with the deponents in the depositions, the dramatic figures in these two plays cite a variety of criteria in assessing suitability. In addition to Olivia's assessment of why she cannot love Orsino (1.5.261–67)—to be considered in more detail later—which includes his character, status, estate, age, and appearance, Thurio and Proteus discuss Thurio's suitability for Silvia in terms of his physical appearance, discourse, valor, birth, and possessions (5.2.1–29). Valentine considers similar categories of criteria when assessing Thurio in front of the Duke: "sure the match / Were rich and honourable. Besides, the gentleman / Is full of virtue, bounty, worth, and qualities / Beseeming such a wife as your fair daughter" (3.1.63–66).[8] In addition to the variety, the kinds of categories deponents and dramatic figures cite ar generally similar. However, while the categories of suitability criteria recorded in the Consistory Court and recited to audiences or read by readers of these two plays are generally the same, the emphasis on the criteria differs between the legal and literary texts. In these two plays, considerations of personal affection, character, and physical appearance play a much more significant role than worth and age in assessing suitability when compared with the assessments in the depositions.

Dramatic figures who identify the criteria that influence their choices can be found in *The Two Gentlemen of Verona* and *Twelfth Night* and in other Shakespeare comedies such as *The Taming of the Shrew*, *Much Ado About Nothing*, and *A Midsummer Night's Dream*. Still, *Twelfth Night* is particularly rich when considering suitability criteria, especially given the number of suitors who are interested in Olivia. Not surprisingly, most of the comments concerning criteria in this play are made by or about her and her suitors regarding either her attractiveness to them or their attractiveness to her. However, not all the dramatic figures involved in wooing Olivia comment on her suitability. Neither Sebastian nor Sir Andrew Aguecheek identify the specific qualities of Olivia that either think make her a suitable partner Similarly, Olivia herself does not comment, although Maria does, on the suitability of Malvolio and Sir Andrew for her, suggesting that she does not seriously consider either as a prospective partner.[10] Readers often provide criteria to support their opinions in regard to the suitability or unsuitability of some of the matches in the play when such silence occurs. Marilyn L. Williamson comments on the lack of profit motive present in the union of Sebastian and Olivia: "Sebastian's marriage to her is a lucky accident which he rapidly accepts, another effect which denies the profit motive" (31). But does the speed with which he accepts her proposal "deny the profit motive"? In addition, although Maria, as L. Caitlin Jorgensen points out, "achieves a marriage with Sir Toby that will take her from a servant's position to one in which she will be mistress of servants" (76–77), Maria remains silent in regard to the specific criteria on which she determines Sir Toby's suitability. Concerning this union, Ann Jennalie Cook argues that "while some of lesser status do wed their social betters, not one of them actively pursues such advancement" (*Making* 62). Was a desire for advancement in social status, for which Maria criticizes Malvolio, a major consideration for her?[11] As the discussion of criteria in the depositions centers on what the deponents themselves cited, here too the discussion of criteria in these two dramas focuses on what the dramatic figures themselves identify as determining suitability.

Before looking at the suitability criteria in these two plays, we should note that the criteria in these two comedies is closer to that in the depositions than to the law, since we do not see dramatic figures worrying about consanguinity, religion, and the like, although Viola suggests that marital status does play a role in her attraction to Orsino: "Orsino! I have heard my father name him. / He was a bachelor then" (1.2.28–29). Although these plays mention more determinants of suitability seen in the depositions than in the letter of the law, once again the emphasis on the specific criteria which determine suitability in the plays does not clearly reflect those mentioned in the depositions. However, in order to compare better the differences and similarities between the legal and literary texts, my discussion of the categories of criteria in the plays follows the order I used with the depositions.

A major difference exists between the two plays and the depositions in terms of the emphasis on worth. As I mentioned earlier, many deponents stressed the economic disparity of a couple as a reason why a match should not go forward. While in both the plays and the depositions financial self-interest as the sole motivator is rare, most dramatic figures, regardless of class, in these two comedies overlook status and economic parity or disparity more than do the witnesses and litigants in the London Consistory Court. Only a couple of the dramatic figures in *The Two Gentlemen of Verona* consider economic resources as crucial in determining the suitability of a match for Silvia.[12] Valentine identifies wealth as the criterion which makes the Duke consider Thurio a welcome suitor to Silvia: "My foolish rival that her father likes / (Only for his possessions are so huge)" (2.4.170–71). However, the dramatic action does not support wealth as a primary determinant. Thurio expresses his disinterest in Silvia because of her lack of affection for him. Her father then reorganizes his priorities deciding that he can measure Valentine's worth differently. Rather than material items, his spirit and birth determine his worth: "Now, by the honour of my ancestry, / I do applaud thy spirit, Valentine, / And think thee worthy of an empress' love: / Know then, I here forget all former griefs, / Cancel all grudge, repeal thee home again, / Plead a new state in thy unrivall'd merit, / To which I thus subscribe: Sir Valentine, / Thou art a gentleman, and well deriv'd, / Take thou thy Silvia, for thou hast deserv'd her" (5.4.137–45).

A dramatic figure in this play assesses suitability in terms of wealth. In his catalog of "conditions," Launce may at first appear to assess the milkmaid's suitability in terms of her domestic abilities rather than in terms of her wealth; yet her wealth is the deciding factor. She can "fetch and carry," "she can milk," "she brews good ale," "she can sew," "she can knit," "she can wash and scour," "she can spin," and "she hath many nameless virtues." Yet he is also aware of her vices: "she is not to be kissed fasting in respect of her breath," "she doth talk in her sleep," "she is slow in words," "she is proud," "she hath no teeth," "she is curst," "she will often praise her liquor," "she is too liberal," "she hath more hair than wit," and she has "more faults than hairs" (3.1.261–360). Although he sees her vices as numerous as her virtues, her wealth makes her faults acceptable. As Speed reads that she has "more wealth than faults," Launce concludes "Why, that word makes the faults gracious. Well, I'll have her" (3.1.357–59). Cook labels his catalog as a "burlesque" of "individuals at this social level": "perhaps the most ridiculous and certainly the most detailed description of a lowly love is Lance's milkmaid in *The Two Gentlemen of Verona* (III.i.271–355) . . . . From Lance comes a catalogue of qualities burlesquing individuals at this social level—domestic skills like milking, brewing, scouring, spinning; personal defects like bad breath, toothlessness, and promiscuity" (*Making* 93–94). Even if one sees his catalog of criteria as a "burlesque," he is the dramatic figure in this play who has the most lines devoted to weighing the qualities which will determine the suitability of his spouse. Alexander Leggatt comments on the practicality of his assessment: "Launce speaks less directly to the lovers, but his own courtship, in which wealth becomes the deciding factor (III.i.293–360), reminds us of the practical side of marriage, hardly touched on by the lovers" (23). Launce's consideration of wealth is more in keeping with the behaviors found in the depositions.

In *Twelfth Night*, regardless of class standing, the figures are mainly unconcerned with the wealth or financial worth of a mate. While Toby mentions Andrew's financial suitability along with other qualities of education and breeding that make him a suitable match for Olivia (1.3.20–43), his comment about wealth can be seen to mark Andrew's suitability for Toby rather than Olivia, since Andrew's monies fund Toby's drinking. In terms of the wealth of Olivia, Stephen Greenblatt comments on the pattern of marrying for wealth in the play: "The lady richly left was a major male wish-fulfillment fantasy in a culture where the pursuit of wealth through marriage was an avowed and reputable preoccupation. Here the fantasy is at its most dreamlike because it focuses not on a widow—the only group whose members actually corresponded on infrequent occasion to this daydream—but on 'a virtuous maid' (1.2.36)" (*Shakespearean* 69). Yet many figures deny or do not cite Olivia's wealth as a criterion when assessing suitability. Orsino denies the importance of Olivia's wealth as the basis of his choice and, since he proposes to Viola, parity in wealth and status is clearly not high on his criteria list. Orsino acknowledges the criteria which attracts him to Olivia while he singles out the one that makes her the most attractive. The source of her purging "the air of pestilence" is not her wealth, but her beauty (1.1.20). As he advises Viola, "Once more, Cesario, / Get thee to yond same sovereign cruelty. / Tell her my love, more noble than the world, / Prizes not quantity of dirty lands; / The parts that fortune hath bestow'd upon her, / Tell her I hold as giddily as fortune: / But 'tis that miracle and queen of gems / That nature pranks her in, attracts my soul" (2.4.80–87). The silence of Sebastian and Sir Andrew in regard to Olivia's wealth and status as determining her suitability may seem all the more surprising in light of the behaviors reflected in the depositions.

One criterion that some dramatic figures use to assess suitability is that of status.[13] Critics often point to the ambiguity of status for the male suitors in *The Two Gentlemen of Verona*. To cite two examples, Ralph Berry writes that " 'Sir' seems a formal term of respect and standing, rather than a precise signification of rank. . . . *The Two Gentlemen of Verona* is an early, and extreme, instance of Shakespeare's playing very freely with time and place: he plays with rank, too. . . . It may be true that the text represents several strata of composition. Still, Shakespeare habitually avoids a system of direct correspondences with English social orderings" (18). Cook also comments on the arbitrariness of status in this play; however, she sees this randomness in regard to the male suitors as appropriate to and indicative of their courting behavior:

> Valentine violates his lord's trust by wooing Sylvia secretly and later offers to hand her over to Proteus—who betrays his closest friend, deceives both the Duke and Thurio, breaks his vows to Julia, forces his suit on Sylvia, and finally attempts to rape her in the forest. The play's farcically improbable events, during which the same girl is casually passed back and forth among all three unworthy suitors, make it comically appropriate to bestow her upon Valentine, reduced to a penniless outlaw chief. In this mad world, rank scarcely matters, although the Duke takes great care at the end to degrade Thurio, to evaluate Valentine, and to recapitulate his own and Sylvia's status. . . . Like his rivals, Valentine no more deserves this—or any—lady than he deserves to be called a gentleman. In such a context, the grotesque social mismatch emphasizes the obvious discrepancies upon which the play's perverse humor depends. (*Making* 55)

As these two critics underscore, the dramatic figures in the play do not point to social status as a criterion when assessing suitability. Neither Julia in her pursuit of Proteus nor Silvia in her pursuit of Valentine and rejection of Proteus articulate their choices in terms of status. Likewise, the male suitors do not stress the status of either woman as determining suitability. Such disregard for status seen in this play differs from the criteria found in the depositions.

In *Twelfth Night*, social status plays a more prominent role as a criterion determining suitability than in *The Two Gentlemen of Verona*.[14] Some dramatic figures measure suitability in part by the position of the partner in terms of maintaining or gaining authority. Malvolio includes a position of authority as a criterion on which he bases his choice of wife; however, Malvolio's interest in authority lies not in marking hers but in calculating what he would attain by becoming the husband of one in such a place (2.5.35–81). In addition, Olivia marries someone who, as she points out, acknowledged both in speech and behavior her authority in the union. Olivia, the countess, and Silvia, the future duchess, marry men below their statuses, which allows them to maintain their positions, unlike Viola who marries a man she "call'd . . . master for so long" (5.1.323). C. L. Barber discounts this possibility in regard to Olivia: "We might wonder whether this spoiled and dominating young heiress may not have been attracted by what she could hope to dominate in Cesario's youth— but it was not the habit of Shakespeare's age to look for such implications" (245–46). The text, however, indicates such a possibility. Sir Toby's earlier reassurance to Sir Andrew foretold Olivia's action: "She'll none o'th' Count; she'll not match above her degree, neither in estate, years, nor wit; I have heard her swear't" (1.3.106–08).[15] While Olivia neither self-consciously comments that her choice of mate depends on her ability to maintain her position nor marries a ninny with a weakness of character in order to retain her dominance, she allows Viola to enter her house only after she hears his words which suggest an acknowledgment of his place in relation to hers; hence, Helene Moglen's comment that "the efficient head of a complicated household, Olivia does not want to surrender her masculine dominance . . . . She is willing to speak with Cesario because he is unthreatening" (16). Olivia admits him and listens to this messenger not only because he is "unthreatening" but also because this messenger specifically acknowledges Olivia's position in relation to his. This reading differs from that of others who identify the cause of Olivia admitting Viola in terms of her attraction to his "audacity . . . to be 'saucy at . . . [her] gates' " (Michael Shapiro 158), his "very youthful appearance" (Richard A. Levin 124), his "youth" (Leggatt 225), his "secret allure" (John Kerrigan 73), or "her adventurous, plucky, give-as-good-as-you-get braggartry" (Ruth Nevo 207).

However, the youth and appearance of Viola do not move Olivia to admit him. After hearing from Maria that a "young gentleman" and "a fair young man" is at the gate who "desires to speak with" her, Olivia still instructs Malvolio to tell the messenger that "If it be a suit from the Count, I am sick, or not at home. What you will, to dismiss it" (1.5.108–10). Even when Malvolio details the insistence of Viola to speak with Olivia, culminating in his assessment that Viola is "fortified against any denial" (1.5.146–47), Olivia still refuses him entrance: "Tell him, he shall not speak with me" (1.5.148). Only upon hearing Malvolio's repeating of Viola's lines suggesting their respective positions—"he says he'll stand at your door like a sheriff's post, and be the supporter to a bench, but he'll speak with you" (1.5.149–51)—does Olivia show any interest in the messenger and asks "What kind o'man is he?" (1.5.152). It is the marker to her authority that finally changes her mind. This interest clarifies and confirms what Toby pointed out in Act 1, scene 3 about her assessment of suitability. By not wanting to match above her, it may suggest she wants an equal match or one in which she takes the upper position. Here, she clarifies that she wants to have the authority in the union. Toward the end of her initial conference with Viola, when Olivia takes a fancy to Viola, she questions him as to his parentage, thereby inquiring into his social status and wealth (1.5.281–83). The timing of this inquiry, after she is interested in him, and her following "five-fold blazon" speech at the end of the scene indicate that economic and social considerations are not on the top of her suitability list. As the speech details, her evaluation of his suitability extends beyond his worth resulting from his parentage into his person, character, and abilities, since she catalogues the markers of his gentility by referring to his "tongue," "face," "limbs, actions, and spirit" (1.5.296).

The play further confirms Olivia's desire for authority in a match in Acts 4 and 5. When she meets who she thinks is Cesario, she points out more directly her desire for authority: "Nay, come, I prithee; would thou'dst be rul'd by me!" To Sebastian's response "Madam, I will," she reaffirms this desire: "O, say so, and so be" (4.1.63–64). In Act 5, after the Priest discloses her marriage to Sebastian, she refers to her sole ownership of her property and finances, despite the joining of their respective estates through marriage: "One day shall crown th'alliance on't, so please you, / Here at my house, and at my proper cost" (5.1.317–18).

John W. Draper comments on Olivia's ability to maintain her autonomy after marriage: "But Olivia, for all her grand passion, apparently does not quite succumb; and, like Mistress Page and Mistress Ford on their humbler social plane, she proposes after marriage to be at least partly her own master; and, with a cleverness for which critics give her little credit, without help of friends or relatives—in fact, in spite of them— she marries herself according to her wish" ("Wooing" 45). The use of the single rather than plural pronouns suggests she is more than "at least partly her own master." Instead, she maintains rather than relinquishes her control.[16] The ease with which Olivia mistakes Sebastian for Viola, a substitution that makes many readers uncomfortable with the ending,[17] may suggest how important this criterion is to Olivia both in accepting Sebastian and in rejecting Orsino.

In *The Two Gentlemen of Verona* and *Twelfth Night*, dramatic figures identify personal affection as a higher-ranking determinant than deponents. William G. Meader points to the primacy of love for unions in Shakespeare's dramas: "Love and the opportunity are all that are necessary to marriage in Shakespeare's plays" (137).[18] Love is a criterion which often appears in *The Two Gentlemen of Verona*. In Act 1, scene 2, when Lucetta and Julia discuss the qualities of Julia's potential mates, they discuss Proteus in terms of the extent to which he has shown his love to her, not in terms of his age, his estate, or his wealth (14–33). Similarly, before she leaves as Sebastian to follow him, Julia again praises Proteus, ironically, for the sincerity of his love, not the value of his estate: "His words are bonds, his oaths are oracles, / His love sincere, his thoughts immaculate, / His tears pure messengers sent from his heart, / His heart as far from fraud as heaven from earth" (2.7.75–78). When she as Sebastian confronts Proteus about the woman he ignores, she again focuses on love as the link between Julia and Proteus: "methinks that she lov'd you as well / As you do love your lady Silvia: / She dreams on him that has forgot her love, / You dote on her that cares not for your love" (4.4.79–82). Likewise, in Act 1, scenes 1 and 3, Proteus talks of Julia in terms of his love for her rather than her estate or character. Only after Julia disguises herself as Sebastian does Proteus comment on other qualities, comments he makes about Sebastian not Julia: "For 'tis no trusting to yond foolish lout; / But chiefly for thy face, and thy behaviour, / Which (if my augury deceive me not) / Witness good bringing up, fortune, and truth" (4.4.65–68). Even though Proteus himself questions what has made him love Silvia—"Is it mine eye, or Valentinus' praise, / Her true perfection, or my false transgression, / That makes me reasonless, to reason thus?" (2.4.192–94)— he determines Silvia's suitability in terms of his personal affection: "but

I love his lady too-too much" (2.4.201). When stressing to Proteus that she has chosen Valentine, Silvia points to the basis of this selection as her personal affection for him, not his character, physical appearance, status, or estate: "O heaven be judge how I love Valentine, / Whose life's as tender to me as my soul" (5.4.36–37). The lack of personal affection, rather than wealth or character, as mentioned earlier, also causes Thurio to give up his suit to Silvia. Despite the Duke's pressure on Silvia to marry Sir Thurio, the Duke cannot "win her to fancy him" (3.1.67). Thurio himself drops his suit to her because of her lack of affection for him: "Sir Valentine, I care not for her, I: / I hold him but a fool that will endanger / His body for a girl that loves him not. / I claim her not, and therefore she is thine" (5.4.130–33). The Duke considers this criterion a "slight" one: "The more degenerate and base art thou / To make such means for her, as thou hast done, / And leave her on such slight conditions" (5.4.134–36).

Dramatic figures in *Twelfth Night* point to love as the basis of their mate selection as well. Cook comments on this pattern in *As You Like It* and *Twelfth Night* in particular: "In two of the middle comedies, not only is rank taken lightly, but so are practical questions of portions and jointures. . . . Not even in comic fictions do married folk live on love alone, although the festive worlds of *Twelfth Night* and *As You Like It* downplay the importance of wealth in affairs of the heart" (*Making* 133–34). Similarly, Malcolmson identifies the primacy of love in determining suitability in this play, noting "the desire of an inferior to be matched with a superior is acceptable as long as it is motivated by love" (39). However, Levin questions the role that personal affection plays in determining suitability for many of the couples in the play: "If Orsino, Olivia, and Sir Toby cannot be said to love their mates, perhaps it is also true that their mates do not love them. Sebastian eagerly accepts his fortune, while Viola and Maria plot theirs" (151). As I noted earlier, Sebastian and Maria remain silent in regard to the criteria on which they base their choice. Yet Viola, at the end of the play, expresses her affection. Rather than provide a catalog of Orsino's attributes as does Olivia, Viola comments on his marital status, as noted earlier, and on her love for him. Levin notes how Viola is silent with respect to any attraction in Act 1, scene 4: "Critics often assume that Viola has fallen in love with the duke. Perhaps she has. All she says at the moment is that she 'would be' Orsino's wife (42)" (122–23). However, in Act 5, scene 1 she is more verbal in this regard. Viola's response to Olivia's query of "Where goes Cesario?" points to her feelings: "After him I love / More than I love these eyes, more than my life, / More, by all mores, than e'er I shall love wife. / If

I do feign, you witnesses above / Punish my life, for tainting of my love" (132–36). Orsino expresses his love for Olivia in similar terms throughout the play. Because his love for Olivia is "as hungry as the sea, / And can digest as much," he advises Viola to "make no compare / Between that love a woman can bear me / And that I owe Olivia" (2.4.101–04). As deponents do in the depositions, Olivia points to this criterion as the basis on which she determines Orsino is an unsuitable match for her, although her lack of affection does not dissuade him. The specific criteria in Olivia's list echoes those found in the depositions, since she mentions such considerations as his worth, age, and character: "Your lord does know my mind, I cannot love him. / Yet I suppose him virtuous, know him noble, / Of great estate, of fresh and stainless youth; / In voices well divulg'd, free, learn'd, and valiant, / And in dimension, and the shape of nature, / A gracious person. But yet I cannot love him: / He might have took his answer long ago" (1.5.261–67). Penny Rixon comments on Olivia's practical view of marriage: "It is noteworthy that here Olivia is appealing to criteria—economic, social and temperamental compatibility—characteristic of a realistic rather than a romantic attitude to marriage" (194). Yet, despite all Orsino's attractive features, Olivia points to her lack of love for him as the basis of her rejection.

In contrast with the deponents testifying in the London Consistor Court, dramatic characters tend to de-emphasize parity of age and to place more emphasis on character as criteria for making a match. While neither of the plays under discussion provides numerical ages for the potential partners, the main couples seem relatively close in age. Cook argues, however, that the circumstances of *Twelfth Night* determine that the ages of Viola, Sebastian, and Olivia must be "at least twenty-one": "In a borderline case like Viola's, the Elizabethan audience would know at once that the voyage which shipwrecks her in Illyria could not have been made under her brother's sole protection, nor could Sebastian independently accept a proposal from Olivia, unless the twins were at least twenty-one. The same holds true for Olivia, who heads her own household after her brother's death and contracts a marriage for herself" (*Making* 32). Meader proposes a younger age for Viola: Viola "claims to have been thirteen when her father died. At that time she was with her brother Sebastian. Possibly they began their sea voyage as a result of their father's death. If so, the age of fifteen would not sit heavily on Viola" (55). In light of the behaviors from early modern London recorded in the depositions, despite the ecclesiastical mandates, the twins and Olivia, who seems more mature than the twins, need not be "at least twenty-one" to accept a proposal or contract a marriage. In fact, the letter of canon law allowed couples to contract marriage after fourteen for the male and twelve for the female. Another difference between the depositions and the plays is that dramatic figures do not reject potential partners because of their ages. Cook notes that "with the ages of wooers," Shakespeare "seems content to work out the consequences of any particular situation according to the requirements of its dramatic context" (*Making* 47–48). Age plays a role, however, in Orsino's advice on the required criteria in choosing a mate, since he advises Viola that men should love a younger woman, which he apparently does (2.4.27–39). This advice suggests the necessity for an age disparity between a bride and groom.

As with personal affection, character plays a more determining role overall in selecting partners in these two plays than in the depositions. However, as in the depositions, sexual honesty of women in these two dramas does not play a large part in making them suitable partners. While Olivia worries that Viola has "set . . . [her] honour at the stake" (3.1.120) and that she has "laid . . . [her] honour too unchary out" (3.4.204), she nonetheless declares her love to Viola in these scenes. Edmund M. Taft comments on how Olivia's desire to express her love is more important than her modesty in Act 3, scene 1: "she leaps over such barriers as modesty, custom, and the fear of disdain because secret suffering is no longer valued but intolerable" (411). In addition, Julia in *The Two Gentlemen of Verona* comments on a woman's choice being influenced by modesty—"Since maids, in modesty, say 'no' to that / Which they would have the profferer construe 'ay' " (1.2.55–56). Yet, in regard to her reputation for honesty, she expresses more concern over how her disguise will affect her reputation in general than to how, specifically, it will influence her suitability for Proteus. She asks Lucetta, "tell me some good mean / How with my honour I may undertake / A journey to my loving Proteus" (2.7.5–7) and "how will the world repute me / For undertaking so unstaid a journey? / I fear me it will make me scandalis'd" (2.7.59–61). Despite her concerns, rather than discourage the suit of Proteus, her disguise helps her to win back his love. Proteus, however, makes a more direct connection by linking love and honor. In reacting to her letter, he comments: "Here is her hand, the agent of her heart; / Here is her oath for love, her honour's pawn" (1.3.46–47). At another point in this play, Speed points to Silvia's concern for her modesty as a possible reason why she did not write to Valentine herself but had him write a letter to himself (2.1.155).

Character is an important consideration in other instances as well. The Duke in *The Two Gentlemen of Verona* ultimately decides that Valentine's character makes him worthy of Silvia: "I do applaud thy spirit, Valentine, / And think thee worthy of an empress' love: / . . . Tak thou thy Silvia, for thou hast deserv'd her" (5.4.138–45). As noted earlier, Valentine's assessment of Thurio in front of the Duke also refers to the attractiveness of his character (3.1.64–66). Issues of character play an ironic role in the courtship of Proteus and Silvia. Proteus advises the Duke that Silvia will lose interest in Valentine if he disparages his character: "The best way is to slander Valentine, / With falsehood, cowardice, and poor descent: / Three things that women highly hold in hate" (3.2.31–33). While he tries to get the Duke to disparage Valentine's character, Silvia is not interested in Proteus in part because of his duplicitous character or, as Agnes Howe said of Thomas Feild, his lack of "honesty": "Thou subtle, perjur'd, false, disloyal man, / Think'st thou I am so shallow, so conceitless, / To be seduced by thy flattery, / That hast deceiv'd so many with thy vows? . . . I am so far from granting thy request, / That I despise thee for thy wrongful suit" (4.2.92–99). While she criticizes his character he praises hers: "But Silvia is too fair, too true, too holy, / To be corrupted with my worthless gifts" (4.2.5–6). Later, she will not look on the letter which she "knows" is "stuff'd with protestations, / And full of new-found oaths, which he will break / As easily as I do tear this paper" (4.4.127–29).

Critics often note the importance of character in determining suitability for figures in *Twelfth Night*. For instance, Malcolmson comments on the importance of character over status: "In the play, a gentleman is 'made' and made loveable not by his title or blood, but by his (or her) will" (33).[19] Some critics assess the determinants of suitability of character of the participants in the love triangle in terms of generosity of spirit, intelligence, femininity, and masculinity.[20] While chapter 3 discusses the importance of the exact content of the verbal exchanges between Olivia and Viola as she woos for the Duke, in regard to this chapter we should note that Olivia explains how Viola's spirit or character attracted her (1.5.296). A dramatic figure in the play offers her own assessment of the character of one of Olivia's suitors. Maria is aware that Andrew's character as a drunk, quarreller prodigal, and fool will not appeal to Olivia despite Toby's opinion of his "good gifts of nature" (1.3.14–33).

Other kinds of suitability criteria that appear prominently in the plays differ outright from those found in the depositions. One main difference is the extent to which dramatic figures point to considerations of physical appearance when choosing a partner.[21] In *The Two Gentlemen of Verona*, Silvia's suitors and Julia often assess Silvia's suitability in terms of her beauty.[22] Rather than commenting on the complexion of her love interest, Julia compares her physical attributes to Silvia's in order to assess her suitability for Proteus: "Here is her picture: let me see; I think / If I had such a tire, this face of mine / Were full as lovely as is this of hers; / And yet the painter flatter'd her a little / Unless I flatter with myself too much. / Her hair is auburn, mine is perfect yellow: / If that be all the difference in his love, / I'll get me such a colour'd periwig. / Her eyes are grey as glass, and so are mine; / Ay, but her forehead's low, and mine's as high" (4.4.182–91). In Act 2, scene 4, Proteus notes that both women are fair: Silvia "is fair; and so is Julia that I love" (2.4.195). Two scenes later, however, he changes his opinion of their physical appearances: "And Silvia (witness heaven that made her fair) / Shows Julia but a swarthy Ethiope" (2.6.25–26). Similarly, Valentine tells Speed that Silvia's "beauty is exquisite" (2.1.52). The Duke again points to the beauty of his daughter in commenting on how it may serve as her dower: "Then let her beauty be her wedding-dower; / For me and my possessions she esteems not" (3.1.78–79).[23] Julia comments on the importance of the physical appearance of Proteus to her, marking that "know'st thou not his looks are my soul's food? / Pity the dearth that I have pined in, / By longing for that food so long a time" (2.7.15–17). In *Twelfth Night*, when Malvolio enters musing on Olivia, even before he finds the letter, his comments reveal his belief that his "complexion" is a source of Olivia's possible attraction (2.5.26).[24] Maria takes this further, making Malvolio believe his appearance, clothing, and demeanor make him suitable. Maria also suggests that the appearance of the messenger affects how Olivia accepts his suit: "If you will then see the fruits of the sport, mark his first approach before my lady: he will come to her in yellow stockings, and 'tis a colour she abhors, and cross-gartered, a fashion she detests: and he will smile upon her, which will now be so unsuitable to her disposition, being addicted to a melancholy as she is, that it cannot but turn him into a notable contempt" (2.5.197–204). As I noted above, Orsino cites Olivia's beauty and not her wealth as the source of his attraction (2.4.80–87), while Viola notes the "complexion" of her beloved when discussing suitability (2.4.26). In addition, part of Olivia's "five-fold blazon" includes a description of the elements of Viola's physical appearance which attracted her. Two items in the blazon are his "face" and "limbs" (1.5.296–97). Karen Newman explains how important this criterion is in assessing the suitability of the marriage of Olivia and

Sebastian, especially in light of critics who find their marriage difficult to accept:

> Critics since Johnson have found Olivia's marriage to Sebastian hard to accept. E. M. W. Tillyard, in discussing the bed trick in *Measure for Measure*, complains of *Twelfth Night*: "it may be useful to ask why popular opinion has objected to the bed trick and not objected to something equally disgusting in *Twelfth Night*, namely Olivia's accepting Sebastian as a substitute lover for Cesario . . . ." What Tillyard and others forgot is that Olivia does not fall in love with Cesario's soul, by which I take him to mean personality or inner nature, but with his "perfections" which crept in through her eyes. The quality of her love is not undermined by winning the appearance of the man she loves, for his identity all along is subsumed in what Viola/Cesario calls her "outside" (II, ii, 17). Through the outside Olivia has "insight" into Sebastian's nature and identity. The epicene figure of Cesario can be compared to a *trompe l'oeil* perspectivist painting. When Olivia sees him from her point of view, she "sees" Sebastian. (*Shakespeare's Rhetoric* 103–04)

Another criterion in this drama includes the ability to play a trick. Maria's wit and her ability to play a trick on Malvolio attract Toby While before the discussion of the trick Feste assesses Maria's wit as an attraction for Toby (1.5.25–27), Toby suggests her adoration attracts him: "She's a beagle, true-bred, and one that adores me" (2.3.179–80). Yet he identifies her ability to pull off a jest as the main consideration when choosing her as his wife: "I could marry this wench for this device" (2.5.182). This "device," her ability to play a trick on Malvolio, is important enough to him to serve as her dowry: "And ask no other dowry with her but such another jest" (2.5.184–85).[25] Fabian identifies the writing of the letter to Malvolio as the basis of the union, suggesting a kind of parity in terms of their shared sense of humor and allegiance: "Maria writ / The letter, at Sir Toby's great importance, / In recompense whereof he hath married her" (5.1.361–63). The fact that Sir Toby considers the device a more important determinant of suitability than money underscores in particular the difference worth played in assessing suitability between the dramas and depositions. As Laurie E. Osborne comments, "Sir Toby does marry her despite her lower station and her relative poverty which would presumably be of some importance to a man who must bilk Sir Andrew for money" ("Letters" 70). Sir Toby's trick of the duel on Sir Andrew also involves the criteria of suitability since Toby coaxes Andrew's participation as a way to demonstrate his valor to Olivia—"there is no love-broker in the world can mor prevail in man's commendation with woman than report of valour" (3.2.35–37)—or at least appear so: "for it comes to pass oft, that a terrible oath, with a swaggering accent sharply twanged off, gives manhood more approbation than ever proof itself would have earned him" (3.4.180–83).[26]

In terms of the specific patterns of suitability criteria found in the depositions and these two comedies, the major difference that occurs in the kinds of considerations when choosing a partner is in the fewer references in the comedies to wealth, status, and occupation. Such a difference raises many questions. Is the reduced role of money the result of wish fulfillment in a fictional world, an assumption that money did not matter? Did people point to money in the courts because it is a criterion that could be measured when assessing the suitability of a partner? Because of the number of references to differences of worth between individuals in the courts in an effort to prevent a match and the fact that many deponents cited the man as falling short financially, were witnesses protecting women from making unsuitable matches? Were they trying to prevent a match in order to protect the reputation of a family? Were they, as the *Woodhall v. Sadler* case, among others, suggests, respecting the clout of the fathers of these women? The latter questions are particularly relevant for *The Two Gentlemen of Verona*. While in *Twelfth Night* couples do not have parental figures to consult, in *The Two Gentlemen of Verona* Silvia, Julia, and Proteus go against their fathers and eventually end up with the partner they originally selected without pointing to considerations of wealth and occupation. Is such an occurrence part of a fictional world? Are unions based on romantic love more satisfying and stable than ones governed by concerns of wealth? As this chapter suggests, to make love the primary motive without a balanced consideration of wealth, status, occupation, and age is more a part of the narrative of the dramas rather than of the depositions. While the basis of partner selection for most dramatic figures in both these comedies is more romantic than worldly, as the next chapter discusses, these two comedies differ in their depictions of courting behaviors. A comparison of the courting behaviors in these comedies with those in the depositions reveals that *Twelfth Night* stands closer to contemporary courting behaviors recorded in the depositions than does *The Two Gentlemen of Verona*.

3

COURTING BEHAVIORS:
TALKING, TOKENS, AND TOUCHING

> he sawe the said Joane Waters and John Newton . . . making love and
> showing great kindenes e*a*ch to other by drincking one to another and
> kissing and embracing together very lovinglye.
>
> (DL/C/219/418ᵛ

> How shall I feast him? What bestow of him?
> For youth is bought more oft than begg'd or borrow'd.
>
> (*Twelfth Night* 3.4.2–3)

While chapters 1 and 2 focus on issues central to the making of marriage—choice and the assessment of suitability—this chapter considers courting behaviors, which might be thought peripheral but can be shown to be crucial evidence for the interpretation of intent and consent.[1] In some cases, deponents did not detail the specific behaviors. Ann Hewse, for instance, testified that Edmund Ellice "made greate meanes to obteyne . . . [Margaret's] love in the waye of marriadge" (DL/C/213/149) but did not recount what the "greate meanes" were. However, in many other cases, litigants and witnesses did identify the specific courtship behaviors and occasionally mentioned as well the locations at which couples courted. Agnes Newman's account of the wooing of Robert Chapman includes many of the behaviors deponents cited. As Agnes, a "servaunt in an Alehowse in Holborn," went "upp and downe the howse abowt her busynes," Robert would "Drinke to her, and fall a iestinge with her after a kynd of love sorte." In addition to his "frequenting" the alehouse, drinking to her, and displaying affection, she recounted other proof of his interest in her, such as "famyliaritye," "comunicac*i*on or conferannce" of marriage, and giving gifts (DL/C/213/416). As this case suggests, the locations of courtships testified to in the London depositions varied from houses of the bride, her family, or her employer to taverns. While the courting of one couple was not atypical in that it occurred in the separate homes of the brothers of a couple, extraordinarily Grace Cooper and Thomas Harrison—like Pyramus and Thisbe in *A Midsummer Night's Dream*—conversed through a "chink" in the wall. In a deposition repeated on 17 February 1598/99, Ellen Pulley alias Pullen detailed how Grace showed her a "Crevis or hole in a wall in her brothers howse w*hi*ch she sayd she had made into . . . Thomas Harrisons brothers howse the twoe howses ioy[n]ing together whear they bothe dwelt" through which she and Thomas talked: "And ther she the same Grace towld her . . . that ther was the place . . . wheare she used to talke w*i*th Thomas Harrison at that hole and he to her And she sayethe that it was so as one of them might well here . . . an other at that hole" (DL/C/215/244ᵛ).[2]

The London Consistory Court depositions and Shakespeare's *The Two Gentlemen of Verona* and *Twelfth Night* contain similar courting behaviors, such as talking together, gift giving and receiving, "frequenting," and drinking and eating together.[3] However, the one behavior that the depositions and the dramas do not include is hand holding. As I explain in chapter 4, this behavior appears to have had a more specific meaning by being part of marriage. Although these legal and literary texts share similar behaviors, the patterns of behavior within them vary between the dramas and the depositions and between the dramas. For example, to examine the behaviors in these two dramas alongside the depositions suggests that *Twelfth Night* stands closer to behaviors identified in the legal sources than does *The Two Gentlemen of Verona*. The wide range of courting behaviors operating concurrently in these depositions and dramas underscores that courtship did not require specific ritualized behaviors to lead to a binding union and that in both kinds of texts individual consent was the basis of marriage.

LONDON CONSISTORY COURT DEPOSITIONS

In examining the courting behaviors that deponents specified, the present section considers several broad categories of behaviors and moves from the most to the least prominent behavior mentioned: talking together, gift exchange, noting love and physical displays of affection, "frequenting," goodwill, drinking, and eating. Even though deponents mentioned gift exchange as the second most common behavior, it receives the most attention here for two reasons: first, because of the attention this behavior receives in social histories of the period; and second, the seemingly ironic and contradictory mention in the depositions. As I have noted earlier, deponents considered a variety of different kinds of courting behaviors to demonstrate the intent of the parties.[4]

Predictably, witnesses and litigants pointed to a couple speaking together as evidence of courtship more than to any other behavior The records note the important distinction between "talking together" as evidence of intimacy and the possible occasion of a contract and the actual words spoken as evidence of a contract. Most of the witnesses who mentioned this behavior included the general topic of a couple's conversation rather than the exact words. Witnesses often pointed out that a couple spoke "in the way of marriage": for example, from a case I cited earlier, at the King's Head and at the Antilope, Mary Hill "heard divers speaches of goodwill in the way of marriage pass" between Joan Praise and Henry Procktor (DL/C/214/268). They sometimes used other similar terms such as "talkinge of love" (DL/C/213/819) to identify the general topic of conversation.

To a few deponents, the specific words a couple spoke were of greater concern, as the case of *Thomas Wye v. Agnes Bushey* demonstrates. In a deposition from Thomas' suit to prove Agnes consented to a contract, a servant to Agnes' father noted that Agnes and Thomas "did often tymes sometymes in her masters kitchen otherwise in the parlor sitt together and conferr . . . very earnestly togithers thone with the other, but what talke they used she could nott here neither ever did she heare the said Master Wye move . . . [Agnes] for marriage" (DL/C/213/832). Thomas visiting Agnes and his speaking to her was not proof enough for this witness; the words themselves mattered more. Agnes herself testified to this effect: "neither did ther ever any speache of her parte . . . passe unto hym or was delyvered by her whereby any Consente of marriadge or good liking thatt wayes mighte arise" (DL/C/213/805). Agnes' statement here is even mor significant in her defense given Thomas' keen concern with the exact words she used in order to make her consent to be his wife. According to Katherine Freame, Thomas "did will . . . [her] to gett some token from . . . Bushye, or take hould of her wordes yf she uttered any wherby, he mighte see and he could gett her to yeild to be his wyff," but she "could never gett . . . Bushy to use any such wordes or geve any tokens" (DL/C/213/831). Thomas' promise to Katherine that if she succeeded in assisting him she "should nott loose by itt" (DL/C/213/829) could suggest how diligently she too tried to get Agnes "to use any such wordes or geve any tokens."

Even though Thomas expressed concern about the specific words spoken and some witnesses mentioned that a couple talked in "private" or "secretly," which may suggest some intimacy, more deponents pointed to a couple talking together, usually noting that it was "in the way of marriage" or such similar terms, as evidence of intent. Since the letter of the law examines the verbal constructions of marital contracts, paying particular attention to the particular verbs and their tenses, it is not surprising that a couple speaking together would hold a prominent place when assessing their intentions. What may be more surprising in light of the letter of the law is the number of depositions which do not record the words spoken and which cite a wide range of courting behaviors, in addition to talking together, to prove intent.

In the courting behaviors that these depositions document, gift exchange—the second most common courting behavior deponents cited—played a central part in demonstrating intent, seemingly providing a more material form of proof of a claim of one litigant on another.[5] Buckingham's advice to Richard in *Richard III* to "Play the maid's part: still answer nay, and take it" (3.7.50) does not accurately reflect the behaviors of women in the depositions regarding gift exchange. Here, women and men were gift givers, gift receivers, and interpreters of the contexts of the giving and receiving.

As I explain in this and the next chapter, whether a person gave a gift or received one as a sign of interest, a pledge of love, or during a marriage, the meaning of the item lay in the context of the exchange and the intent of the giver and the receiver rather than intrinsically in the specific item; a gift of a pair of stockings did not demonstrate in itself a lesser or deeper commitment than the gift of an ear pick. Deponents read the context of the exchange to assess, for example, whether a gift exchange was a voluntary act of goodwill or a binding contract. John R. Gillis underscores the importance of context in determining meaning: "It was not the value of the gift, but the giving and the acceptance that mattered" (31). Diana O'Hara sees this ambiguity of meaning as consistent with the ambiguity of the process of marriage. Her comments about "the nature of the gift and the circumstances of giving" based on sixteenth-century records from the diocese of Canterbury are also accurate when applied to the behaviors in London: "As a language for conducting and defining relationships, its versatility was, it seems, appropriate to the essential ambiguity of matrimonial negotiation" (*Courtship* 57). In the London Consistory Court depositions, witnesses and litigants pointed to this ambiguity. Elizabeth Orton testified that she "hard itt spoken in the howse that

Captayne Wye has sent . . . [Agnes] tokens of good will butt howe they were received or what answeare was geven upon them she never harde" (DL/C/213/832). As Elizabeth implies, the intentions of the giver and the receiver were central to determine meaning. The evidence in these depositions regarding the fluidity of meaning in giving, then, supports the conclusions of some social historians whose research focuses on sets of records from areas other than London.[6]

This fluidity in the meaning of gift giving and receiving in the process of courtship and marriage is particularly ironic and seemingly contradictory. That is, given the importance of marriage in contemporary ideology, economics, and politics, one might expect that the signs of consent to a marriage would be more clearly defined. Ironically, rather than consent being evident from a certain gesture or lying intrinsically in a certain gift, which could clarify intentions, the depositions indicate that the interpretations of the context in which a suitor gave a gift generally determine intent; women and men wer offering their own interpretations. This argument based on the evidence in these London records differs from that of Eric Josef Carlson who argues that specific gifts could "demonstrate intent": "While no gifts 'proved' consent in a legal sense, betrothal tokens were strong circumstantial evidence, for people recognized that such tokens wer qualitatively different from mere courtship gifts. When such a ring was given and received there could be little doubt what was intended" (*Marriage* 127).

The gender imbalance in gift giving in these records supports the findings of social historians examining records from other areas for this period. While women could and did take the initiative in giving, court papers from other areas demonstrate that women usually did not take the lead. For instance, in his study of gift giving recorded in the Durham Consistory Court depositions for 1560 to 1630, Peter Rushton concludes that "it was comparatively rare for there to be a balanced exchange of tokens, and women rarely opened negotiations by giving them, because women's tokens did not have the same initiatory force" ("Testament" 26). O'Hara also comments on "the unevenness of the exchange" in giving in the Canterbury Consistor Court depositions, by noting that "women usually acted in response to their suitors, either in returning tokens and, by implication, terminating negotiations, or in reciprocation, reassurance and positive encouragement" (*Courtship* 65). Her comments are certainly appropriate for the actions of women in the London Consistory Cour depositions. Here, too, more women "acted in response" to a gift given by their male suitors.

I differ from O'Hara, however, in assessing female activity in gift exchange. As I noted above, O'Hara suggests that women played an active role in this exchange through their receiving and returning gifts. I argue that those roles in the London Consistory Court depositions involved more than just returning or reciprocating gifts in a central way—women often offered their own interpretations of the giving and receiving. Sometimes these interpretations included a calculation of the worth of the gifts sent by them or their suitors seemingly in order to quantify the extent of their obligation or relieve themselves of an obligation by indicating an equal exchange of goods.

The conclusions of this study differ from Ralph Houlbrooke's, as well as O'Hara's, on the point of autonomy for women and men in interpreting the contexts of exchange. Houlbrooke comments on the role men and their witnesses played in determining the meaning of gifts: "Men and the witnesses they produced often did their best to blur still further what seems to have been the always hazy distinction between tokens of 'good will' and symbols of binding agreement" (*Church* 61). However, "men and the witnesses they produced" were not the only individuals doing "their best to blur" the distinction. As these London depositions document, women and the witnesses they produced were offering their own interpretations of the meaning of the gifts and the exchange as well. Unlike Houlbrooke, O'Hara sees this lack of autonomy to interpret the context of giving as including both women and men. She argues that, regardless of gender, gift giving represents another level in which "the pressures and controls of society and the values and concepts of community confront the individual":

> If we consider, for example, the passage of tokens between individuals, the form and value of the token, its symbolic representation and the modes of behaviour associated with its reception, we are immediately forced to recognize that this was not an intimate, private affair, but a regulated and ritualized means of entering into a marriage, and forming ties between kin groups. Formalizing the entry into marriage, the gift of tokens can be seen to operate as a kind of pressurizing ritual and represented, therefore, one aspect of control by kin and community. (" 'Ruled' " 26)

The number of London depositions which offer a variety of readings of gift giving and receiving suggests less a "pressurizing ritual" representing social control than a moment in the process of courtship when individuals were able to interpret the context of courtship for themselves.

As I have noted in the introduction, I also read the patterns of gift exchange differently from Laura Gowing who focuses on the framework of the exchange. I have focused on a shorter time frame (1586 to 1611) and been able to include material from DL/C/215 and DL/C/216, two deposition books for 1597 to 1601, which wer recently made available for consultation. Further, I have looked mor closely at the material items themselves appearing at different stages of the courtship process, particularly in the differences between gifts people gave before, during, or after marriage. Suitors gave the majority of gifts in the extant London Consistory Court depositions during or after a marriage, a pattern I examine in chapter 4. Here, we need to glance at the patterns of giving before a marriage; despite their reduced use at this stage, they nevertheless could point to intent and to the progress of a courtship.

The diversity in the items people gave before a marriage underscores the role context played in determining meaning. Two depositions from different cases show us the diverse items exchanged and that both women and men were gift givers, receivers, and interpreters of their meanings as well, patterns which are found in a plethora of depositions. In one case, Ann Hamond gave her fellow servant Thomas Phillipps several different items as tokens of her goodwill. In a deposition repeated on 11 June 1602, for instance, Jane Collett recounted how she had seen Ann deliver to Thomas "twoe angells of gould at Soper lane end and after that five pownd*es*... in gowld and silver ... at the gowlden key dore in Cheape side in an evening." Later, Ann sent Thomas "a peece of black velvett rowled upp close together seeing to be ... a good bigg peece more then a yard as she thinckethe and then a ryng of gowld" as "tokens of her good will and love to him and he recyved the same thanckfully." Jane also testified that "in token of ... [Ann's] great good will and Love" to Thomas, Ann gave him "xl^{li} in ... silver uppo*n* a sondaye night" (DL/C/216/400^v-401^r). Ann's gifts to Thomas of money, cloth, and a ring underscore the diverse gifts presented prior to a marriage and that a woman interpreted the context of exchange.

The variety and number of gifts Thomas Wye gave to Agnes Bushey again points to the fluidity of meaning surrounding premarital gifts and the need for careful, specific interpretations of the intentions of the parties and the contexts of the exchange. Such interpretations often included evaluating the economic worth of the items and sending another "in recompense." In doing so, individuals seem to be quantifying the extent of their obligation. Katherine Freame testified that "she carried ... [Agnes] dyvers gyft*es* from

Master wye viz a payer of watchett Jersye stockinges, a paier of mayden heare garters a blew silke girdle a lether purse wroughte with gould, ii faier wrought smockes, . . . which . . . [Agnes] with much adoe received . . . telling her that she would take them, butt nott in the way of any marriadge" (DL/C/213/829). Despite the gifts, as Katherine testified, Agnes never did "graunt hym any goodwill in that waye or agree in any respecte to his suite" (DL/C/213/829). Instead, Katherine's testimony suggests that Agnes carefully weighed Thomas' gifts and counterbalanced for an exchange that would not allow him to have any claim on her. "Only att one tyme" did Agnes send Thomas a gift, "a cutt worke bande," but as Katherine points out, only "in recompence of some parte of his gyftes he had before tyme sent her, but nott in respecte of marriadge as this respondent verily thinketh" (DL/C/213/831).

Many individuals in the depositions noted the worth of the items as part of their readings. To cite a representative example, Joan Mortimer specifically quantified the value of the objects Richard Campion gave her and offered him another "in recompence," noting the similar worths of the objects:

> on a tyme when the said Richard had occasion . . . to goe into the Cuntrye, she did lend hym a hand kerchiffe and a payer of cuffes, and then did paye hym his money namely three shillinges fower pence againe, which he had layed owtt for the gloves and wascoate received . . . by . . . [her] And she beleiveth that att a nother tyme she gave hym a shirte bande, which coste . . . [her] two shillinges six pence in recompence of the girdle which he delyvered her . . . which severall thinges he received thanckfully. (DL/C/214/11)

The exchange of similarly valued objects and the phrase "in recompence" indicate that she was not financially obligated to him. Joan may have hoped to suggest that by not being under a fiscal obligation to Richard she was not under an emotional obligation as well. Yet such testimony nonetheless points to an economic relationship. In a different case, Agnes Newman's testimony that Robert Chapman was not out of pocket for her suggests that she did not "owe" him anything, neither fiscally nor emotionally: "neither hath he ever spente more of [her] . . . then she her selfe hath agayne requited . . . nor is he a pennye the worse for . . . [her] then he was" (DL/C/213/416). Even if she intended to nullify the existence of an emotional relationship between them, the testimony still points to a fiscal exchange, once again underscoring the difficulty in interpreting the exchange and the intentions of the givers and receivers. These depositions offer another way to read gift exchange to that offered by Natalie Zemon Davis. In a study of the gift in sixteenth-century France, Davis argues that "among the most important [features] are techniques and manners for softening relations among people of the same status and of different status and for preventing their closure" (9). In the late sixteenth- and early seventeenth-century depositions for the diocese of London, a gift could serve to close off relations between two people.

While many people noted the economic value of gifts, Ann Hyde added another condition to her interpretation of a gift she received. Ann recounted how she "deny[ed] to recyve" a pair of gloves, which, in her opinion, "weare not worth above v or vi^s" (DL/C/215/112^v–113^r), that Alexander Hollinworth sent her, saying that "she had gloves of her own to wear" (DL/C/215/113^r). After she refused to receive them, John Griffith, she reported, "threw the sayd gloves unto her lapp and left them with her" (DL/C/215/113^r). Part of her reading included her pointing out that "she never sent to him for any gloves nor ev[er] . . . spake to him for any." While such qualifications appear in the depositions in explanation for possession of a gift, what is more unusual is her noting that although she still had the gloves, she "never wor them" (DL/C/215/113^r). Here, she suggested that wearing the gift indicated more consent than possessing it. Such fine distinctions further complicate the meanings of both the gift and the exchange.

While deponents interpreted the meaning of a gift and the context of giving and receiving, patterns emerge in these records for the gifts people gave before, during, and after marriage. Prior to marriage, women and men most often gave each other items of clothing or personal accessories. The depositions contain some nineteen different accessories and items of apparel from pins to stockings to waistcoats which parties gave prior to marriage.[7] In addition to the items I mentioned above, Elizabeth Cole testified that Martin Mullens gave "hir a pair of gloves at two severall tymes at each tyme a pair in token of good will" (DL/C/214/170).[8] Other items individuals gave include "a velvett purse layd on with silver lace" (DL/C/215/94^v),[9] "a payer of sheers which he fownde" (DL/C/213/188), and "an orenge and thereon the figure of a harte made in Cloves" (DL/C/215/260^r). (See Figures 3.1 and 3.2 for contemporary examples of purses and shoes.)

Money was the second most common gift prior to a marriage. In some cases, someone sent it to buy something. James Flussher sent Margaret Hall money "to buy frindge to her petticote" (DL/C/214/565) and "for hose and shoes to hir feet" (DL/C/214/433).[10] More often, however, the money served as the

Figure 3.1 Early seventeenth-century purses, © Museum of London.

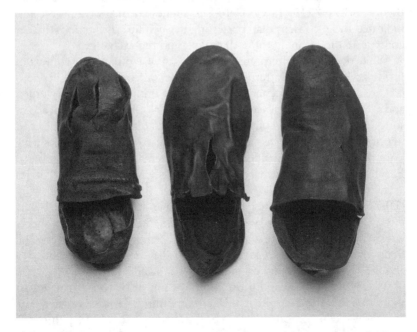

Figure 3.2 Late sixteenth-century and early seventeenth-century women's shoes, © Museum of London.

gift itself. The scarcity of coinage during this period gave it special value.[11] The sums varied from pennies to pounds, as Ann Hamond's giving suggests. In addition, John Goodall gave "xii^d" to Alice Boyce (DL/C/213/188), John Swinsted gave Elizabeth Brode alias Ibotson "a peece of gowld of half a Crowne befor the sayd Contract or talke . . . of marrage" (DL/C/215/95^r), Robert Chapman gave Agnes Newman an "angell of golde" (DL/C/213/419), and Thomas Feild gave Agnes Howe "ii or iii peeces of gowld" of "xx^s peece" (DL/C/216/47^v and 48^r).

Even with a monetary gift, deponents calculated its worth through the context of the giving and receiving and the intent of the parties. Since the standard measure of the value of money was itself variable,[12] it may not be surprising that deponents determined worth by the context of the exchange rather than by the value of the specific coin. Some deponents were quick to explain the intent behind the giving and receiving of money. Susan Fidgett indicated that Thomas Baines intended to buy her love through purchasing "wyne and oth*er* thing*es*" for her, but she was careful to point out his intentions wer not complicit with her own: Thomas "hath divers tymes beestowed money in wyne and oth*er* thing*es* wh*i*ch . . . [she] beeleeveth he beestowed for her . . . love butt was nev*er* intreated to it by . . . [her], but all wayes did it voluntarily" (DL/C/214/172). She suggested that since she "did not intreat" him, she was not obligated to him. In another case, Robert Scarre interpreted his gift of "three peces of golde of xx^s a pece" to Helen Tinckham as a loan "for he never had any intent to marry her" (DL/C/218/304). In yet another case, a deponent explained the giving of money in terms of safe keeping. Ann Fuller "intreated" Henry Crampe "to keepe xxx^s of hers wh*i*ch he thinckth and beleveth she left w*i*th him for feare of being robbed of it and not for any thing ells" (DL/C/215/510^r).

Rings were the third most common gift prior to marriage.[13] While the depositions indicate that people more often gave rings during rather than prior to marriage, giving them as a courtship gift indicates that a ring in and of itself did not always enjoy special status as technical proof of a marriage. In addition to a gift people gave before, during, or after a marriage, people also gave rings (including plain gold, jewel, and memento mori rings) as funeral gifts. In his catalog of the rings in the Victoria and Albert Museum, Charles Oman discusses the difficulties in classifying "love rings," further underscoring that their meaning was not intrinsic. For as Oman notes, "it is the use and not the shape which distinguishes the wedding and betrothal ring"

(*Catalogue* vi). He writes that

> In dealing with some of the other principal types of love rings it is necessary to abandon any attempt to arrange them according to their uses as wedding rings, betrothal rings, or love tokens. It should be remembered that many rings which have been used for the above purposes must be scattered unrecognised among the other parts of the collection, especially among the decorative rings, simply because there is nothing in their appearance to show the special purpose which they have served. It is not possible, for instance, to distinguish any separate class of wedding rings, as the present uniformity of use belongs only to recent centuries. It does not, however, appear to be true that the use of a plain gold wedding ring was due entirely to the spread of Puritan ideas in the 17th century. (*Catalogue* 20)

In his catalog of rings in the British Museum, O. M. Dalton makes a similar point regarding how people used them, a point which again agrees with descriptions in the London Consistory Court depositions: "The love-rings in the Collection are naturally numerous, and the number is really greater than would at first appear, since many rings, which from their type or the nature of the subjects engraved on them were probably made for other uses, have been transformed into love-rings by the addition of amatory mottoes, such as *mon coeur avez* or *per bon amor*" (xlvii). Henry Bowles tried to give Susan Jason alias Jackson a ring, as she was "ready to go to my lady Wroathe," but after Henry put the ring into her hand, she "refused it and put it from her and left it at her howse in her parlour windowe" (DL/C/219/312ʳ). Other men gave women rings of gold (DL/C/217/11–15), a hooped gold ring (DL/C/214/386), and a ring with a "posie" in it (DL/C/214/179–80); unfortunately, the defendant here only referred to the posie rather than spelling out its content.

Love letters figured prominently in very few cases. Although, in his discussion of courting behaviors from 1300 to 1840 in England, Alan Macfarlane notes a "widespread" giving of letters: "One of the most acceptable 'gifts' from a lover was a letter . . . . Yet such letters seem to have been a widespread institution in England from at least the sixteenth century. Indeed, so widespread were they that . . . a special genre grew up of 'model' love letters" (*Marriage* 301–02). Sadly, the few depositions from the London Consistory Court that mention letters do not provide detailed accounts of their contents. Given their rarity in the depositions both before and after a marriage, it is difficult to determine how the court weighed written expressions in relation to other evidence. Exceptionally, the suit of *Joan Carewe v. Ralph Yardley* provides details regarding how these litigants weighed this evidence, the context in which he wrote the letters, the content of his love letters, and the context of exchange. Because of this rarity in the depositions, I quote fully from the case. In his defense that a contract did not exist between Joan and him, Ralph "being," as he said "a fond youthe and not wele advised what he did," claimed that the six letters he wrote to Joan were only "letters of protestacion of Love and frendshipp" (DL/C/218/251): he "did write all the six letters exhibited unto this Court with his owne hand and subscribed . . . his name unto them and five of them he delivered him selfe unto Joane Carewe . . . and the sixt he sent unto her by an other And he sayethe he did write them then out of his affection . . . he then bore unto her but never intended any contract of . . . matrimonie therby nor by any of them or by any thing in them" (DL/C/218/254). Despite his interpretation of the letters not being binding, Ralph tried to buy them back, not, he said, out of fear that someone could use them to confirm a contract, but out of fear that his master might use them to harm him:

> he . . . Considering how that many maisters went about to hinder their servantes when they came nere out of their yeares and to hinder their servantes of their freedom uppon slight occasions And he . . . knowing nothing worse in suche a Case then love letters greatly feared least . . . Joane Carewe should iniuriously give his . . . maister some . . . advantage that waye, . . . but yet . . . he never feared any contract of matrimonie that could be claymed of him [he] . . . promised to give her the same Joane v^{li} within a yeare after he was free and v^{li} more within a yeare after that if she would give him . . . all his letters againe. (DL/C/218/253)

Ralph's worries appear to lie in his concerns regarding his apprenticeship. Ann Jennalie Cook notes the disadvantages of a male apprentice marrying without his master's approval:

> Ironically, about the only legal advantage for anyone marrying without permission accrued to women servants who "purposely mary to free themselues: because our lawes doe free a maide that is maried from her seruice to master and mistresse." The same gender differentiation applied also to apprenticeship: "If a man prentice in London marry, he shall be forced to serve of his time, and yet loose his freedome [the right to practice his craft in the City] . But yf a woman prentice marry, shee shall onely forfayte hir libertie, but shall not be forced to serve." (*Making* 79)

The testimony of Joan's mother, Sara, differed from Ralph's. She claimed the amount he promised was "x^{li} when he should come out of his apprentisshipp if she the same Joane would deliver him his letters back againe and promis never to truble him about any Contract or Claime of marriage." Although Joan was "very unwilling to yeald," her mother persuaded her to agree, so they set up the delivery at "Colmanstreet end." Despite Ralph's "fears" of his master, he did not attend the meeting (DL/C/218/290).

Deponents cited how a party felt for or acted around another fewer times than gift giving. They, not surprisingly, pointed to love existing between the parties twice as much as liking. While Ralph Yardley testified that he loved Joan Carewe (DL/C/218/251), in another case a witness deposed that "Love and affection" existed between Thomas Cartwright and Gertrude Stafford (DL/C/218/360). The specific behaviors within this category include the term "familiarity" which deponents sometimes used. As I cited earlier, Thomas Clemence pointed to the "very kynde familiarite" between Richard Thomas and Alice More (DL/C/218/539).[14] It seems appropriate to include "familiarity" in a category including physical displays of affection, because when deponents used this term it usually suggested a level of physical intimacy between the parties. As Henry Hall deposed, "he hath seen" Francis Norman and Alice Webster "very familiar togither and sene him . . . kisse her many tymes eache showing kindnes and love to the other" (DL/C/219/249ᵛ).

As the above quotations indicate, deponents sometimes pointed to intimate physical contacts between the parties as proof of an emotional commitment or intent of the parties. Edward Bolton's deposition is one of the few that includes a reference to "love signes." He testified that he saw Ann Fuller and Henry Crampe "ticke and toye and shewe love signes betwene them as with kissinge and embrasinge of eche other in such sorte and as [he] . . . and his said Brother and his servant did knowe and wele perceyve the goodwill that was betwene the partyes litigantes" (DL/C/215/526ᵛ). Deponents mentioned premarital kissing more than embracing when describing a couple's physical contact prior to a marriage. The suit between John Newton and Joan Waters contains the most extraordinary physical demonstration of intent in these records for this period. George Ireland testified that "Waters was then very much affected to . . . Newton in the way of marriage for yt shee . . . did then with her lips sucke . . . Newtons necke in a manner of kindenes whereby shee made 3 red spottes arise wherupon . . . Newton asking her what shee ment by it shee answering said yt shee had marcked him for her owne" (DL/C/219/418ᵛ).[15]

Deponents cited "frequenting" fewer times than emotions or intimate physical acts. Since speaking is the most prominent courting behavior and deponents did not cite letters often in the depositions, obviously, suitors visited, "frequented" each other in order to speak together. Since some witnesses pointed to "frequenting" as a separate category of evidence of courtship, I count these references as a separate category as well—rather than assume their presence in the most prominent behavior—in order to represent more accurately the patterns in the depositions. To cite one of many examples, John Ridle testified that "by reason of the often coming of . . . Raphe Grimes to . . . Joyce Griffin he . . . did suspect . . . ther would be a matche of marriage betwene Joyce Griffin and [Raphe]" (DL/C/218/439–40).

In a few cases, "frequenting" sometimes involved spending the night. The testimony of a witness could imply that an individual's presence at a house overnight indicates an emotional commitment: John Grice testified that "Raphe Grimes went home with . . . Joyce and laye at her howse that night in London" (DL/C/218/443). Others, however, were more careful to point out the circumstances surrounding the person's presence, particularly noting at whose invitation the person was present. As one witness testified from a different case, "Maste Wye would oftentymes . . . use to come and make merry in her said masters howse with . . . Bushye, but throughe whose meanes he gott to lodge in her masters howse she knoweth nott neither whether . . . Bushey gave her consent" (DL/C/213/832). Here, Agnes' consent to Thomas' stay, rather than his presence alone, would be proof of their intent. Such qualifications could clarify whether an individual accepted or encouraged a suitor.

Deponents cited goodwill more than drinking and eating. W could label the other courting behaviors in this chapter as evidence of "goodwill." Although one might argue that this term is simply a catchall phrase or a matter of semantics, to forty-eight deponents, goodwill was a category that could help prove or disprove the intent of the parties. Given the number of deponents who pointed to its presence or absence in recounting courtships, I include it as a separate category to reflect better the behaviors in the depositions. According to Katherine Freame, Thomas considered goodwill to be a valuable asset: "she hath hard master wye say that he would nott for his parte lose . . . Bushies good will nore sell itt for a thowsand pownde" (DL/C/213/831). Thomas valuing it, according to this witness, as equal to "a thowsand pownde" suggests it means more than liking. Deponents often linked it to marriage. In Deborah Woodhall's testimony, goodwill meant her consent to marry: "Sadler was a Sewter to . . . [her] for her good will in marriadge and therein did oftenmove her" (DL/C/213/824). The testimony of Arthur Newman pointed to a similar meaning, especially since he used the words "goodwill" and "consent" equally. He "asked . . . William dickers if ever he had given his Consent or goodwill to Thomas Thornewerk to marrie his dawghter or no," and William "answered that he had only given his goodwill to Humfrey Grene" (DL/C/215/252ᵛ). Whether goodwill meant personal affection or consent to marry, to several witnesses it served as evidence of a commitment prior to marriage.

Drinking and eating follow goodwill in the order of frequency of courting behaviors in the depositions, with drinking appearing in four more depositions than eating. In terms of the former, fifteen examples exist of deponents noting that a couple went to a tavern to drink together. Yet other deponents explained the intentions of the parties who participated in this activity together. One mother's response indicated that sharing a drink with someone could convey liking or consent. When asked to share a drink with a suitor to her daughter, Joan Wise responded "that she would thrust a knife into him if she went to drinck with him" (DL/C/215/81ᵛ–82ʳ). In eleven cases, the parties drank to each other. For instance, Samuel Firthe "hath sene" Elizabeth Willson and James Harrison "drinck very kindely the one unto the other" (DL/C/215/360ᵛ). The surviving depositions contain an almost equal number of instances in which deponents noted that parties either shared a drink together or one drank to another. As I shall clarify in chapter 4, this pattern differs from the references to drinking as evidence of marital consent.

Deponents cited eating together fewer times than drinking as evidence of courtship. As with gifts, deponents interpreted the contexts of sharing a meal differently. While George Ireland pointed to John Newton's presence in Joan Waters' home as evidence of her intent, she further explained the circumstances of their "dinner in bed": "being big with child," which she had conceived with her now deceased husband, "and not well and . . . Newtons brother and sister were there with him and stayed there and supped with . . . [her] in her chamber she being in her bed and they sate on or by the bed syde and eate their meate upon the bed" (DL/C/219/426ʳ). Joyce Griffin appeared to deny that a shared meal was evidence of an emotional commitment on her part since she pointed to the event as a single occurrence for which she did not pay: Ralph Grymes "one only time dyned" at her house "but it was at his owne proper Costes" (DL/C/218/371). In many more cases, however, eating together was the occasion during which deponents noted other kinds of proof. To cite a typical case, the familiarity of the couple at meals rather than the fact that they shared a meal indicated their intention to marry: "Henry Proctor and Johan Purk als Praise did twise or thrice resort to the [Antilope in Smithfield] . . . and thear dined and supped togith*er* sundry times . . . when and whear . . [Robert Whooper] heard and saw them confer of marriage beetween them selves and used one an oth*er* very familierly . . . as though they had intent to be married togith*er*" (DL/C/214/266).

TWO SHAKESPEAREAN COMEDIES

A detailed reading of the courting behaviors in the London Consistory Court depositions can help to inform our reading of the courting behaviors dramatized in *The Two Gentlemen of Verona* and *Twelfth Night*. The courting behaviors differ between the depositions and the dramas and between the two dramas themselves. Despite the differences, these literary and legal texts emphasize individual rather than group consent as the basis of marriage; such an emphasis places these two Shakespearean comedies—despite their individual differences—closer to actual social behaviors, as identified in the legal sources, than to literary fantasy. Like the depositions, these two plays usually do not focus on first meetings (although in *Twelfth Night*, we see the first meetings of Olivia and Viola, and Olivia and Sebastian).[16] These plays concentrate mainly on the three most prominent courting behaviors seen in the depositions: namely, speech, gift exchange, and meetings. Since these three behaviors also differ in the two plays, I shall discuss them separately. Unlike in the depositions, drinking and eating together neither indicates nor sets the scenes for much courtship in either play at least among the main couples.[17] The matter of intimate physical contact prior to marriage is relevant to both plays, and here I shall begin.

The omissions of intimate physical contact prior to marriage in these two plays differ from the depositions and from other dramas of the period. Michael Shapiro notes the extensive enacting of physical contact that occurred in other plays of the period: "Elizabethan professional troupes did not hesitate to dramatize moments of physical intimacy, and apparently did so with greater naturalism and intensity. J. G. B. Streett's catalog of examples suggests that English Renaissance plays call for considerably more kissing, caressing, and fondling than earlier scholars wished to acknowledge" (146). Unlike other plays in the period, *The Two Gentleman of Verona* and *Twelfth Night* do not dramatize scenes of "caressing or fondling." Instead, *The Two Gentleman of Verona* discusses the effects of love on the physical appearance and behavior of the individual suffering from love pangs. Proteus, for example, comments on how his love for Julia changed him: Julia hath "Made . . . [him]

neglect . . . [his] studies, lose . . . [his] time, / War with good counsel, set the world at nought; / Made wit with musing weak, heart sick with thought" (1.1.67–69). Likewise, Speed's catalog of Valentine's "special marks" of love include that Valentine "learned (like Sir Proteus) to wreathe . . . [his] arms like a malcontent," "to walk alone," "to sigh," "to weep," "to fast," and "to speak puling" (2.1.17–25). Harold Jenkins comments on Valentine's passion and how it reflects that of Orsino:

> In Valentine, of course, we recognize the typical victim of the passion of courtly love. He tells us how he suffers "With bitter fasts, with penitential groans, / With nightly tears and daily heartsore sighs." That these groans and sighs survive in Orsino is clear when Olivia asks "How does he love me?" and the messenger replies, "With adorations, with fertile tears, / With groans that thunder love, with sighs of fire." (77)

Yet a difference occurs here between these two men in that dramatic figures do not comment on the physical effects of love to Orsino to the same extent as to Valentine in *The Two Gentlemen of Verona*. Viola is the source for another description in *Twelfth Night* about the physical effects and manifestations of love when she notes that Olivia's silences indicate love: "methought her eyes had lost her tongue, / For she did speak in starts distractedly. / She loves me, sure" (2.2.19–21). Rather than the plays including specific physical acts demonstrating intimacy, *Twelfth Night*, much more so than *The Two Gentlemen of Verona*, includes the exact words couples used, a specificity of language that is missing from the narratives in the depositions.

The Two Gentlemen of Verona dramatizes speaking, gift giving, and frequenting particularly through writing. One could argue that the emphasis on writing in this play may account for the omission of other courting behaviors such as eating or drinking together and physical displays of affection. One could further propose that such an emphasis, which is very different from that in the depositions, may in part be due to the fact that this is a literary text. However, if such were the case, the emphasis on writing would occur in other early modern literary courtships as well. And one could certainly not make such an argument for all the courtships in *Twelfth Night*. Instead, in terms of lovers communicating, *Twelfth Night* relates more to actual social behaviors as identified in the depositions.

Speaking becomes especially important to the wooers in *The Two Gentlemen of Verona* given the constraints upon visiting each other. Yet rather than through face-to-face meeting, communication in this play is often done through written words—love letters, sonnets, and songs.[18] As Jonathan Goldberg notes, "In *The Two Gentleman* [*sic.*] *of Verona*, desire is textual" (76).[19] Proteus, for instance, advises Thurio that he "must lay lime, to tangle . . . [Silvia's] desires" though "wailful sonnets, whose composed rhymes / Should be full-fraught with serviceable vows" (3.2.68–70). He even details the kinds of vows the sonnet should contain and how Thurio should compose (3.2.72–76). Proteus also advises that after Thurio's "dire-lamenting elegies" (3.2.81), he should communicate his love through a song (3.2.82–85). The song praises Silvia: "She excels each mortal thing / Upon the dull earth dwelling" (4.2.50–51). Other suitors communicate their love through written words as well: Julia sends a letter to Proteus, Launce's catalog of the virtues and vices of his milkmaid is called a "letter" (3.1.372), and Silvia goes so far as to have Valentine writing her love letters to him. In terms of the latter, unlike Olivia in *Twelfth Night* who asks Viola to "Come to what is important" (1.5.194) in her "speech" (1.5.174), Proteus and Valentine express their praise and love for Silvia in written form. In a poem from Valentine to Silvia that the Duke intercepts, Valentine cannot himself "lodge where (senseless) [his thoughts] are lying" (3.1.143). Although she does not receive it, the missive nonetheless suggests, as do the many written sentiments in the play, how writing replaces face-to-face courtship and becomes the vehicle through which individuals frequent each other. Although Silvia refuses the letter, she asks Valentine to write to "the secret, nameless friend" because she judges it to be "very clerkly" and "very quaintly writ" (2.1.98, 101, and 115). She nonetheless stays with this form of wooing by asking him for another letter written "more movingly" (2.1.121). Furthermore, one could argue that the picture which Proteus requests from Silvia is another text composed of lines in the courtship process.

Gifts also play a more central role in the wooing in *The Two Gentlemen of Verona* than in *Twelfth Night*.[20] In the play as they are in the depositions, both women and men are gift givers and receivers. The main courtship presents are love letters, songs, and sonnets although other items include a picture, rings, a dog, and possibly a glove. In regard to the prevalence of letters in the play, Frederick Kiefer notes, "No other Shakespearean comedy contains so many letters; no other devotes so many scenes to the composition, delivery and reception of love letters" (65). Unlike in the depositions, money does not become part of the exchange.

The gift giving is similar to actual behaviors in the depositions in regard to the gender imbalance and the rarity of a simultaneous exchange prior to marriage. In regard to gender differences, men give more gifts in *The Two Gentleman of Verona* as they did in the depositions. Proteus sends Julia a letter; Valentine and Proteus send letters to Silvia; Valentine tries to send a poem to Silvia; Proteus gives Julia a ring which he then sends to Silvia; Thurio arranges for musicians to entertain Silvia; and Proteus sends Silvia a dog. Fewer instances occur here of a woman's giving a gift; Silvia sends Valentine a letter and Proteus the picture he requested, and Julia gives Proteus a ring and a letter. Another similarity is the atypicality of a mutual exchange of presents before marriage. While Julia initiates an exchange of rings— "Keep this remembrance for thy Julia's sake" (2.2.5)—Proteus turns it into a mutual exchange—"Why then we'll make exchange; here, take you this" (2.2.6). While, as I remark in the subsequent chapter, some critics read this exchange as a marital contract, I read it as marking their goodwill. Julia supplies her intent when she delivers the ring she gave Proteus to Silvia: "This ring I gave him, when he parted from me, / To bind him to remember my good will" (4.4.97–98).

The play contains another instance of a mutual gift exchange before marriage. However, this instance is extremely unusual in both the dramas and the depositions since the giver unknowingly gives and receives the same gift simultaneously. Although earlier Valentine would write letters to Silvia, she could not send him a letter in return. Speed speculates that through "modesty," "want of idle time," or "fearing else some messenger, that might her mind discover," she was unable to give him a similar gift (2.1.155–57). Unusually, she creates a situation in which Valentine immediately receives as he gives since Valentine "sues to her; and she hath taught her suitor, / He being her pupil, to become her tutor. / O excellent device, was there ever heard a better? / That my master being scribe, to himself should write the letter?" (2.1.130–34).

While this gender imbalance in gift giving echoes that in the records, gift giving in this play differs from the depositions in terms of the timing, of assessing value, and of the role of the go-between. Unlike the depositions, the dramatic figures, as in *Twelfth Night*, exchange more gifts prior to marriage and do not assess their value to prove or disprove a marriage or return one of like value to make an equal exchange.[21] In addition, the gifts take on more importance since messengers such as Julia and Proteus woo in ways different than requested. Julia points out how she will try to impede the progress of Proteus' suit to Silvia: "I am my master's true confirmed love, / But cannot be true servant to my master, / Unless I prove false traitor to myself. / Yet will I woo for him, but yet so coldly, / As (heaven it knows) I would not have him speed" (4.4.103–07).[22]

Because presents play a prominent role as expressions of intent both in literary and legal texts, one could argue that they play a mor prominent role in this drama—the majority of the gifts are written expressions of love; they literally contain meaning inherently *in* themselves. Inga-Stina Ewbank points to the primacy of writing in expressing love in this play: " 'Lines' are made the vehicle, indeed the essence, of 'love' and 'life' in this world, even as the 'hand' that writes is the chief agent and evidence of the 'heart' that feels" (42). For example, in a letter from Julia to Proteus, Proteus' overview of the contents of the letters indicates that the letter details Julia's intent: "Sweet love, sweet lines, sweet life! / Here is her hand, the agent of her heart; / Here is her oath for love, her honour's pawn. / O that our fathers would applaud our loves / To seal our happiness with their consents! / O heavenly Julia!" (1.3.45–50). Proteus is so concerned that his father will discover Julia's intent that he lies about its authorship claiming it is from Valentine. In addition to containing the meaning in itself, a letter also serves in the play to help interpret the meaning of a gift. Proteus sends Silvia a ring accompanied by a letter (4.4.85–86). Another gift in the play may also suggest that meaning lies in the gift. Because "the hangman boys in the market-place" (4.4.54–55) stole the dog Proteus wanted Launce to deliver to Silvia, Launce ends up offering his own dog, Crab, figuring that since his dog is "as big as ten of" Proteus' that he is "therefore the gift the greater" (4.4.56–57).[23] On the one hand, Launce's own comments that because the dog is bigger it is better suggests that meaning lies in the item itself. On the other hand, Launce's view that he can substitute one dog for another suggests that the specific dog does not determine its meaning. As Silvia's response to Crab indicates, one dog may not be just like another: "Marry, she says your dog was a cur, and tells you currish thanks is good enough for such a present" (4.4.48–49).[24]

However, the dramatic action of the play more often demonstrates that, as in the depositions, the context of the giving must be read to understand intentions. One can argue that the context of giving and receiving determines the meaning of the letters. Even though the letters appear to have intrinsic worth because they can be seen literally to contain the intentions of their givers, in most cases the play does not include their contents. Instead, the dramatic action focuses mor on how the receiver interprets the receipt of the gift and its contents rather than presenting the contents for the reader or theatregoer to hear directly. In addition, Silvia and Proteus' discussion of the intentions behind the giving of the picture further underscores that, as in the depositions, the context of the exchange and the intentions of the parties determine the meaning of the material object. Proteus requests her picture to woo it—"to your shadow will I make true love" (4.2.122). Silvia reinterprets the meaning of this gift not to underscore his constancy and devotion to her but to underscore his falseness: "I am very loath to be your idol, sir; / But, since your falsehood shall become you well / To worship shadows, and adore false shapes, / Send to me in the morning, and I'll send it" (4.2.125–28).

Much of the criticism regarding the intentions of a gift giver in *The Two Gentlemen of Verona* concerns the subsequent fate of the ring Julia gave to Proteus. The original and subsequent exchanges of the ring emphasize once again the importance of the context of the exchange. When Proteus first suggests sending his ring to Silvia, Julia reads this giving as a sign of Proteus' lack of love and more generally the "contrariness" of love (4.4.79–84). This exchange turns into another since he sends a letter and the ring in hopes of a picture in return (4.4.85–87). The symbolism of the ring changes at the end of the play where it becomes a symbol of constancy, not only of Julia's constancy to Proteus but also Proteus' pledged constancy to Julia: "I have my wish for ever" (5.4.118).

The play's many comments on how to interpret the receipt of a gift also emphasize the role context plays to determine intention. Valentine provides advice on how to interpret a woman's reaction to receiving gifts. After the Duke tells Valentine that the woman he is wooing "did scorn a present that . . . [he] sent her" (3.1.92), Valentine advises him on how to read her reaction: "A woman sometime scorns what best contents her. / Send her another; never give her o'er, / For scorn at first makes after-love the more" (3.1.93–95). This advice underscores the response rather than the particular item as containing the meaning. In addition, Speed's catalog of the signs proving Valentine's love for Silvia after Valentine finds her glove at the beginning of Act 2, scene 1 points to Valentine's reaction as more important than the item, especially because the play does not specify the conditions under which she left the glove.

Mostly, however, as I noted above, dramatic figures offer interpretations of a gift when it is a letter. When Lucetta accepts the letter from Proteus to Julia in Julia's name, Julia points out how receiving a letter affects her modesty (1.2.41–47). Although Julia wishes she "had o'erlook'd the letter" (1.2.50), she outlines how she could receive it without any taint to her honor: "What fool is she, that knows I am a maid, / And would not force the letter to my view! / Since maids, in modesty say 'no' to that / Which they would have the profferer construe 'ay' " (1.2.53–56). Yet Julia herself acts differently from how she suggests she should. Although she tears up the letter claiming, "This babble shall not henceforth trouble me" (1.2.99), she immediately regrets her actions: "O hateful hands, to tear such loving words; / Injurious wasps, to feed on such sweet honey, / And kill the bees that yield it, with your stings! / I'll kiss each several paper, for amends" (1.2.106–09). Her self-criticism emphasizes that the meaning of a gift lies in the context of exchange. Here, the manner in which she received the letter indicates her intentions.

The sender also scrutinizes the manner in which Julia receives the letter. Speed interprets the way in which Lucetta, who he assumed was Julia, received the letter as proof that Proteus will "hardly win her" (1.1.128). Her lack of financial generosity to him for delivering it is indicative of her lack of emotional generosity: "I could perceive nothing at all from her; no, not so much as a ducat for delivering your letter; and being so hard to me that brought your mind, I fear she'll prove as hard to you in telling your mind. Give her no token but stones, for she's as hard as steel" (1.1.130–35). Proteus interprets her lack of speech upon receiving the letter as the fault of the messenger rather the message (1.1.145–47). Since Proteus believes the person who delivers the letter affects its receipt, he employs Julia to deliver a letter and a ring to Silvia because her "face" and "behaviour . . . Witness good bringing up, fortune, and truth" (4.4.66–68). However, when he sends his next letter, this time to Silvia, the post does not have any influence. Although at first Julia delivers the wrong letter to Silvia, the exact letter Silvia receives does not matter: "I will not look upon your master's lines: / I know they are stuff'd with protestations, / And full of new-found oaths, which he will break / As easliy as I do tear his paper" (4.4.126–29). Meaning lies neither in the item nor in the letter; instead, the receipt of the item depends on the identity of the sender Silvia's response to the ring further indicates her refusal to accept anything from Proteus: "The more shame for him, that he sends it me; / For I have heard him say a thousand times / His Julia gave it him at his departure: / Though his false finger have profan'd the ring, / Mine shall not do his Julia so much wrong" (4.4.131–35).[25]

"Frequenting" in *The Two Gentlemen of Verona* occurs under strained conditions. While Proteus, Valentine, and Thurio all visit Silvia, given her father's choice of Thurio as a suitable partner for her Proteus and Valentine must woo under cover. Part of this cover is in the choice of gifts and, in Proteus' case, having Julia woo for him. In addition, Silvia's father limits her accessibility; so too, as Proteus points out at the beginning of the play, Proteus' father blocks his visiting Julia. Julia must disguise herself in order to be near her love.

With the constraints that the fathers put on these wooers, letters, as I noted earlier, serve as a form of displaced visiting. That is, Proteus and Julia start the play expressing love through letters rather than seeing each other, while Silvia and Valentine woo through the subterfuge of letters. Even when Proteus sends a messenger to Silvia instead of visiting her personally, his messenger delivers a written suit, rather than delivering his words orally as Cesario does for Orsino in *Twelfth Night*.

While *Twelfth Night* has similar categories of courting behaviors as those in the depositions and in *The Two Gentlemen of Verona* (speaking together, gift giving and receiving, and "frequenting"), the patterns of behavior within these categories vary more from the earlier comedy than from the depositions and as such place this play closer to actual social behaviors that deponents identified in the depositions. Speaking to one another and the exact words couples use play an important role in showing intent. Unlike in *The Two Gentlemen of Verona*, wooing for most couples is through face-to-face rather than written interaction. Rather than weighing down Cesario with numerous gifts for Olivia, Orsino advises Cesario what to say when wooing: "O then unfold the passion of my love, / Surprise her with discourse of my dear faith; / It shall become thee well to act my woes" (1.4.24–26). In addition to the words, Orsino thinks the sound of Cesario's voice will also persuade Olivia to accept his suit (1.4.31–34). Orsino was correct in thinking that face-to-face rather than written speech is the more effective manner by which to woo Olivia, but the exact words and the speaker of those words matter as well.

Twelfth Night contains more specific language than the previous play or the depositions in terms of what was said during courtship, particularly in the courtships of and by Olivia. The face-to-face wooing between Olivia and Viola deserves careful attention since it informs the individual consent to the pairings in the final act, and, as Jenkins points out, the wooing in Act 1, scene 5 is the most prepared-for scene in all of Shakespeare: "there is no encounter in Shakespeare, not even that of Hamlet with the ghost, which is more elaborately prepared for" (80).

The content of the speeches in wooing Olivia demonstrates a conflict between Olivia's definition of woman and the one that Viola and Orsino hold. Before we see Olivia, Orsino and Valentine establish the current definition of woman and her place within their society. Man is a worshipping, unrequited lover, and woman—whether it derives from the Petrarchan or Pauline tradition—is a "self-less," silent image. The opening lines of the play establish Orsino as the conventional

Petrarchan lover. Motivated by Olivia's rejection, he languorously enjoys the "sweet pangs" of unrequited love: "O, when mine eyes did see Olivia first, / Methought she purg'd the air of pestilence" (1.1.19–20). In Act 2, scene 4, he defines himself as a "true lover," because he worships an image: "For *such as I am, all true lovers* are, / Unstaid and skittish in all motions else, / Save in the constant *image of the creature* / That is belov'd" (17–20, emphasis mine). As critics often comment, Orsino is not in love with the woman herself but with his own self-generated image of her.[26] As an image, Olivia has no independent identity, and Orsino continues to view her in these terms. He reveals his deification of her when they meet in Act 5: "Here comes the Countess: now heaven walks on earth" (95) and "You uncivil lady, / To whose ingrate and unauspicious altars / My soul the faithfull'st off'rings hath breath'd out / That e'er devotion tender'd" (110–13).[27] Juliet Dusinberre notes the restriction of such worship: "To see a woman as a goddess is to silence her as a human being" (140). His Petrarchanism, however, has to be modified so the marriages at the end can occur, since Petrarchan love—except for Spenser's—is usually incompatible with marriage. The unmarried state of Viola and Orsino, Orsino's need to see Viola in her female attire, and the language in his final speech may indicate how little his, as well as Viola's, Petrarchanism has been modified.

Valentine's description of his reception at Olivia's house reinforces this definition of woman. By defining Olivia as an image, Valentine forms an identity for woman that simultaneously shapes and further constructs his knowledge of what a woman should be: "I might not be admitted, / But from her handmaid do return this answer: / The element itself, till seven years' heat, / Shall not behold her face at ample view; / But like a cloistress she will veiled walk" (1.1.24–28). In these lines Olivia is an unspeaking image. Valentine reports that he received no words from Olivia; she seems to have no voice of her own. Through her isolation and her veil, she seems to lack an independent identity.

Olivia's identity as an image dissipates when Viola comes wooing in Act 1, scene 5, for in this wooing Olivia puts forward a different definition. Olivia's power of speech enables her to shatter the construction of woman as image and to reconstruct another. Marilyn L. Williamson points out the particular power women gained through language during courtship: "The language of courtship in itself conveys power on the woman who is wooed by the male suitor, but Shakespeare and his contemporaries encoded the language of love so that for them the woman was especially powerful in such a

relationship" (27). With this power, Olivia provides a gender definition in which she can be active and retain autonomy.

Paradoxically, Olivia reveals her identity while she denies it. She has
veiled herself just before Viola enters, thereby conforming to the conception of woman as an image. However, in the verbal exchanges
between Viola and Olivia, Olivia reflects the directness of many
women in the depositions, despite differences in status. As Viola continues in the Petrarchan mode by planning to woo "with my speech in
your praise" (191), Olivia steps off the pedestal, out of her stereotype,
overturning the convention: "Come to what is important in't: I for-
give you the praise" (193–94). She not only refuses the praise but also
denies the importance of poetry: "It is the more like to be feigned;
I pray you keep it in" (197–98). By regarding poetry as fictitious and
unimportant, Olivia turns the Petrarchan courtship on its head. Carol
Thomas Neely's comments on women who mock Petrarchan love
obtain for what Olivia ultimately achieves:

> By debunking Petrarchanism, they expose the emptiness of male ideal-
> ization and the unrealiability of male vows of undying love. They are
> able to seize control of courtship, to insist on the reality of female sex-
> uality and shrewishness, and to affirm for themselves and other women
> a complex identity beyond the Petrarchan stereotypes. (6)

Olivia resists a language that constricts woman's power, since it
appears that she is the center of the male-devised structure when that
structure actually restrains her power. The illusion of the woman's
exalted place within this code is central to its power. As Michel
Foucault observes, "Power is tolerable only on condition that it mask
a substantial part of itself. Its success is proportional to its ability to
hide its own mechanisms. . . . For it, secrecy is not in the nature of an
abuse; it is indispensable to its operation" (86). Olivia here reveals
that she is aware of its mechanisms and offers an alternative definition.
She wants the suit of her wooer to be based, not on passion, but
"reason" (201), reason here suggesting autonomy.

Although Viola goes on to read the text by Orsino, Olivia continues a heretic. She refuses the current definition of being a worshipped
image and mocks the conception of woman as picture: "we will draw
the curtain and show you the picture. [*Unveiling*] Look you, sir, such
a one I was this present" (236–38). Her self-consciousness in becoming an image enhances its anti-Petrarchanism. Of this moment of
unveiling, Geoffrey H. Hartman comments, "I was, not I am; by pre-
tending she is a painting, just unveiled, the original I is no longer

there. . . . There is no 'present': no absolute gift, or moment of pur
being. Yet a sense of epiphany, however fleeting, is felt" (51). As
Hartman points out, regardless of duration, an epiphany occurs. The
"original I," however, does not disappear as Hartman believes;
instead, the epiphany contradicts Orsino and Valentine's view of
women. Olivia further mocks Petrarchan structure by becoming the
sonneteer herself: "I will give out divers schedules of my beauty. It
shall be inventoried, and every particle and utensil labelled to my will.
As, item, two lips indifferent red; item, two grey eyes, with lids to
them; item, one neck, one chin, and so forth" (247–52). Petrarchan
sonneteers are for the most part obsessed with cataloging the physical
attributes of their beloveds, reducing a woman to only the sum of her
parts. Besides parodying literary convention by being both poet and
subject, Olivia omits elaboration and so undercuts convention even
further. Rather than having eyes like the sun, her eyes are like pans, a
description which hardly conforms to Petrarchan standards. Charles
Tyler Prouty notes the lack of idealism in her scheduling of her
beauty: "Beauty has thus been reduced to an inventory such as one
might find appended to an *inquisition post mortem* or in a testamen-
tary paper such as a will. The conceit that Olivia is here employing
punctures, of course, any idealization of love" (120–21). However
when Olivia confesses her love for the page, she adheres to the ver
ideology she previously denied. She uses neo-Platonic theories to
describe how she falls in love, thereby suggesting the method of the
Petrarchan lover as well as echoing Orsino's depiction in the opening
of the play: "Methinks I feel this youth's perfections / With an invis-
ible and subtle stealth / To creep in at mine eyes" (300–02). Yet the
fact that she declares this love and that she sends Viola a ring undercut her conformity to Orsino's definition. As Williamson notes, "The
courtship of Olivia is structured so that she is never really the
Petrarchan lady, for she quickly begins to pursue Cesario" (31).

In the second courting scene, Act 3, scene 1, Olivia's comments on
love and Orsino again undercut Petrarchan posturing: " 'Twas never
merry world / Since lowly feigning was call'd compliment" (100–01).
While in Act 1, scene 5 Olivia expresses her love in neo-Platonic theories, here she concerns herself with what her beloved *thinks*. Within
thirty-nine lines, the words "think" and "thought" occur twelve
times. As a lover, Olivia does not insist she knows what the beloved
feels, but what Viola "thinks" of her (140–43). Oivia disrupts mor
than Petrarchan conventions here. Both her position of lover (rather
than beloved) and her insistence on *reason* (rather than passion)
emphasize the head. However, the Christian Pauline tradition states

that woman is the body of man, thereby underscoring subservience and the heart: "For the husband is the head of the wife, even as Christ is the head of the church: and he is the saviour of the body" (Ephesians 5:23). Here Olivia disrupts both literary and Christian patriarchal traditions. Olivia, however, then sabotages this disruption by shifting to an emphasis on passion as the basis of her love: "I love thee so, that maugre all thy pride, / Nor wit nor reason can my passion hide" (153–54).

Despite the possibility for directness, Viola woos in the conventional Petrarchan fashion. Viola's question—"The honourable lady of the house, which is she?" (1.5.169)—reveals that she sees Olivia as her master does: namely, as an object. For "the lady of the house," the house's lady, indicates that Olivia has no identity beyond possession of the house. Despite Olivia's denial of being a possession, Viola persists in defining her in terms similar to those of Orsino: "Most radiant, exquisite, and unmatchable beauty" (171). In addition, Viola's tools include an "excellently well penned" speech of praise, to which she is most sensitive (174–75), and the posture of a devoted worshipper. Viola can only argue for love in Petrarchan terms, since the way to love is "With adorations, fertile tears, / With groans that thunder love, with sighs of fire" (259–60). To Viola, whether male or female, one loves in the way the patriarchal Petrarchan convention allows— with "thriftless sighs" (2.2.38). Though "sighs" suggest she here takes the male role, they hardly count for an independent voice with which to form an identity.

The image of the yearning lover in her "willow cabin" speech further underscores the sincerity of Viola's adherence to the gender definition put forward by Orsino and Valentine. As indicated by the absence of a subject pronoun in this speech, Viola's wooing is more active than the Duke's wooing, but it continues in the same Petrarchan fashion. Although Viola inverts the Petrarchan behavioral posture by becoming the wooer, she nonetheless reveals her subscription to this pose: the sighing lover is the truest expression of love. Likewise, Viola's conformity to Orsino's definition of woman appears in her soliloquy where she laments, "How easy is it for the proper false / In women's waxen hearts to set their forms! / Alas, our frailty is the cause, not we, / For such as we are made of, such we be" (2.2.28–31). Moreover, although Viola denies that she is a wooer by stressing that she only plays a role—"I can say little more that I have studied, and that question's out of my part" (1.5.179–80)—she woos Olivia just as she woos the Duke in Act 2, scene 4, when she represents herself to him as he himself sees Olivia—as a silent image. To the Duke, she orally describes herself as "Patience on a monument" (115). This tableau-like description recalls Valentine's picture of Olivia in the very first scene. The "sister" has neither a past— "And what's her history? / A blank"—nor a voice with which to express her self—"she never told her love" (110–11); instead, she is frozen and silent. To Viola and to the Duke, this is "love indeed" (116).

Like *The Two Gentlemen of Verona* but unlike the depositions, in *Twelfth Night* dramatic figures exchange most of the gifts prior to a marriage. Rather than the catalog of "love-tokens" that appears in *A Midsummer Night's Dream*—"bracelets of . . . [his] hair, rings, gauds, conceits, / Knacks, trifles, nosegays, sweetmeats" (1.1.29, 33–34)— or the list of tokens for sale in Autolycus' song in Act 4, scene 4 of *The Winter's Tale* (220–32), this play includes five love tokens given prior to a marriage—a jewel, ring, picture, pearl, and love letter. While this play contains an array of different kinds of gifts, once again money figures less prominently as a courting gift preceding a marriage, unlike in the depositions.[28]

In addition to the kinds of items, this play differs from *The Two Gentlemen of Verona* in terms of who gives the majority of courtship gifts. Significantly, a woman, Olivia, gives almost all the gifts, and, as the depositions suggest, her giving is not solely the result of her social status.[29] That is, even though she is a countess, she gives tokens as a single woman who has never been married. Like the women in the court records, Olivia is both a suitor and the object of a suit; she is both a gift receiver and giver. While Olivia worries about "How shall I feast" Cesario? "What bestow of him?" (3.4.2), the play's drama- tized courting behaviors contain more of the latter. In Act 1, scene 5, for example, she tries to give Cesario money (287) and then sends her ring to "him" (304–10). In Act 3, scene 4, in her final courting scene with Cesario, she gives him a picture of herself (210–11). In Act 4, scene 3, she gives Sebastian a pearl.

Although Olivia offers and gives most of the gifts in the play, men give some gifts as well. Orsino sends Olivia a "jewel" (2.4.124). Despite a love so intense that it can "bide no denay" (2.4.125), this jewel is the only gift he sends Olivia. Yet we neither see her receive it nor learn that she does. Whether this nondelivery is a dramatic over- sight or a way for Viola to sabotage his wooing of Olivia is left to speculation. That he sends Olivia only one token which she perhaps does not receive serves as yet another indicator, especially in light of the behaviors narrated in the depositions, of the lack of commitment and emotional and sexual force of his courtship. William G. Meader's point—that in giving "a 'jewel' . . . meaning both the object given and the beloved's chastity asked for in return" (146)—suggests the gift may hold some sexual force. If so, such a meaning could explain why Viola would not deliver it.

Compared with the previous play and the depositions, *Twelfth Night* limits both the interpreting and the negotiation of obligation. The interpretations by Olivia and Viola of the ring she sends to Viola and by Malvolio of the letter are the main instances of the former in this play. A difference exists between the depositions and these two dramas since the plays do not dramatize individuals quantifying the exchange in financial terms and delivering items in return of similar economic value. As economic worth did not play a large role in determining suitability of a partner for the dramatic figures, so too the economic value of the gift does not play a role in quantifying the obligation of the giver or receiver.

Unlike many of the women in the depositions, Olivia neither negotiates the value of a courtship gift that she received in order to prove or disprove a contract nor sends return gifts of quantified value. In Act 1, scene 5, Olivia pretends to have received a ring from Orsino, a ring she claims was left with her against her will. Of course, it is her own ring that she sends as a token to Cesario (304–10). Even though Orsino never sent it, the explanation she gives Malvolio for returning the ring nonetheless shows her interpreting a "gift" and negotiating the exchange: "Run after that same peevish messenger / The County's man: he left this ring behind him, / Would I or not; tell him, I'll none of it. / Desire him not to flatter with his lord, / Nor hold him up with hopes: I am not for him. / If that the youth will come this way to-morrow, / I'll give him reasons for't. Hie thee, Malvolio" (1.5.304–10). That is, Olivia says she "returns it" so that Orsino will have no claim on her. The remorse she later expresses for sending the ring was not about the act of giving but from the way she gave it, for using "a shameful cunning" to get him to accept it (3.1.113–18).

In addition, Olivia interprets the value of a gift that she gives Cesario—which is not ultimately refused—in Act 3, scene 4. Here, the interpretation is of its personal rather than economic value. In her final courting scene with Viola, she gives her a picture of herself. Her interpretation suggests this gift has meaning in itself: "Here, wear this jewel for me, 'tis my picture: / Refuse it not, it hath no tongue to vex you" (3.4.210–11). Roy Strong explains that miniatures were meant to capture the person in a more relaxed state than in a formal portrait:

> Miniaturists actually only ever paint what they see before them. An elementary fact this may be, but it accounts for the extreme power of these portraits which is only matched in their sense of revelation by

early photography. The limner did no preparatory drawings; we see the fruits of an immediate encounter between a painter and his sitter placed only a few feet away from him. This must account for the sparkling spontaneity and vivacity of so many of them, as though their subjects were caught mid-stream in conversation—which must often have been the case. (*English* 9)[30]

Yet, while the limner was to catch the motion and spontaneity of the person, Olivia does not draw attention to the spontaneity of the miniature but the lack of it since she points to its stillness, its fixed silence. Ironically, in the very act of giving the gift, Olivia deconstructs her conformity to the definition of a woman as an image.

In addition, Malvolio focuses on the potential personal benefits resulting from the gift, rather than on its economic worth. As with the letters in *The Two Gentlemen of Verona*, here too the meaning of the item and the intentions of the sender are supposedly contained within the gift itself. Yet the letter becomes the center of negotiations concerning intent, particularly since the expressions and requests are par of a trick.[31] The use of a love letter in this play is more sophisticated than in *The Two Gentlemen of Verona*, especially since here we have the contents of the letter, which allows us to interpret his interpretation. As Toby predicted, Malvolio is quick to interpret the identity and the intentions of the assumed giver of the letter: "He shall think by the letters that thou wilt drop that they come from my niece, and that she's in love with him" (2.3.165–67). Malvolio's earlier action in Act 2, scene 2 of "dropping" the ring Olivia tells him to return to Viola may partially account for his lack of suspicion regarding the identity of who sent the "dropped" letter: to drop a gift is a form of delivery. While he earlier showed his contempt for the gift through this form of delivery, in this reverse situation he ironically shows great regard for the gift found on the ground. His reading of the context of the gift and of the gift itself expresses his emotional commitment and intentions to Olivia, specifically his political and sexual desires.[32] In this play, the anti-love letter Malvolio writes to Olivia—"*you wrong me, and the world shall know it*" (5.1.301–02)—rather than the "love letter" is a more accurate marker of the intentions of the sender. When it comes to written versus oral expressions of love in *Twelfth Night* face-to-face communication is the more successful form of wooing.

While Sebastian and Malvolio do not concern themselves with the expected personal cost of receiving a gift from Olivia,[33] Viola does. Unlike her brother, she considers the value of the exchange. She refuses the money in Act 1, scene 5—"I am no fee'd post, lady; keep your purse" (288)—and the ring in Act 2, scene 2. In the latter refusal she points not to its specific economic value but to the personal costs for her and Olivia: "I left no ring with her: what means this lady? / Fortune forbid my outside have not charm'd her! / . . . / She loves me, sure; the cunning of her passion / Invites me in this churlish messenger. / None of my lord's ring? Why, he sent her none. / I am the man: if it be so, as 'tis, / Poor lady, she were better love a dream" (16–25).[34] Once again, a female figure in the play interprets the meaning of a gift and the context of the giving just as women and men do in the depositions. Some critics believe the ring has intrinsic worth. Michaela Roell argues that the shape of a ring informs its symbolic meaning: "the 'O-thing' or 'no-thing'. . . objectifies Olivia's surrender of her sex and sexuality" (48). Although Meader's argument of the ring's meaning differs from Roell's, his comments indicate—as do hers—that the ring's meaning is clear: "Viola feels that the ring signifies a request for betrothal by signs and that by accepting it she would have assented to a betrothal" (178–79).[35] However, here, as in the depositions, the context of the exchange and the intentions of the giver and receiver determine its meaning. The play leaves the meaning of the ring more open to interpretation than these two critics allow.

"Frequenting" is a courting behavior which differs in *Twelfth Night* from that in the previous drama and in the depositions. It is not as prominent as evidence of intent in this play as in the depositions despite the many courtships which occur, in part because one of Olivia's suitors and another couple dwell in her house and another suitor is part of her staff. Living in the same house, as demonstrated in the depositions, is not enough to prove intent; instead, the source of the invitation must be considered. For example, since Olivia did not directly invite Aguecheek to stay with her, his presence in her house does not demonstrate her acceptance of his suit.[36]

The depositions and the dramas both contain a wide range of courting behaviors operating concurrently. Yet a common thread weaves through the multiplicity of behaviors in the different categories and different texts—the need for individual consent. The following chapter and postscript explore further the kinds of evidence dramatic figures and deponents cited to determine individual consent during and after a marriage.

4

Contracting Couples: Vows, Hand Holding, and Gift Giving

he heard the sayd Alice confesse that she had receyved a pece of silver which was broken betwene them to bynd a contract of marriage betwene them which if it had byn gold she sayd it would have bownd but by reason it was but silver she sayd it could not bynde and she sayd that therefore the contract was voyd.

(DL/C/219/250ʳ

A contract of eternal bond of love,
Confirm'd by mutual joinder of your hands,
Attested by the holy close of lips,
Strengthen'd by interchangement of your rings.

(*Twelfth Night* 5.1.154–57)

Under the letter of canon law in early modern England, as I discussed in the introduction, couples could marry using verbal contracts without exchanging vows from the Book of Common Prayer in a church in the presence of a minister and witnesses.[1] The matrimonial enforcement suits in the surviving London Consistory Court depositions contain disputed marriages of individuals who married by contract away from the church and, in fewer numbers, by the ceremony in the Book of Common Prayer inside the church. In evaluating the validity of a marriage, the courts considered a variety of evidence—mainly, the exchange of vows, hand holding,[2] gift exchange,[3] kissing, and pledging—when determining whether a marriage occurred and both parties consented to it. Some of this evidence supports the existence of marriage, and some supports the plausibility of marriage. While the above list indicates the number of times—from most to least—deponents cited a behavior the order of what deponents cite happened during a marriage varies slightly: usually, the couple held hands, exchanged vows, kissed, gave gifts, and then pledged each other. The personal response of Helen

Johnson represents this typical order: William Taylor, holding Helen "by her righte hande," said "I will*i*am tak the hellen to my wyffe to have and to hould for better for worse till death us departe and therupon I geve the my faithe my hand and my troathe." Then, Helen, "houldinge hym the s*ai*d Will*i*am still by his hande," said "I Hellen take the Will*i*am to my husband to have and to hould from this day forward for better for worse till death us dep*a*rte and thereto I geve the my faithe my hande and my trothe." Then, "they kissed ech other." Helen deposed that she then broke "a gould geniou in twayne and gave . . . William Taylor one p*a*rte and kepte thother to her selfe; and then he gave her for his p*a*rte a pece of gould of halfe a crowne" (DL/C/214/59). Occasionally, deponents pointed to a few other types of evidence when assessing individual consent, such as the amount of alcohol consumed, whether parties were forced to marry, overall demeanor, the manner in which the vows were spoken, and the pitch of the voice of an individual while speaking the vows. Although, as I noted in the introduction, we cannot know the complete course of litigation or even the outcome of most matrimonial enforcement suits, we can discover what deponents understood as significant in providing evidence of consent and how deponents interpreted this evidence. In this chapter, I focus first on the signs of consent as the London Consistory Court depositions register them. I then turn briefly to consider how these marrying behaviors relate to *The Two Gentlemen of Verona* and *Twelfth Night*. These two plays replicate the significance of marital consent found in these depositions, and they (like the depositions) ultimately affirm the letter of contemporary ecclesiastical marriage law.[4]

Canon Law

Because the formation of marital contracts was a key step in legal and social practice, it is important to review the relevant legislative theory. The legal history of marriage contracts is a complex topic. The continuity and change of medieval ecclesiastical legislation regarding marriage has been the focus of excellent studies, particularly by Charles Donahue, Jr., R. H. Helmholz, and Michael M. Sheehan. Here, I would like to provide a brief outline of the basic tenets of the legislative theory, particularly in terms of the formation and status of verbal marital contracts, in order to understand better the marriage contracts recounted in the London Consistory Court depositions and in Shakespeare's dramas.

The medieval Roman canon law maintained that consent was the basis of marriage.[5] This law regarded the exchange of words by a couple—the boy at least fourteen and the girl at least twelve years of age—in the present tense (*verba de praesenti*) or in the future tense (*verba de futuro*) followed by sexual intercourse as a valid marriage, absent such fundamental impediments as being within prohibited degrees of consanguinity and affinity, under age, already married, incompetent, or permanently impotent.[6] The law also recognized conditional contracts, which became binding once the stipulated condition had been fulfilled. Ideally, these verbal contracts should be made before witnesses. Yet, while the Roman Catholic Church changed its marriage laws after the Reformation, England still held on to the former canon law that defined these contracts as a valid marriage. Paradoxically, as Helmholz outlines, "the English Church clung to a part of the medieval Roman canon law which the Roman Catholic Church itself discarded" (*Roman* 69). As he details, "Medieval canon law had allowed a man and woman to enter into a binding and indissoluble marriage merely by exchanging words of present consent. No public ceremony, no publication of banns, no approval of the couple's family, no sexual consummation were required. Only a contract, made by *verba de praesenti*, between two consenting parties was necessary" (*Roman* 69). Henry Swinburne, a longtime judge of the Prerogative Court at York, stresses "the only want of Solemnity doth not hurt the Contract" (195) for "Spousals *de praesenti* are as indissoluble as perfect Matrimony solemnized and consummate" (236). Solemnization was more a matter of publicity than a requirement for a valid marriage.

The Church of England urged couples to solemnize their marital contracts within specifically defined times, dates, and places. Ecclesiastical legislation dictated that marital contracts should be solemnized or church marriages should take place between the hours of 8 a.m. and 12 noon, within the dates the ecclesiastical calendar allowed, after the reading of the banns on three successive Sundays, and in the parish church of the bride or groom or both. The complex ecclesiastical calendar offered couples specific times in which to marr in church that varied year-by-year depending on the date of Easter According to ecclesiastical legislation, the three forbidden seasons of marriage were Lent, Rogationtide, and Advent. As David Cressy notes, "Altogether the Anglican ecclesiastical calendar, inherited from Roman Catholicism, marked 144 days as unsuitable for marriage ceremonies. Formal inhibitions against marriage affected almost 40 percent of the year" ("Seasonality" 2).[7] In light of these restrictions, "The three peak periods for marriage," as Ralph Houlbrooke notes, "fell in October-November (by far the biggest), April-June and January-February" (*English* 85). The purchase of a license allowed a couple to forgo the publicity of the reading of banns and to change the place, date, and time of a marriage. Canon 62, codified in 1604, suggests the importance the church placed on these prescripted times, dates, and places: ministers who married couples during unseasonable hours and in prohibited places without first attaining a license or dispensation faced a three-year suspension (Edward Cardwell, *Synodalia* 282). According to the church, a couple should not consummate their vows until they married in a ceremony conforming to the church's regulations. As Houlbrooke notes, "In the Church's view, full consummation of a marriage was not permissible until after solemnization in church, preceded by triple banns to ensure adequate publicity for the couple's intentions" (*English* 78).[8] While the 141 canons approved in 1604 indicate what the church held important, they did not alter the ecclesiastical laws governing marriage. As R. B. Outhwaite comments, "the canons governing entry into marriage contained nothing new; they merely codified existing regulations" (*Clandestine* 8). However, a couple need not meet these conditions in order to contract a valid marriage in early modern England.

A variety of labels regarding these contracts exist to represent a variety of situations. Here I distinguish *verba de praesenti* contracts, which are sometimes referred to as betrothals, handfastings, trothplightings, and spousals, as a valid, binding marital contract from a promise to marry, which I here use to refer to a conditional or future contract.[9]

LONDON CONSISTORY COURT DEPOSITIONS

Predictably, deponents often provided details regarding times and dates of marital contracts and church ceremonies in assessing whether a marriage occurred and both parties consented to it. In terms of the time of day, while several contracts, like church marriages, occurred before noon, many more contracts took place in the afternoon or evening. Rather than general references to the morning, afternoon, or evening, deponents usually supplied more specific times, often pointing to hour increments: "about one or ii a Clock in the after noone" (DL/C/215/295[r]); "about 3 or 4 of the clocke in the afternoone" (DL/C/219/420[r]); and "about eight a Clock at night" (DL/C/ 215/203[v]). In addition to the time of day, contracts allowed couples more variety and convenience in terms of the time of year in which they married—two people could marry when they wanted without worrying about a license. Deponents provided times of church ceremonies as well. When the union of a couple married in church was in dispute, deponents often cited the time the ceremony occurred as partial evidence of consent. In the depositions that provide the times of church marriages, they often took place between the canonical hours of 8 a.m. and 12 noon. Deponents also cited some couples who married in the church at noncanonical times. Ann Keningham alias Terrill testified that she married "James Tirrell in the body of Greenewiche Churche right against the pulpett . . . betwene five and six a Clock in the morning" (DL/C/218/121).[10]

Some deponents included the locations of contracts as partial evidence of consent. Contracts were less restrictive than church marriages in terms not only of the times of day and of year but also of the locations. Without the purchase of a license, ecclesiastical legislation dictated the church in which the couple could marry. The lack of a legislated location for a contract allowed one couple to perform multiple contracts in multiple locations. Henry Jackson and Jane Browne, according to a few witnesses in the case, performed a *verba de praesenti* contract in three different locations. In a deposition repeated on 27 October 1597, Thomas Bushe recounted how Henry and Jane contracted themselves first in the orchard of Jane's stepfather at Cliffe in Kent (DL/C/215/10ʳ); six weeks later, at John Fisher's house in Rochester (DL/C/215/9ᵛ); and a fortnight later, extraordinarily on Gadshill while on horseback on the road from Rochester to London: "a they came Ryding over gad*es* hill . . . Henry Jackson being uppo*n* horse a lone rode very close unto [Thomas] . . . Jane being behinde him . . . and then tooke her the same Jane by the hand and rehearsed the . . . same or the like word*es* of Contract" (DL/C/215/10ʳ). In addition to contracting in the orchard and on horseback, another example of a contract that occurred al fresco is the marriage of Thomas Baines and Susan Fidgett, who contracted matrimony when she was in "the ffeild*es* to dry clothes" (DL/C/214/171). The extant depositions indicate that litigants preferred to marry indoors rather than out regardless of the season. While deponents offered details regarding location to demonstrate their own presence and credibility as a witness, these specific details also indicate the amount of evidence considered when assessing consent.

Couples contracted themselves in locations similar to those in which they courted. The depositions identify houses as very popular places for a couple to contract themselves followed by taverns or inns.[11] Unlike with courtship, the private houses mentioned in the depositions indicate that no clear pattern exists in terms of at whose house a couple marry. In depositions that specify relationships, contracts occurred at the houses of the parties themselves, their parents, a brother, a brother-in-law, kinsman or kinswoman, friends, and masters and mistresses. For instance, one couple married in the house of the bride's father in the parish of Langdon Hills, Essex (DL/C/215/197^v), while another couple married in a "victualing howse" in Kingston-upon-Thames in Surrey (DL/C/216/307^v). The variety of locations for contracts suggests again that individual consent of the marrying parties was more important than where they married.

Deponents were seldom specific about the exact location in the house or tavern in which the litigants marry. However, some cases include information regarding the location of the room in the house. I include the individual references to underscore further the different kinds of information considered when determing contract validity and assessing consent. Some witnesses identified the room in which a contract occurred by its function—the hall (DL/C/215/12^r) or the kitchen (DL/C/215/107^r)—or pointed to the location of the room in the house—"an upper roome" or chamber (DL/C/216/312^r), a middle room (DL/C/215/93^v), or a lower room (DL/C/219/420^r). Some deponents provided even more details by noting the room's position in relation to the back or front of the house (DL/C/213/335), to stairs (DL/C/215/96^v), or to a specific place such as Smithfield (DL/C/219/418^r).[12]

Evidence that a contract occurred can also include such details as a couple's position in the room at the time of the contract. The range of details varies here from where a couple were in the room—"in the middle of the roome" (DL/C/216/294^r)—to a couple's position in relation to a feature such as a window or chimney.[13] Some deponents also included how the couple were placed in relation to furniture in the room—as they sat at a table (DL/C/219/83^v)—or in relation to each other—Richard "sittinge and Katherin standinge somwhat afor him but more towardes the right hand than the lefte" (DL/C/214/553) and "she . . . [was] sitting in his lapp" (DL/C/215/121^r). Such details as the latter could certainly suggest intent and consent.

Deponents pointed to the presence of people rather than written accounts more often as witnesses whether a couple married in or away from church.[14] As in the case of Thomas Baines and Susan Fidgett, having "nobody beeing then present but them selves" (DL/C/214/171) at a contract could quickly turn into a "he said/she said" situation. The number of witnesses present at nonchurch marriages in the extant depositions from the London Consistory Court was not large. Deponents varied on the minimum number of witnesses that they believed the law required. In defense of the validity of his contract with Ann Hyde, Alexander Hollinworth told Elizabeth Dune that "he had two wittnesses, and that ii wittnesses were as good as two hundred" (DL/C/215/107ʳ). Some deponents thought more were needed. When John Hardinge asked Thomas Cordie to be a witness to his contract with Margaret Hardinge, Thomas replied that "we will have more wittnesses," and he "called John devenishe the brother of . . . Margaret then in the howse and one Agnes Layland a mayd servant in the howse to be witnesses with him" (DL/C/215/197ᵛ). The location of a contract could influence the number of witnesses available. As Helmholz comments, since many couples contracted themselves at home, the contracts were "seldom witnessed by more than a few people" (*Marriage* 154).

It is impossible to determine the gender of witnesses or their relationships to the litigants at contracts and church ceremonies, since many depositions specify neither; instead, deponents sometimes listed names or often included such phrases as "dyvers others" or the assembled congregation. At one contract, Margaret Swinerton testified that William Greene and she "in a howse in East Smithefild by the tower of London in the presence of divers wittnesses did Contract them selves togither in matrimony" (DL/C/215/181ᵛ). Such common phrasings by deponents indicate that individual consent of the marrying parties was more important than the presence of specific kin.

When deponents identified a relationship between a litigant and a witness, the relationship of a witness to a couple varies widely. While legislation did not exist dictating the specific relationship of witnesses to the couple, social historians note patterns in depositions from other areas of early modern England. For example, Diana O'Hara points to the importance of the presence of "kin" in the depositions from the diocese of Canterbury in 1540 to 1570: "Those groups which congregated at such betrothal ceremonies, and which were by implication an integral part of the social system, were composed predominantly of biological and 'fictive' kin, and where larger groupings manifested themselves they might nevertheless form an identifiable sub-group" (" 'Ruled' " 22–23). The relationships of the witnesses to the couples at marriages mentioned in the London Consistory Court depositions for 1586 to 1611 differ from the familial and kinship participation O'Hara outlines for the diocese of Canterbury in 1540 to 1570. In the few instances in which deponents identified the relationship of a witness to the couple, they almost always did not point to the witness as family. Such a pattern may not be that surprising given the patterns of migration to and mobility within London.[15] That witnesses wer usually not family relations also suggests the variety of locations in which people contracted themselves. That is, when a couple contracted themselves in a tavern, they sometimes called on the people who happened to be present to be witnesses.

Most often the role of the witness was more important to the union than her or his gender or relation to the bride or groom. As mentioned above, canon law in England did not require witnesses to contract a valid marriage. However, the church recommended that people were present to witness the event, especially at contracts at which a minister usually did not officiate and a register book did not record the event. The eagerness with which William Carnaby volunteered to be a witness indicates an awareness of the important roles witnesses played in determining whether a contract occurred. William "sayd Sibill let me see you ioyne hand*es*" with Alan Browne "by way of contractm*ent* that I may be a witnes thereof what soever shall happen hereafter" (DL/C/219/23ᵛ). Deponents suggested that witnesses were as important at church ceremonies as at contracts. A minister alone was not enough for some. Thomas Curtys invited Elizabeth Mathewe and "other of hys neighbours" to be present the next morning when he and Alice Twissleton would solemnize their contract (DL/C/213/170).

Litigants themselves also called for witnesses to their union, sometimes even highlighting a witness' role during their vows. Frances Edmondes called on those present to "bare wittnes that I doe here take this man John Stubbes to be my husband and I doe for sake all this for his sake and ther unto I plight him my faiethe and trothe" (DL/C/216/337ᵛ). Witnesses sometimes played a more direct role than observing a contract, by offering advice to the bride in mid-contract. According to George Ireland, after William Addison read a contract to Joan Waters, William directed Joan to consider her actions carefully, warning "her to take heed what shee did and to Consider well before shee sette her hand to the said writing for it was a contract w*hi*ch was not for a day or a moneth but for terme of life and shee answered shee knewe what shee did" (DL/C/219/409ʳ–409ᵛ). Likewise, Elizabeth Maberly, a widow, cautioned Frances Edmondes "to take hede what she did saying it is not for a . . . day or a yeare but for one of . . . yo*ur* lives" (DL/C/216/337ᵛ). While one of the advantages of a minister marrying a couple was to have a witness, so too witnesses sometimes served in that capacity by leading couples in their contracts or advising the marrying parties. Leading a couple through their contract could help them use the most explicit language of consent. Master Hawton "willed" Christopher Dawson "to take the peece of gowld againe" from Marion Crompton and give it to her again and "therw*i*th all give her his hand his faieth and trothe for ev*er*." Christopher followed his direction: he took the gold from her redelivered it to her, took Marion by the hand, and said, "I give yow this meaning the gowld and my faiethe and trothe for ev*er*." Then, Hawton directed Marion that she "must doe as muche to him." Marion then took a "gowld ring fro*m* of her finger and putt it uppo*n* one of *Christ*ofer dawsons fingers saying here *Christ*ofer and I doe give the this ring and w*i*thall my hand my faieth . . . my trothe for ev*er*" (DL/C/217/13).

Since canon law dictated that present consent by individuals who did not violate the church's requirements was the essence of marriage, the main task of the church courts was to determine whether both parties individually consented. In determining individual consent to marriage in the London Consistory Court, the particular words used for the vows were significant for many who sought redress. Edward Hyde "renounce[d]" his suit with the widow Joan Ellis, for example, after he was "p*er*swaded by his Counsell that the wordes wh*i*ch so were spoken betwene them will not Reache to a contract of matrimonye nor bind them" (DL/C/213/417). Witnesses and litigants were often careful to detail the exact content of the remembered vows. They most often recount *verba de praesenti* rather than *verba de futuro* or conditional contracts.[16]

Before considering the contents of the vows deponents recounted, we need to consider the overall form of the marriage contracts, since couples who contracted themselves away from church experienced a wider range of choice regarding the forms a marriage could take. The effects of the forms of the contracts in early modern England are far reaching. Alan Macfarlane comments on the extent to which this form emphasizes the individual: "It is difficult to envisage a more subversively individualistic and contractual foundation for a marriage system" (*Marriage* 129). While, as the first chapter suggests, parties were not "subversively individualistic" throughout the courtship process, the form the contracts could take allowed for individualism. That is, verbal contracts allowed couples more control than church ceremonies, since they provided them with more options in terms not only of where and when they married but also the content of their vows at their marriage. Economically, contracts were less expensive as well. Significantly, contracts allowed the woman more autonomy since they offered her the opportunity to officiate and control the ver form the marriage took, particularly controlling the language, which would not likely occur during a church ceremony—the woman need not be married by and in the presence of a "father" to contract a binding marriage. In addition, contracts offered men and women more autonomy than a church ceremony in terms of the order in which they spoke their vows. Yet the order in which the parties spoke the vows in contracts often echoed the order in the Book of Common Prayer ceremony, since the groom usually began. However, a few contracts occur in the depositions in which women vowed first, and these women were the never married as well as widows. In a contract between Frances Edmondes and John Stubbes which occurred in an upper chamber in an Inn, a witness testified that Frances took John by the hand, saying "I doe take yow . . . to my husband and theruppon I give yow my faiethe and trothe And . . . that she would for sake ffather and mother and all the world and betake her selfe only to him the same John." After loosening their hands, John took her by the hand, saying "I doe take yow . . . to my wief and I doe for sake all other women for your sake" (DL/C/216/312^r). In another case, after refusing Martin Mullens' goodwill for several months, Elizabeth Cole, speaking the vows first, contracted herself to him. She took him "by the hand and said unto him, . . . theise very woordes and none other . . . hear is my hand . . . in faith for ever whither my mother will or noe and then the said Martin answeared thear is my hand and my faith for ever and I will never forsake thee" (DL/C/214/170).

Most of the testimony—in the London Consistory Court depositions from matrimonial enforcement suits recounting marriages—focuses more on issues regarding the consent of the parties during verbal contracts than on matters regarding banns or licenses. Very rarely did witnesses at a contract fail to recall some account of the words. Even those who could not remember the exact words usually pointed to their understanding of present consent being exchanged. "After some secret talke and loving familiarytie" between John Swinsted and Elizabeth Brode alias Ibotson, William King saw John "howld . . . Elizabethe by the hand and he having a gowld ring in his other hand sayd unto her theis woordes with this ring I the wedd and so put the ring uppon one of . . . Elizabethes fingers" (DL/C/215/96^v–97^r). Yet although he could not remember the exact words, this witness still stressed that their language indicated present consent: "now by vertue of his othe he doethe not remember but he sayethe he . . . did then perswade him selfe that by the speches they then used they bothe had purpose and meaning to be married togither" (DL/C/215/97^r). Sometimes, a lack of specificity occurs regarding the exact words of the vows, since some testimony includes phrases surrounding the vows such as "theise woordes or the like in effect" (DL/C/214/269) and "used wordes to this effect" (DL/C/219/145^v). Yet such phrasings do not negate the value of the word patterns in the vows. The many witnesses who recounted similar verbal patterns in contracts with only slight variations indicate an awareness of the need for the vows to express consent even if they could not remember the exact words used. Depositions containing a contract almost always point to an exchange of vows. The balanced number of words used and the language chosen in the vows when both parties spoke suggests equal consent. While vows differed slightly from contract to contract or between the individuals during the contract, with the appropriate variations based on the sex of the speaker the marrying couple usually echoed each other word for word, as the contract between Grace Cooper and Thomas Harrison represents: "Thomas Harrison gave . . . Grace his right hand and howlding her by the right hand sayd I Thomas take the Grace to my wief and I will have the to my wief and no other woman, and therto I plight the my trothe and then they . . . losing hand*es* . . . Grace . . . tooke . . . Thomas by the right hand . . . saying And I Grace take the Thomas to my husband and I will have the to my husband and no other man and therto I plight the my trothe" (DL/C/215/243ᵛ).

Deponents commonly demonstrated a self-conscious awareness of the language needed to make a valid contract. Such comments as those by George Archer that "what a contract is he sayethe lett the Lawe Judg" are very rare (DL/C/216/280ᵛ). The case of *Alexander Hollinworth v. Ann Hyde* provides some rich evidence concerning knowledge of what makes a contract. In a deposition repeated on 13 February 1597/98, Elizabeth Dune testified to John Griffith's knowledge. While she, John, Edward Hyde, and Ann were all in the kitchen, Edward inquired "what are the word*es* that make folk*es* suer together." John then took "Edward by the hande sayed theise word*es* ffollowing doe make folk*es* suer together, And therew*i*th . . . John . . . houlding . . . Edward by the hande sayed, I John take the Jane to my wedded wyffe till death us departe and thereto I plight the my trothe, and then the woman to saye the like word*es* againe make folk*es* suer together quoth the sa*i*d John Griffen" (DL/C/215/106ᵛ). Griffith's knowledge of what made a contract was not just theoretical. He took an active part in the *verba de praesenti* contract of Ann and Alexander. At John Hyde's, Ann's uncle's, house in the parish of St. Mary Axe, Alexander said to her:

> I Alexander take the Ann to my wief and therto I plight the my trothe And then they loosing their hand*es* Griffin bad them ioyne hand*es* againe and willed her to say the like word*es* the sayd Griffen repeating them over unto her whearuppo*n* . . . she . . . so ioyned hand*es*

againe . . . with . . . Alexander and sayd I Ann take the Alexander to my
husband and therto I plight the my trothe And . . . after that
she . . . and . . . Alexander kissed eache other.

Ann testified that she did not intend to contract herself to him and
"that she never suspected that . . . those wordes above sayd should any
wayes tye her with . . . a Contract untill about a weeke or a fortnight
after" (DL/C/215/109ᵛ), but Griffith knew. According to Ann, he
asked her and his wife "if they could tell what wordes made a Contract
of mariag." Upon their denial, Griffith displayed his knowledge by
"then repeating . . . the wordes which she . . . and . . . Alexander had
contracted by as he sayd and then had used uppon Newyears evening
together as are above sett downe he towld her . . . and his said wief
that those wordes made a Contract of marriag" (DL/C/215/110ʳ).

Some deponents used the legal terms when discussing a contract.
Not surprisingly, some of these deponents were associated with the
legal profession. The testimony of William Addison who "is a Clerke
and serveth one Master Bryars a Counsellor of Graies Inne and so
hath done about 3 yeares" (DL/C/219/410ᵛ) includes a legal distinction: "the contract was simple and not condicionall"
(DL/C/219/411ᵛ). What may seem more surprising is the number
of witnesses not serving a counselor at the Inns of Court who also
demonstrated knowledge of contemporary law. The ability of witnesses in early modern England to distinguish between a *verba de
praesenti* and *verba de futuro* contract in these records differs from
what others find in records from areas outside the London diocese. In
discussing contracts in depositions of matrimonial cases from the
Consistory Court in Durham for 1560 to 1630, Peter Rushton notes
a general inability to understand the difference between the two contracts: "in the popular view there was no distinction made between
promises to marry and actual contracts of marriage (in medieval law
words '*de futuro*' and '*de presenti*')" ("Testament" 28).[17]

In the London Consistory Court depositions for 1586 to 1611,
many witnesses and litigants showed an awareness of what was legally
required to make a valid marriage and even self-consciously called attention to the exact legal forms used by a couple. In a personal response
repeated on 21 November 1588, Margaret Callowell pointed out that
the vows exchanged must contain mutual consent to be binding: "she
saiethe that neither at the tyme or place articulated nor ells where at anie
tyme she and . . . John Le Sage have made or contracted togither a true
and leafull marriage neither by wordes of the presente tyme nor others
expressions reciprocallye theire mutuall consentes neither have they

ever betrothed them selves togithers and muche les made recitall thereof" (DL/C/213/452). Her testimony indicates knowledge of the contemporary law concerning verbal contracts by her reference to present time. Other deponents showed an awareness of this legal necessity. A few examples are representative. Elizabeth Sebright testified that she "did not at any time contract matrimonie by wordes of the present time with . . . Robert Wyn" (DL/C/216/213ʳ), and Agnes Hawke deposed that "neither in the monethes and yeere mentioned in the firste article neither before nor since . . . she . . . and . . . John Bawcocke have either privatelye betweene them selves or before anie witnesses whatsoever . . . contracted . . . matrimonie togithers by wordes of presente tyme" (DL/C/213/470).[18] Edmund Hawes, when faced with a contract between his stepdaughter and Lawrence Grimshawe, questioned Lawrence about the form of contract they used. Both the question and the answer reveal the knowledge of both Edmund and Lawrence of the law: "is your contract made betwene your selves condicionall to holde yf her frendes will do any thing for her or else to breake of yf they will not." Lawrence answered, "it is not condicionall but absolute she is my wife and I am her husband" (DL/C/219/136ʳ).[19]

In addition to using the language "wordes of presente tyme," deponents suggested an awareness of the need for individual, present consent to marry in two other ways: (1) the use of "I take"; and (2) exchange of faith and troth. Most contracts included both the taking of another and the exchanging of faith and troth. It was both taking and giving that made the marriage. The testimony of Peter How is a typical example of how taking another and plighting of faith and troth were evidence of consent, since the lack of it indicated that a contract between Agnes and Thomas did not exist: Peter "thinckethe if . . . Agnes . . . did nott give her faiethe and trothe . . . unto . . . ffeild . . . and take him to her husband ther is no contract betwene them" (DL/C/216/78ʳ–78ᵛ). Similarly, William Sadler's testimony that he and Deborah Woodhall did "plighte and geive eche to other their ffaithe and trothe and take one another for husbande and wyff" (DL/C/213/762) demonstrates the taking of another and plighting of faith and troth as evidence of consent. Although the contracts usually included the verb to "give" faith and trothe more than to "plight" or "pledge," Alexander Hollinworth was very concerned that Ann Hyde said "plight" during their contract, so concerned that he extraordinarily had her redo her vows. After Alexander took Ann by the hand, he said "I Alexander take the Ann to my wief, and ther to I plight the my trothe . . . and then they unioyned their handes And . . . Ann Hide tooke . . . Alexander . . . by the hand

and sayd . . . I Ann take the Alexander to my husband and ther to I pledge the my troth and then Master Hollingworth sayd, nay good sweete hart speake the wordes againe and say plight," which, according to this witness, she did (DL/C/215/121ʳ). Deponents cited "faith and trothe" most frequently to complete the vows, with "faith trothe and hand" and "trothe" alone being used almost equally and "faithe and hand" and "faith" alone hardly used.[20]

A few deponents indicated a similarity of the vows in contracts to those given in the Book of Common Prayer. Martin Ingram argues that more and more couples were turning to church unions to marry in order to have a more permanent record. "Given the social and economic importance of marriage," as Ingram explains, "it was desirable for all concerned that a single, incontrovertible act should signal entry into the married state; and the church ceremony, duly recorded in the parish registers, really made spousals redundant" (*Church* 133). On the one hand, one could argue that to indicate a similarity in vows may reflect a desire for a more permanent record. In most of these cases that note this similarity of wording, deponents cited the Book of Common Prayer as the source of the vows without the vows being given. In recounting a marriage contract, John Nutting explained how the contract occurred "according to the wordes of the book of Common praier viz . . . [he] did take . . . Susan for his wife and . . . Susan did take . . . [him] for her husband, plighting theire faith and troth to . . . marry together and thence forth to live together as man and wife" (DL/C/219/362ᵛ). On the other hand, the scarcity of these references may suggest a lack of concern for these deponents for a written record, since in the contracts included in the London deposition books for this twenty-five year period, only a few deponents pointed to the similarity of the vows of the contract to the words of the Solemnization of Matrimony included in the Book of Common Prayer.[21]

Deponents very rarely mentioned that vows had been written down, and the few that did even more rarely detailed the circumstances surrounding the transcription. Similar to letters individuals exchanged before or after a marriage, even in the rare cases that mention written vows deponents considered the circumstances surrounding the transcription and the consent of individuals to the transcription as well as to the contents. *John Newton v. Joan Waters* contains more circumstances surrounding the transcription of the vows than most cases that mention written vows. Even the context of her signing her marriage vows was open to interpretation. I will discuss some of these circumstances in more detail later in this chapter, since the amount of alcohol Joan consumed was an issue in determining her voluntary consent. In terms of the impetus for the writing of the vows themselves, according to George Ireland, a gentleman from Grey's Inn, Newton "did desire . . . [Ireland] to make and drawe the forme of a Contract of marriage between him and the said Waters in writing which he . . . having had some foreknowledge of their said meeting and intent had drawne and provided afore" (DL/C/219/419^r). During a contract that took place in the Queen's Head Tavern in Smithfield, he "drewe out 2 papers in one wherof was written these wordes viz I John take the Joane to my wedded wife *etc* verbatim as in the . . . wordes of matrimony in the booke of Common prayers is sette downe and in the other paper were written these wordes for the woman viz I Jone take the John to my wedded husband and as in the said booke of Common praier out of which . . . [Ireland] had wrote the wordes verbatim is sette downe" (DL/C/219/419^r). After an exchange of vows, John and Joan signed the sheets containing their individual vows, and George gave John Joan's paper and Joan John's paper.

The manner in which a party spoke her or his vows also could indicate the extent of consent. Once again, witnesses offered their own interpretations of what it meant if a litigant said or did not say the vows. In the marriage of William Busshopp and Frances Edmondes, two witnesses identified the manner in which she spoke her vows in addition to her saying the words as evidence of consent: Frances "being more foreward willing and more redy to speake after the minister the wordes of matrimonie then . . . William Bisshopp was" (DL/C/216/354^v), and she "spake the wordes of matrimony playnely after him . . . and more playne and more boldly then . . . William Bisshopp" (DL/C/216/359^r). In another case, Edward Bolton claimed that Ann Fuller's silence while Henry Crampe spoke his vows points to her agreement: Ann "all the while the wordes were speaking semed contented and well pleased therewithe nott disagreinge to any of the wordes or interrupting hym in hys speakinge" (DL/C/215/526^r).

Only a couple of witnesses pointed to the pitch of voice during the vows. In the case of Carr and Vaughan, Richard Phillips identified the tone of Alan's voice and his manner as further evidence of his unwillingness to marry Helen: "Carr was verye unwilling to have bin married unto . . . Vawham yf he Could have Chosen but had rather have byn gone owte of the Chamb[er] then have bin there as it seemed to him . . . [Carr] spake so faintly heavelie and so unwillingly and not Cheerefullie at all But was werrie pensive and sad"

(DL/C/215/85ʳ–85ᵛ). In another case, a witness commented on the strength of the voices as an indicator that no one forced the couple to marry: the "word*es* of contract . . . were uttered neyther very lowd nor w*i*th any soft voice but in suche mann*er* as men usually talke togither and this r*es*p*on*dent was w*i*thin halfe a yard of the sayd Thomas and Elizabeth at yt time when he so heard them speake and M*ist*res Sprigge stoode at the windowe in the same roome and they at the other ende about some 6 or 7 yard*es* of . . . from her" (DL/C/219/20ʳ). In two other cases, witnesses commented on the strength of the woman's voice during the contract: Elizabeth Cage "did repeate the word*es* of contracte w*i*th as muche bouldnes . . . as any woman in the like case com*m*inge to the churche use to doe" (DL/C/213/190) and "at suche time as . . . Sara was to speake the word*es* of Contract she spake . . . w*i*th so lowe a voyce and as it seemed w*i*th suche feare and trembling as that . . . M*ast*er Eaton . . . did speake unto her to speake Lowder and either to speake freely w*i*thout feare or ells not at all" (DL/C/217/45). Reminiscient of what King Lear says about Cordelia, if one wanted out of a contract, a voice "ever soft, / Gentle and low" could be "an excellent thing in woman" (5.3.271–72).[22]

In addition to the vows, the giving or taking of a hand was a significant sign of consent during a marriage. As John R. Gillis notes, "The clasping of hands, the contemporary way of striking any kind of bargain, had a similar binding power" in regard to marriage (44). In addition, Roy Strong comments on the symbolism of clasping hands in this period in his discussion of a 1588 miniature by Nicholas Hilliard in the Victoria and Albert Museum: "Clasped hands recur in emblem books from Alciati onwards as symbols of Concord and plighted faith" (*Artists* 97). Almost all depositions which include a description of a marriage mention hand holding either at a contract or church wedding. In these many references to hand holding, giving, or taking, deponents rarely specified which hand, suggesting that the exact hand a person offered was less important than the gesture itself.[23] In a few instances, the giving of the hand served as the primary indicator of consent. Master Sanders believed that the joining of hands made the union. As George Ireland testified, "Sand*er*s tooke both . . . Newton and Waters hand*es* and ioyned them together and said Thus I make you man and wife" (DL/C/219/419ʳ).

While Ireland's testimony points to hand holding as the primary proof of consent, many more depositions document that hand holding, giving, or taking itself did not make a union but was an important gesture to confirm consent. In denying that a contract occurred, Alice

Danson explained that no words went with the hand holding: "Botherod willed . . . [her] to give unto him her hand which she did and in a shorte tyme after departed and she sayth that there passed not any other woordes deduced in this article of her parte" (DL/C/213/348). To this litigant, her defense indicates that words and hand holding needed to go together to form a contract. Some depositions include that a couple took each other's hand, thereby suggesting equal consent and initiative. However, the most common behavior was for the man to give his hand or take the woman's hand first before vowing, although witnesses noted a couple of examples in which the man did this immediately after saying his vows. This behavior is reminiscent, of course, of the Solemnization of Matrimony in the Book of Common Prayer. In a few cases in the depositions in which a minister officiated or someone facilitated a contract, the minister or person directed the groom to take the hand of the woman. George Nicholls "repetinge the wordes of matrimonye as theye wer in the . . . service booke which he then had in his hande caused his brother to take . . . Elizabeth Cage by the hande and saye as . . . [he] repeted" (DL/C/213/178). Witnesses reported a few instances in which women offered to give their hands first. In a passage I cited in chapter 2, Susan Jason alias Jackson gave her hand first in an account of her contract with Henry Bowles: "I am . . . content and do give you my hand and my hart in token of my love and consent . . . and then . . . Henry did accept thereof and sayd to her I give you my hand and my hart" (DL/C/219/314ᵛ). In addition, Elizabeth Cole "took . . . [Martin Mullens] by the hand" and said "hear is my hand . . . in faith for ever whither my mother will or noe." Martin responded, "thear is my hand and my faith for ever and I will never forsake thee" (DL/C/214/170).

The testimony of several witnesses from different cases concerning other hand gestures litigants made, in addition to those at the start of the vows, emphasizes this gesture's importance in confirming consent. The lack of such additional details surrounding kissing and pledging can be seen to underscore the significance of this particular gesture even further. In many cases, the hand gestures made befor the second party gave her or his vows came under scrutiny by witnesses. A significant difference does not appear in the number of cases in which the witnesses noted if a couple continued to hold hands when the second person said her or his vows or whether a couple released their hands and reclasped them. In addition, witnesses mentioning that couples held hands after their marriages seems to suggest mutual consent: the "contract being so done and made . . . Henry Jackson and Jane Browne went out at dores and walked hand in hand upp the street" (DL/C/215/12ʳ). Similarly, in another case, Elizabeth Willson, unable to speak, took James Harrison by the hand in confirmation of his statement that they were married. When Elizabeth's brother, Jeffrey, found James sitting at her bedside weeping, Jeffrey told him that he "was the cause of her sicknes and willed him to be gon." James' response—"good brother Jeffery be contented and not angry with me for Coming to her for she is my wief and I her husband . . . before god"—was supported by Elizabeth taking his hand: "Elizabeth being very sick and weake scarce hable to speake putt her hand out of the bed when he sayd that she was his wief, and tooke him by the hand seming to affirme the same" (DL/C/215/346ʳ). In another instance, a mother showed her approval of the match by giving Ralph Yardley her daughter's hand: Ralph "came home . . . to her howse at tower hill and towld her . . . that he had byn a suter to her dawghter for marriage but quothe he all this while I have byn but an usurper of her I praye yow now give her unto me whearuppon she . . . tooke her sayd dawghter Joane by the hand and Layd her hand in . . . Raphes hand and so ioyning ther handes together she . . . sayd I praye god blesse yow" (DL/C/218/289).

Deponents cited gift giving to confirm individual consent to a marriage fewer times than exchanging vows or hand holding. Nonetheless, gifts given during or after a marriage could play a practical role of material proof, a role that may explain why suitors mentioned in these records exchanged more gifts during or after a marriage than before. This pattern raises a central difference in my reading of token exchange in the London Consistory Court depositions compared to that of Laura Gowing. She argues that "a set of more material transactions gave premarital commitment an economic context" (159). However, since the depositions indicate that more gifts were given during or after a marriage, the emphasis on the "economic context" shifts from before to the moment when and after a couple marry.

Parties were sometimes more explicit about their intentions when giving a material item during or after rather than before a marriage. What O'Hara notes for the Canterbury Consistory Court depositions is also accurate for the patterns of giving and receiving in some of the London Consistory Court depositions: "Although early promises of marriage are not always easily distinguishable from the stage of formal betrothal, the contractual nature involved in the giving of the token was, at times, made explicit" (*Courtship* 75). In the case of *John Nicholls v. Elizabeth Cage*, the extant depositions point to the groom's concern to perform a valid contract, a concern that drove him to perform a second contract. William Nightingale's testimony suggests John's awareness of the need for material proof of a contract: John "in confirmacion of his contracte gave Elizabeth a peece of gould which was as John Nicholls told . . . [William] a spurr riall: and because Elizabeth had noe token for John againe he toke . . . a pynn of her" (DL/C/213/185).

However, neither the act of giving or receiving a gift during or after a marriage nor making intentions explicit seems to have made a marriage less open to question. As I explained in chapter 3, in the matrimonial enforcement suits from the London Consistory Court for 1586 to 1611, the meanings of the gifts themselves given before, during, or after a marriage, the intentions of the giver and receiver, and the context of the exchange were open to interpretation. In regard to gifts that parties exchanged during or after a marriage, these interpretations were crucial to determine whether the item served to confirm a marriage and expose consent. This fluidity in the meaning of gifts seems even more ironic at this stage in the marriage process. That is, if a suitor gave a certain gift clearly associated with marriage, then the intentions of the giver and even the receiver would be clear and assist in determining consent to a union—to receive a ring, rather than a pair of gloves, would symbolize a marriage. However, depositions record that parties gave rings, money, clothing, and personal items before, during, and after marriage. The variety in the kinds of gifts indicates that their meaning was not necessarily conveyed by the objects themselves even for those items given to confirm a marriage. Further support of this interpretation is found in the witnesses who pointed to the lack of gift exchange as proof that a marriage did not occur. In their testimonies, they referred to the lack of gift exchange in general rather than to the giving or receiving of one item in particular. Two representative examples include: Alice Hawkyn said that "there was never anie token taken by . . . [her] of him the said William Wrenall nor anie gyven by her to him" (DL/C/213/602), and Agnes Hawke testified that "neither hath she . . . in anie of the said monethes articulate . . . or at anie tyme sithens receaved of . . . [John Bawcocke] anie guifte or token whatsoever nor he of her either in signe or token of anie suche contracte or for anie cause or matter whatsoever" (DL/C/213/470). O'Hara's conclusions about the particular gifts exchanged before, during, and after contracts in the depositions from the diocese of Canterbury reflect the patterns found in the depositions from the diocese of London: "Individual items were never exclusively concerned with any specific occasion or strategy. Instead they were disposed throughout all stages in the development of marriage, and the entire range of strategies employed" (*Courtship* 81). In addition, the number of deponents who calculated the worth of the gifts individuals gave during or after a marriage underscores the fluidity in their meaning, since to assess value indicates that deponents interpreted the context of the gift exchange in order to quantify one party's obligation to another. Moreover, the different interpretations deponents made of the intentions of the giver and the receiver further underscore this fluidity. My conclusions about gifts bestowed to confirm marriages in the matrimonial enforcement suits in the records from the diocese of London differ from those of Rushton based on matrimonial enforcement cases from Durham. In suggesting a "general rule about marriage tokens," he writes, "usually a contract was made by a man offering a token (of his good intentions) and a woman accepting it and returning her 'word to marry'. There was no need to reciprocate in kind because the token evoked a return of faith by its receipt and acceptance" ("Testament" 26). As the depositions from the London Consistory Court indicate, women were not only reciprocating and even initiating confirmation gifts, but also interpreting the contexts of giving and receiving.

The case of *Alexander Hollinworth v. Ann Hyde* serves as a rich example of the different kinds of items parties gave to confirm a marriage, demonstrates how differently individuals read giving and receiving, and displays Ann, as seen in chapter 3, calculating the worth of items given. Ann, who denied a contract occurred, cataloged the gifts Alexander sent her "after the pretended Contract." In her deposition, she very carefully detailed her intentions or the manner in which she received them and quantified their value, seemingly to quantify her obligation to him. After the "pretended" contract,

> she receyved . . . at severall times bothe the ringes mentioned in this article that with the stone by Griffins wife and thother by Griffin him selfe, the one ring being . . . not worth . . . iiii⁵ . . . and thother is a Counterfitt stone as she hath byn synce towld and . . . it cannot be worth . . . above a noble . . . she receyved the bracelett of pearle and bugle from Master Alexander by Griffen worth . . . about xviii⁵ . . . all which . . . she receyved at the great importunite of Griffin and his wief synce the time of the pretended Contract a forsayd they still telling her that it was but a folley to Carrie them back for . . . Master Alexander would throw them a way. (DL/C/215/114ᵛ–115ʳ)

Even after she explained her intentions in receiving each item, she again stressed her intention: "she utterly denyeth that ever she receyved any of those tokens in token . . . or Confirmac*i*on of any Contract of marriage betwen them but only as she hathe after answerd at the grat importunite of the sayd Griffin and his wief" (DL/C/215/115^r).

Ann also carefully explained her intentions behind "sending" Alexander gifts. John Griffith "snatcht" one token from her bosom: "she one day wearing a silke flower in her bosom Griffin came to her and snatcht it fro*m* her and so went forthe at the dore And the next day when she asked him for it he sayd he had given it to . . . M*aste* Alexander who sayd he would weare it in his hatt as long as it would howld togither but she denyethe that she ever sent it or bad Griffin deliv*er* it." Ann admitted that she sent Alexander a "gallie pott of Conserve of roses" to "Comfort him" (DL/C/215/113^v) and a "peece of gowld . . . of ii^s vi^d" and included her intentions in sending these gifts: she only sent them after John told her "how extreame sick . . . Alexander was and how he tooke on as thowgh he would dy . . . because he could not here fro*m* her" (DL/C/215/115^r). As with the "confirmation" tokens she received, she here qualified her intentions in sending the items and her lack of knowledge of how Alexander interpreted her gift giving: "she did not send any of theis tokens uppo*n* Confirmac*i*on of any Contract of marriage but only for the Causes above by her sett downe butt w*i*th what intencion he receyved them she sayethe she cannott tell" (DL/C/215/115^v). While Ann vehemently denied that she willingly received or sent the items as tokens to confirm a contract, Alexander nonetheless sent the rings and "bracelett of pearle and bugle" as confirmation gifts, and he and John read the receipt of the silk flower, the money, and the "gallie pott" as the same from her.

Like Ann Hyde, many deponents focused on the context of exchange and on their intentions in giving and receiving. To cite just a few of many examples in which deponents read the giving or receiving of a gift as not confirming a contract, Ralph Stonbanck admitted he gave the plaintif some money, but he disagreed with the common reading of what it meant. While "Ann ffinall Lay in Childbed," he "went twice or thrice unto her And . . . gave . . . Ann a peece of gowld of x^s but not in confirmac*i*on of any form*er* contract of matrimonie" (DL/C/217/209). In a deposition repeated on 19 February 1602/03 from another case, Susan Peele testified that the "payer of gloves" that John Fitzwilliams gave her "neither could be either given by him, or taken by her . . . in confirmac*i*on of any Contract of matrimonie betwene them for she sayethe ther nev*er* was any Contract betwene them" (DL/C/216/299^r). In yet another case, a defendant and a witness identified the primary use of the

Figure 4.1   Sixteenth-century earscoop/toothpick and pins, © Museum of London.

item and interpreted the meaning of its receipt differently. Susan Atkinson deposed that she "receaved" a "crowne of gold and an eare picker of silver" from John Payne "but in no consideracion of marriage to be had betwene the*m*" (DL/C/213/344). (Figure 4.1 contains a marvelous example of a contemporary earscoop/toothpick carved in the shape of a sea-serpent.) Although Susan claimed that receiving these items did not indicate any "consideracion of marriage to be had betwene them," Matthew Lips read her acceptance differently: John "did give unto" Susan "a frenche Crowne and a tothepiker of silver, . . . which . . . Susan did thankfully accepte and take in token of there contracte" (DL/C/213/331).[24] As the earlier-cited deposition from Ann Hyde indicates, deponents reading the context of exchange included assessing the economic value of a gift. To cite two cases from many additional examples, Susan Peele noted that the gloves John Fitzwilliams sent her were "worthe . . . ii^s vi^d and no more" (DL/C/216/299^r). In a deposition from a different case, John Mullens testified that Thomas Thorpe sent Elizabeth Jackson a "prayer booke" worth "viii^d" (DL/C/219/15^r). However, Elizabeth assessed the value of the prayer book differently, testifying that it was worth "4^d" not "viii^d" (DL/C/219/25^r).

As with the courting gifts I discussed in chapter 3, despite the fluidity of their meaning, patterns in the items parties gave during or after a marriage emerge in the depositions. With respect to the kinds of items parties gave during marriages in the extant London Consistory Court depositions, Gowing, who studied gift exchange in these records for a longer chronological period, argues: "At the moment of contracting, couples exchanged rings or broken pieces of gold" (159). My conclusions in this study concerning the kinds of items parties gave during marital contracts in the extant London Consistory Court depositions differ from hers. "Rings" and "broken pieces of gold" do play a prominent role, since rings and coins (usually unbroken) were the two most popular gifts individuals gave during a contract in these depositions. However, in the matrimonial enforcement cases from these depositions for 1586 to 1611, "rings" and "broken pieces of gold" were not the only gifts parties exchanged during a contract as Gowing indicates. To mention items from four different cases, in addition to the earlier-cited case of John Nicholls taking a "pynn" from Elizabeth Cage, deponents testified that parties gave a "petticote" (DL/C/213/170), a "tothpicker" (DL/C/213/332) or "eare picker" (DL/C/213/344), and a pair of "gloves" (DL/C/213/762) to confirm a marital contract. The most frequent gifts in these depositions to confirm a marriage are first rings, then money, and then clothing and personal items.

Deponents identified rings as the item individuals gave most often as confirmation gifts (forty-six deponents from twenty-two cases). The prominence of the ring in the Solemnization of Matrimony ceremony in the Book of Common Prayer could be seen to explain why more rings appear in the depositions as the gift given during or after a marriage than were given before. It may even appear that the ring itself symbolized marriage.[25] Houlbrooke supports this position, writing, "No other sort of gift was so closely associated with marriage in the eyes of the law" ("Making of Marriage" 344). When recounting contracts that they mentioned echo the ceremony in the Book of Common Prayer, deponents sometimes called attention to the giving of a ring during a contract as similar to the giving of a ring during that ceremony.

Some deponents suggested that a ring had intrinsic meaning. In a contract between John Swinsted and Elizabeth Brode alias Ibotson, the ring seems to symbolize the contract itself. Because the ring did not usually play such a central part during an exchange of vows in these depositions, I cite the contract itself. According to Ann Done, John

> having the ring in his hand sayd here Elizabeth . . . take this ring and with this ring I the wedd with my body I the worshipp and withall my worldly goodes I the indowe and theruppon I give the my hand my faiethe and trothe and so putt the ring on her finger and . . . tooke her by the hand saying he never ment to have other wife then . . . Elizabeth till deathe them departed And . . . Elizabeth sayd unto . . . John Swinsted howlding him by the hand And so doe I likwise give yow my hand my faiethe and trothe so long as I live. (DL/C/215/94ᵛ)

In a different case, according to Agnes Bushey, Thomas Wye may have seen a ring as symbolizing a marriage. On the one hand, his gift of "a Jett ringe" to Widow Bushey did not in itself symbolize marriage, since he gave her many other items and a similar ring to both her "mother in lawe" and "a mayde" (DL/C/213/832). On the other hand, his eagerness to get hold of her rings may point to their special meanings—it is "a litell gymmewe" [gimmal] ring and "her weddinge ringe" that "he tooke . . . from her" that she denied was evidence of a "contracte of marraidge" (DL/C/213/805). The gimmal ring is especially provocative here, since this kind of ring was made of double hoops and bezels, the latter of which was usually in the form of clasped hands (see Figures 4.2 and 4.3).[26] If this ring contained the usual clasped hands, it would be suggestive of a contract and as such may signal Thomas' intentions in taking it. That a ring could symbolize a contract may explain Mistress Jacob's immediate assumption when she found one in her maid's chest. When she confronted Richard Houghton about his gift of the ring to her maid, he answered that she "had it of me to keepe." Mistress Jacob then questioned him on his intentions, "did you not give it her to the end to make her your wife,"

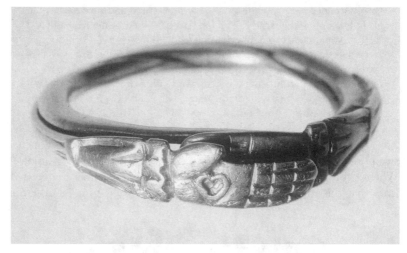

Figures 4.2 and 4.3 Sixteenth-century gimmal ring with inscription, "As handes doe shvt so hart be knit," © Museum of London.

which Richard denied: "I gave it her to no such . . . purpose but onelye to keepe till I called for it againe for I meane to have it" (DL/C/214/542).

But the meaning of a ring was not intrinsic, since, as I noted earlier individuals gave rings as courting gifts, gave other gifts to confirm a union, and interpreted the context of gift exchange. Couples had neither to marry in church nor to follow the ceremony in the Book of Common Prayer to have a valid marriage, and this may help explain why parties did not give rings exclusively while marrying and why a ring was not in itself the symbol of marriage. In a contract between Thomas Powell and Katherine Garnett alias Armsted that took place in an upper room at the tavern "knowne by the sign of the White Lyon" in Hoxton, St. Leonard Shoreditch, individuals interpreted the meaning of a ring differently. In a deposition repeated on 12 February 1601/02, Robert Meridithe deposed that Katherine's desire to have Thomas' ring was the beginning of the contract: Katherine

> espying a ryng . . . of gowld uppo*n* . . . Thomas Powells finger . . . sayd unto him will yow bestowe that ring uppo*n* me whearunto . . . Thomas . . . answrd her saying I will uppo*n* Condicion that yow shall be my wief whearuppo*n* . . . Thomas Powell . . . tooke a Cupp of wine in his left hand and tooke her by the right hand w*i*th his right hand saying I doe drinck to yow uppo*n* this Condicon that yow shall be my wedded wief and then she tooke the Cupp and sayd she would pledg him uppo*n* the same Condicion that he should be her husband and she . . . would be his wief and then he tooke the same ryng of his finger and deliv*er*ed it unto . . . Katherin saying uppo*n* Condition that yow shall be my wedded wief . . . I doe give yow here this ryng and she then tooke the same ryng of him being a gould ryng w*i*th a deathes head uppo*n* it saying and uppo*n* that Condition that I will . . . be yo*ur* wief and yow shall be my husband I doe take it of yow. (DL/C/216/292*v*-293*r*)[27]

After the contract, Katherine pointed to the death's head ring as conclusive proof of their union (see Figure 4.4 for a contemporary example). When Thomas Turke "espying a gowld ryng . . . uppo*n* her finger sayd unto her, this ring I know this was Thom*as* Powells ring," Katherine

Figure 4.4 Early seventeenth-century death's head ring, © Museum of London.

identified it as "the ring that knitt the knott betwene Thomas Powell and me . . . and that made . . . us man and wief" (DL/C/216/251ᵛ). Katherine later spoke with Elizabeth Chadborne, and she pointed to the ring again as that which married them. When Elizabeth asked Katherine if she were married, Katherine "answered that she was and with that pulled of her glove and showed her . . . a gowld ring uppon her finger saying here is my wedding ring." To Elizabeth, the ring was not proof enough for she asked Katherine "if she weare married indede" and "if she weare married in . . . the Churche." Although Katherine's answer reveals that to her the ring made a marriage that was equal to one in church—"with that ring she was married" (DL/C/216/234ᵛ)— Elizabeth read the exchange of the ring differently. In another case, the testimony of John Sharp further illustrates that a ring in itself did not symbolize marriage. After Richard Thompson and Helen Butt held hands, a stranger dressed like a minister asked Richard

> for a ring, and . . . Tompson answeared that hee had none, and thearupon the other man whom . . . [he] supposeth to be an hostelier stooped down and made a ring of a rush and wolld have given it them but they took not the same for the straunger tolld them it mattered not for any ring and so the same straunger pronounced the woordes of marriage beetween . . . Richard Tompson and Hellen Butt as is sett down in the Book of comon prayer and . . . the said straunger tolld them . . . that they wear as sure togither as could be. (DL/C/214/118)

Even though the minister's asking the groom for a ring seems to suggest it was a necessary part of the ceremony, his telling them, according to John, that a ring "mattered not" indicates that it was not.

While individuals most often gave a ring as a confirmation token, a ring's value lay in the timing of the gift and the intentions of the giver and the receiver than in the kinds or numbers of rings. During a contract, Thomas Curtys gave Alice Twissleton "for confirmacion of his contracte three ringes and a petticote" (DL/C/213/170). As I cited in chapter 3, Charles Oman notes, "it is the use and not the shape which distinguishes the wedding and betrothal ring" (*Catalogue* vi). Twenty-four depositions contain details of eleven different types of rings beyond simply pointing to a "ring" or a "gold ring," as in the above case in which Thomas gave Katherine "a gould ryng with a deathes head uppon it" (DL/C/216/292ᵛ). To cite another example, at a contract between William Greene and Margaret Swinerton, he gave her "a hoope ring of gowld" while she gave him "a iemowe [gimmal] ring of gowld in Confirmation of the same Contract of matrimonie betwixt them" (DL/C/215/181ᵛ). Parties gave memento mori, signet,[28] and other types of rings as courtship and marriage confirmation gifts. The identifications of rings as confirmation tokens in the depositions varied from the simple to the more elaborate—"a ring of gold" (DL/C/219/362^v), "a little small ring of gowld" (DL/C/218/322), "a ringe of gould as above taken to the value of xii^s and no more" (DL/C/216/253^r), "a hoped round gould ringe" (DL/C/213/160), "a gowld ring inamuled" (DL/C/218/122), "a ringe of gold w*i*th a Dyamond in it w*hi*ch she at the first refused saying it was to youthfull for her to weare" (DL/C/219/313^v), and a ring in which "ther was made an R an O and a K for bothe their names" (DL/C/214/552). This reference to the carved letters is unusual in the depositions. Even though posie rings were popular at the time, surprisingly, deponents did not include testimony regarding the posies in rings. Such posies as "Ile neuer be his, whose ring this is" or "In the my choyse, I do reioyce" (Harley MS 6910, 160^v) could help clarify the intentions of the parties.[29] While the testimony of John Sharp I cited earlier includes a rare example of a rush ring (DL/C/214/118), Ann Keningham alias Terrill's description of a ring she gave to James Terrill makes it more memorable than others: "at the time when they weare so contracted giveing him a seale ring of . . . gowld w*i*th the picture of a white dogg upp*on* it w*i*th the eares tipped w*i*th silver" (DL/C/218/122). Maybe, as the epigraph suggests, the associations of gold being more binding than silver because it was more valuable indicate why so many witnesses pointed out that a ring was gold.

The number of people who borrowed a ring underscores that the specific type, ownership, or value of a ring was not as important as the intentions of the giver and receiver in assessing individual consent. In the contract between John Swinsted and Elizabeth Brode alias Ibotson in which the ring played such a central role, John did not purchase a certain kind of ring, but borrowed it. In a deposition repeated on 11 February 1597/98, Richard Done deposed that John "towld him that he would gladly have a wedding ring whearuppo*n* [Richard] . . . caused his wief . . . to borrow a wedding ring for the . . . same John Swinsted w*hi*ch his wief did and deliv*er*ed it unto . . . John" (DL/C/215/93^r). At another contract at the Queen's Head Tavern in Redcross Street between the above-mentioned Richard Thompson with a different woman, Phillipp Stacie, Richard "borrowed . . . a ring of one of the women who wear in the companie . . . and did put the same upon . . . Phillipp Stacies finger" (DL/C/214/112). While he returned the ring and bought another "the next day" (DL/C/214/116), the ring at the contract served to demonstrate consent.

Parties gave money in almost as many instances as rings. The difference between the number of deponents citing rings rather than money as a confirmation gift is a small one, since forty-two deponents in twenty cases pointed to money as the gift to confirm a marriage while forty-six deponents in twenty-two cases mentioned a ring. Statements as general as Thomas gave Grace "a peece of gowld after they had contracted them selves" (DL/C/215/244ᵛ) from witnesses at marriages are more unusual than statements that report the exact value of the money. In fact, witnesses were more specific about the amount of money than they were about the kind of ring parties gave as marriage gifts. While thirteen depositions include "gold," twenty-nine depositions out of the forty-two contain references to ten different amounts of money. Out of these twenty-nine depositions, deponents identified parties giving x^s or the Elizabethan Angel in thirteen depositions from five cases, making it the most common amount deponents specified. To cite two examples, Robert Archer gave Bridget Iles a "peece of gowld of tenn shilling*es*" (DL/C/216/327ᵛ), and Richard Thomas gave Alice More "an Elizabeth Angell" (DL/C/218/550). Other amounts deponents specified include "a pece of gould of halfe a crowne" (DL/C/214/59), "a french Crowne" (DL/C/213/334), and "a spurr ryall" (DL/C/213/180). The giving of a "spur ryall" (the name referring to its reverse design of a spur-like rose) in this case is provocative given its rarity in Elizabeth's reign. This coin did not become official until 1605 (George C. Brooke 195). Thus, 69 percent of the depositions that mention money as a confirmation token include a specific amount beyond pointing to "gold," while 52 percent of the depositions that mention a ring as a confirmation token include a description beyond a "ring" or a "gold ring."

The amount individuals gave did not necessarily determine the depth of commitment. However, as an epigraph to this chapter suggests, Henry Hall testified in 1610 that the value of the coin Francis Norman gave to Alice Webster mattered, since to Alice gold meant something very different from silver: "he heard the sayd Alice confesse that she had receyved a pece of silver w*hi*ch was broken betwene them to bynd a contract of marriage betwene them w*hi*ch if it had byn gold she sayd it would have bownd but by reason it was but silver she sayd it could not bynde and she sayd that therefore the contract was voyd" (DL/C/219/250ʳ). Alice's differentiation of the value of the metal was fiscally prudent, since gold was more economically valuable than silver. As the table in John Craig's *The Mint* indicates, gold was valued at approximately twelve times that of silver at the time of the 1560–62 recoinage. The value of gold increased in 1610 to approximately thirteen times that of silver (414 and 415). Unlike Alice, most deponents did not make such distinctions.

In a few cases witnesses noted that one party bowed or broke a coin. In these cases, people overlooked the legislation enacted in 1576, which stated that clipping and any other impairments to coinage were a treasonable offense (C. E. Challis 280).[30] Two cases in the depositions mentioned bowing. In one instance, Edward Brookes gave Susan Powell "a bowed peece of gould" (DL/C/213/749) to confirm their contract. In the other instance, before John Stubbes gave Frances Edmondes an "angell of gowld . . . in confirmacion of . . . their Contract" (DL/C/216/312r), he bowed it in his mouth: "then he . . . bowed an angell of gowld in his mouthe and sayed unto her and in token of this Contract of marriage betwene us I doe give yow this peece of gowld" (DL/C/216/315r).

Rather than bowing, some depositions reveal an expectation that the couple split a coin between them, each member keeping half in confirmation of their union. Rushton comments on the symbolism of such sharing: "the bond between the couple was expressed by the equal division of a single object" ("Testament" 26). In three matrimonial enforcement suits, a person received a broken coin as confirmation of a contract, in one case the bride stopped a witness from breaking the coin immediately before the contract, and in another case witnesses pointed to an expectation that the groom should break a coin during the contract.[31] The very few instances in which a person broke a coin or a witness to a marriage expected such a behavior to happen further qualifies Gowing's above-mentioned point that "At the moment of contracting, couples exchanged rings or broken pieces of gold" (159). In the latter two instances—the woman halting the breaking of a coin and the expectation that one was to be broken—deponents identified the broken coin as an indicator of someone keeping his or her word. In a 1606/07 case, Master Hawton, a witness at the contract, "asked a peece of gowld of Christofer dawson that he might break the same and divide it betwene Marrian Crompton and him as . . . a token of their being man and wief togither and ther unto Marrian Crompton said no the gowld is better whole then broken I will be as good as my word" (DL/C/217/19). Similarly, in the case of Margaret Perry alias More against Richard Warren, the deposition reveals an expectation for money to be broken as part of the contract. Mistress Johnson asked Richard to "breake a pece of gold betwene" him and Margaret in order "to bynde the matche." Since Richard "sayd he had not a pece of gold," Mistress Johnson "willed him to breake a vi[d] betwene them."

However, Richard said "he wold breake no money his word should be as sufficient as if he broke money" (DL/C/219/86ᵛ). In one of the depositions from this case, that the witness cannot remember the "ver word*es*" Margaret spoke at the contract underscores this expectation further. Although "he was at the further p*a*rte of the roome undressing him selfe to go to bed," he had no trouble recalling what his wife requested immediately thereafter: "he well remembreth that . . . [his] wife would have had . . . Richard Warren to breake a pece of gold betwene him and the widowe and to give her ye one halfe and kepe thother and . . . Warren sayd he had not a pece of gold there and thereuppon . . . Margaret sayd what nede we any gold I dare take his word for I am p*er*swaded he will not go from his word" (DL/C/219/81ᵛ). His memory may point to his own understanding of what should happen after a contract. Although in these two cases a bride and a groom prevented this from happening, in three cases a litigant broke a coin: Helen Johnson broke "a gould geniou in twayne and gave . . . William Taylor one p*a*rte and kepte thother to her selfe" (DL/C/214/59); Richard Thompson broke "a shilling in two and . . . gave the said woman the one half and kept the oth*er* half to him self" (DL/C/214/116); and Francis Norman "did breake a peece of silver of viᵈ a sunder," giving Alice Webster "a peece" (DL/C/219/201ʳ).

Individuals gave clothing and personal items in fewer instances to confirm a marriage than as courting gifts; yet many people gave such items. Twenty-two deponents from eleven cases mentioned people giving nine different kinds of items to confirm a marriage. In keeping with their wide use as presents for wedding guests, funeral attire, rewards for service, and signs of a pledge, gloves are the most popular item in this category. William Sadler gave Deborah Woodhall "in confirmac*i*on of their contracte a payer of gloves" (DL/C/213/762), while Susan James gave John Nutting "a paire of gloves . . . in Co*n*firmac*i*on of the said m*a*tromo*n*i*a*ll contract" (DL/C/219/362ᵛ). In addition, "since the saide Contract," Frances Edmondes testified that John Stubbes "in signe of his love toward*es* her and in further confirmac*i*on of the saide Contract as shee beleeveth sent her a paire of gloves" (DL/C/216/303ᵛ). Grisill Mills, a witness in this case, described the gloves and assessed their value as "being worthe as she thinckethe at least iiiˢ 4ᵈ for they had iii gowld laces uppo*n* them" (DL/C/216/313ʳ). While John sent her a pair of gloves, Frances sent him "a peece of Crimson rybbyn knitt in a square knott w*hi*ch she Called a trew lovers knott" (DL/C/216/338ʳ). In addition to gloves and a "peece of Crimson rybbyn," some of the other clothing and personal items include a "petticote" (DL/C/213/170), "pynn"

(DL/C/213/185), "tothepiker of silver" (DL/C/213/331) or "eare picker of silver" (DL/C/213/344), "a flower made of greene sylke" (DL/C/215/121ᵛ), a "kirtle" (DL/C/216/330ʳ), a "gowne" (DL/C/216/327ᵛ), and "a Cote garded beinge. one of her ma*jestes* lyverie and a velvett Capp" (DL/C/213/765).

A few deponents identified more unusual gifts than rings, money, and clothing and personal items. Alice Deacon, echoing the property rights of a husband under the letter of the law, offered her "bodye and good*es*" after she plighted her faith and troth (DL/C/213/764). In the case of Richard Warren and Margaret Perry alias More, Richard identified more specifically the "good*es*" he was giving Margaret. At supper in a house called the "blacke spreadeagle," after Margaret consented to marry Richard, he gave Margaret "this howse in token that we are man and wife," and offered her "other howses more" (DL/C/219/81ʳ). The most shocking gift, however, was that of a daughter. In the case of Susan Atkinson versus Thomas Barnerd, after the contract, Thomas gave her "a pece of gold in token thereof," and "for that she had nothing else to geve (as she then sayd) gave him . . . her eldest doughter" (DL/C/213/327). In the four extant depositions from this case, only one includes this account.[32]

A few litigants gave letters after a marriage, but, unfortunately, deponents did not usually recount their contents. The suit of Alexander Hollinworth against Ann Hyde provides a wealth of details concerning letters they exchanged after a *verba de praesenti* contract. John Griffith's testimony tantalizes in terms of the contents of the letters Alexander sent Ann; he pointed out how one of the letters was read to him at his examination yet did not include the contents in his deposition: "this le*tter* annexed to the matter whearuppo*n* he is now examined being shewed him and read over unto him at this his examinac*i*on . . . or suche a one to that effect . . . he . . . brought fro*m* M*aster* Hollingworth . . . and deliv*ere*d to M*ist*ris Ann Hide . . . w*h*ich she read over her selfe ev*er*y word her selfe" (DL/C/215/123ᵛ). However, he did mention that in it Alexander called Ann "sweete wief" (DL/C/215/121ᵛ). While he cannot recount the contents of the letter that Alexander sent to Ann, he recalled the contents of a letter Ann sent to Alexander, contents that Ann did not write or think of herself: John

> willed her to write ii or 3 word*es* in answer of the same le*tter* and she answerd that she Could not write well butt willed him . . . to goe gett ii or 3 word*es* written what he . . . would and she sayd she would sett h[er] hand to it whearuppo*n* he . . . went toward*es* Leaden Hall and

ther procured one for to write the wordes which are under written
to this letter articulat viz Sweete husband if it lye in me I would doe
any thing I could, And then he . . . brought it to . . . Ann Hide againe
and she tooke it and read it what he . . . had so gotten written and
when she had so read the same wordes she wrote her name to them as
now it is viz Ann Hide. (DL/C/215/123^v-124^r)

Ann, who denied the contract, told a different story regarding how
her signature appeared on the bottom of the letter. In her account,
John tricked her into signing. Given how unusual it is to have such
splendid details, I cite fully from her deposition. After reading a letter
from Alexander, John, according to Ann,

was very earnest with her to send an answer unto it . . . which she
refused to doe . . . but uppon his importunitie she sayd that if he had
gotten ii or three wordes written which she lyked of for an answer she
would putt her hand to them . . . and ther uppon . . . Griffin kept
the letter him selfe and about an howr after one Ann whose other name
she knoweth not . . . who is Chamber mayd unto her sayd uncle and
the sayd Griffin being in the parlour together [Hyde] . . . came into the
parlour to them and ther the sayd Ann and she . . . falling in talke
togither of writing she . . . asked . . . Ann wheather she Could write or
no she answ[ered] that she had forgotten then [Hyde] . . . asked her
wheather she Could write her name or not and so eache of them fell to
byd eache other write their names and ther lying many papers uppon
the table table fowlded upp . . . the Chamber mayd wrote her name
uppon one of the papers and she . . . being . . . about to take a peece of
paper to write her name . . . Griffin had folded this letter as it semed so
close together as she sayethe she did not see any one word that was
written in it and so putting it to her . . . she wrote her name as she
thought uppon a blanck paper and so soone as she had so written her
name Griffin tooke it upp and asked her . . . if she knew what she had
putt her hand unto and she sayd . . . no she knew not any thing she had
putt her hand unto then sayd he I will deale playnely with yow and
show yow what yow have putt your hand unto and so opended this
letter and delivered it unto her . . . and bad her reede what was written
next before her name whear she founde written theis wordes, Swete
husband if it lye in me I would doe any thing I could, and under neathe
this a little way she then founde she had written her owne name as now
it is. (DL/C/215/118^r-118^v)

Upon Ann expressing her offense at the trick, John "swore with a grat
othe" that after showing it to Alexander, he would "take it and burne
it" (DL/C/215/118^v). Since the letter appeared in the examination,
John violated his oath.

Witnesses also cited kissing and pledging as behaviors that could prove individual consent to a marriage, although with less frequency than hand holding and gift giving. Once again, the deponents provided different readings of what these behaviors meant. Deponents, predictably, mentioned kissing as a sign of emotional commitment and intent. They often pointed out that the couple kissed "eache other" seemingly to underscore further their individual consent: "they kissed eache other in signe and token of this contracting them selves in marriage togither" (DL/C/219/86ᵛ). As such, it is hardly surprising that Margaret Callowell explained that a kiss was not mutual and that it was not confirmation of mutual affection when denying a contract occurred: "John Le Sage then kissed her . . . who was neere him But knowethe not by what affection he did it and declareth that she did not kisse him againe" (DL/C/213/453). The point when two people kissed during the marriages recounted in the depositions varied little. They usually did so after the exchange of vows and before the gift giving or pledging.

Pledging, or drinking to someone, was another gesture that deponents included as evidence of individual consent to a marriage, although they cited it fewer times than hand holding, gift exchange, and kissing. The witnesses who included pledging in their accounts of the contracts usually placed this gesture after hand holding and kissing and before gift exchange. Here, what one put in the cup did not matter as much as what one did with the cup. Witnesses often pointed out how each party acted separately, thereby underscoring individual consent to the marriage. To cite a representative example, Thomas Halle and Margaret Horne "dranke one to the other very lovingly and frendly and were familiar togither after supper . . . in suche manner as parties that have contracted matrimonie togither use to be" (DL/C/219/206ᵛ).

Witnesses noted other kinds of behaviors as evidence to prove individual consent, including alcohol consumption, force, understanding, and a person's demeanor during and after a marriage. The wide range of evidence deponents and the court considered in assessing individual consent further underscores it as the basis of marriage. Many cases include evidence concerning the amount of alcohol litigants consumed immediately prior to or during a marriage in order to assess a party's knowledge of and consent to a marriage and the clarity of the witnesses' memories. Such questions regarding alcohol are particularly relevant when the litigation concerned a contract rather than a church wedding, since many contracts occurred in taverns or during a meal. Joan Waters tried to defend herself against a contract by pointing to her lack of understanding in regard to the contents of a document she signed after noting how long they had been drinking. After they "had byn drinckinge wyne in the said taverne three howers or more," someone "shewed forthe a little noate or writinge" to her and she "not knowinge what ye contentes of the same were did as she beleeveth at ye request of some . . . then present sett her hand to ye said noate." Not until two or three days later did she learn what she had signed: "she fownd the note at home Caused her boye to reade it and then she perceyving they had deceyved her was muche greved and burnt the note" (DL/C/219/426ʳ). This explanation as well as the rest of her defense did not convince a judge, who ruled that she and John Newton solemnize their contract, which they did.[33]

Two other cases illustrate the role alcohol consumption played in the question of voluntary consent. The depositions in *Christopher Dawson v. Marion Crompton* contain specific details about Marion's sobriety. Ed Payne noted that Marion "was at the time of the Contract aforesayd very sensable and temperate in her wordes and behaviour and did contract her selfe . . . voluntarily as above save only by the direction of Master Hawton who was her especiall good frend" (DL/C/217/15) and that she "was not Compelled to drinck mor then she would and desyred her selfe" (DL/C/217/17). *Richard Thomas v. Alice More* also includes testimony regarding the sobriety of the litigants. John Manwood testified that while at "the Guild hall gate," they "drunck ii quartes of muskadell and no more . . . they being in number five but . . . Alice drunk very little not half a pynt at the most at that taverne." After which, she and Richard reportedly contracted themselves before going to another tavern at which they drank again: "at the son at Criplegate," they "drunck . . . on quart . . . of muskadell a pynt of basterd and a pynt of ippocras they being five in number still." He also deposed that neither Richard nor Alice were drunk, pointing out that Alice "spoke soberly and modestly and went home as well as she was when she came into his . . . company neither was her understanding witt or iudgment decayed or diminished any thing at all for . . . . yf she had byn distempered she would nott in his . . . iudgment have come back from her mothers howse" (DL/C/218/538). Similarly, Robert Scott deposed that Alice and Richard were "not drunck," noting, like John, "Alices memorie understanding witt and Judgment was then as in former time it was wont to be and not any thing distempered" (DL/C/218/553). Robert Sadler, a witness for Alice, suggested that Alice's "iudgment" may have been "decayed," since he heard Richard "confesse before ye Lord Maior of London" that at the time of the contract with Alice he "carryed" her to two taverns where "they dranke good score of wine" (DL/C/219/8^r).

Witnesses sometimes testified as to whether someone forced the consent of another. In terms of force, deponents pointed to fear of another most often. To cite a representative example, in three extant depositions in *John Nicholls v. Elizabeth Cage* the witnesses all recounted Elizabeth's denial that she contracted herself to John "for feare or by constrainte" (DL/C/213/185). In other cases, deponents noted whether someone's consent resulted from their confinement. Ed Payne noted that the presence of Marion Crompton at her contract with Christopher Dawson indicated her consent, since "she was not held by any body but might have gon awaye when she would" (DL/C/217/16). In *Alan Carr v. Helen Vaughan* (as I noted in chapter 1), the question of whether Alan voluntarily consented to the union hinged on whether he was held against his will by being locked in his chamber all night. Helen explained how Alan came to be locked in his room. The night before the "solemnizac*io*n of the fore sayd marriage," Alan went to bed in his chamber and locked his door. Agnes Loveday, at the request of Helen, asked him "to lend her the key of his Chamber dore to lock the kitchen dore of the howse of her mayster M*aster* Richard Phillipps." Alan gave Agnes the key who passed it on to Helen, who "kept it till seaven of the Clock the next morninge at w*hi*ch time the sayd Allen Carr called for the sayd key." At "eight of the Clock in the forenoone," she "beleveth the sayd Chamber dore was unlocked and sett wide open so that the sayd Carr might have gon forthe of the Chamber if he had would" (DL/C/215/76^r). Richard Phillips confirmed her account that Alan was not being held against his will. After his wife heard "some noyes abowt the howse," he got out of bed and "going into his p*ar*lor looked owte of the windowe toward*es* M*aster* Car*r*s Chamb[er] and he sayth he did see M*aster* Cars Chamber dore shake and he . . . Called up his men in the howse who went abowt the howse and returned againe and sayd ther was no bodie." Rather than call for help, according to Richard, Alan told him that "it is some dogg or hogg at the kitchen dore" (DL/C/215/86^r). In keeping with this account of Alan's freedom, Helen said that after talking to Lady Dixie and her mistress, Mary Phillips, he "yealded and Consented to marrie" her, "bothe before and after the minister was com*e* thither that ioyned them together in holy matrimonie" (DL/C/215/77^r). The location of Alan's room in relation to the overall structure of the house and to that of their neighbors became a central part of the testimony to determine whether his confinement forced his consent. The details regarding the location of his chamber were crucial in determining whether he would have been heard if he cried for help. Helen reported that his room "was not suche a solitarie place as in the sayd article is induced" (DL/C/215/76ʳ). Similarly, the master and mistress of the house deposed that the location of his chamber would not have prohibited him from being heard. As Richard testified, their "howse indeede standes some what alone," but was "not so farr but with Crying out he might have byn heard" (DL/C/215/86ᵛ). Even though Mary noted that Alan could have been heard and was thus not confined against his will, she suggested that Helen nonetheless forced his consent through fear' of repercussions rather than confinement (DL/C/215/87ʳ). Helen's own account of her discussion with him through the door before the marriage may identify the cause of his fear: she "sayd that she would cause the same Carr to be hanged althoughe she weare hanged with him unles he would marrie her" (DL/C/215/76ᵛ).

Some deponents offered testimony regarding the understanding of a bride or groom. Ann Hyde, for instance, claimed "she spake the wordes in ieste" (DL/C/215/106ᵛ), since she did not understand the words of contracting: "she towld . . . Alexander that she did not knowe that those wordes made a Contract neither did she suspe[ct]. . . that those wordes did Contract her neither . . . was she requested to contract her selfe but only to speake the wordes she not knowing what they ment" (DL/C/215/110ʳ). Deponents also pointed to the maturity of Frances Edmondes when discussing her participation in a contract. To cite one example, Nicholas Sheffeild testified that Frances "seemed to be bothe of . . . Lawfull age and of discreation enoughe" (DL/C/216/359ʳ).

A few deponents also considered the demeanor of a couple when assessing individual consent. Not surprisingly, deponents noted affectionate behavior in addition to kissing during and after a contract as evidence of consent. In one representative case, after a contract between Richard Warren and Margaret Perry alias More, Richard was "imbracing her in his armes and setting her on his knee and kissing her and suche like daliance by the space of an howre" (DL/C/219/81ᵛ). Other witnesses identified other behaviors as indicating consent. While George Nicholls noted Elizabeth Cage's "kynde of maydenly bashfullnes" as evidence of her consent (DL/C/213/188), contrastingly, in a different suit, Thomas Clemence identified the forwardness of Alice More as partial evidence of her willingness to marry Richard Thomas (DL/C/218/546).

As I noted earlier, the Church of England urged couples to solemnize these marital contracts within specified times, dates, and locations. The time between a contract and its solemnization recounted in the depositions varied greatly. A solemnization could follow the contract on the same day—"after the promisses beefore sett down about five a clock in the morning the same day . . . [she] was at hir dowghters marriage at Islington Church" (DL/C/214/174)—or it could occur on the following morning—Master Greene, who conducted the contracting between Alice and Thomas, "appoynted them to be married the nexte morninge followinge" (DL/C/213/170). While in another case "a fortnnight or iii weke*s*" after a contract, the groom appointed the marriage should take place "on the sonday following" (DL/C/219/153ᵛ). For another couple two years passed between the contract and the church ceremony (DL/C/215/30ʳ).[34]

As I also noted above, the church advocated that a couple should solemnize a verbal contract after the reading of the banns on three separate Sundays or holidays in the parish church of one or both of the parties. The roles banns played in the church ceremony need not be fully reviewed here.[35] The banns were a way in which couples publicized their intentions to marry and from the church's perspective, as Cressy notes, they acted as "a safety device to prevent those who were ineligible from attempting the passage into matrimony" (*Birth* 306).

The readings of banns are another kind of evidence in the depositions that litigants and witnesses interpreted when assessing consent. Houlbrooke comments on how the denial of consent regarding the reading of the banns undercut their purpose: "even an announcement which might have been expected to provide the clearest evidence of intention could prove quite useless in this respect" (*Church* 62). A few citations from cases in which deponents mentioned banns can suggest the ways in which they appeared in the London Consistory Court depositions. While a witness may simply report the reading of the banns (DL/C/213/799), in another case a deponent revealed her attitude to this form of publicity. The mother of one woman preferred the reading of the banns to securing a license. After John Swinsted "sayd unto Mist*r*is Hurtly I will marrie yo*ur* dawghter Eliz*abeth* in a morning w*i*th a licence," she th*e*n said "no I will have my dawghter lawfully asked in the Church and sayd she would not pyn her dawghter uppo*n* his sleve" (DL/C/215/95ᵛ). In some cases, the banns served as further evidence of the intentions of the couple. The deponents testified as to the intentions of each party by identifying at whose initiative the banns were read and whether both parties consented to their reading. In terms of the former, Alice Haines deposed that she heard Tide Clear and Elizabeth Spakman "asked in the Church but by whose meanes they wer so asked she cannot tell" (DL/C/214/382). In terms of the latter, in the case of *Katherine Massey v. William Wright* William testified that "the bannes of matrimony wear . . . thrice asked beetween them both in St Botulphes Church w*i*thowt Allgat and in St Giles w*i*th owt Crepulgate by . . . [his] consent" (DL/C/214/329).

By purchasing a license, a couple could forgo the reading of the banns and change the time, date, and location of a marriage.[36] Individuals seeking a license were, as Outhwaite notes, "to be carefully questioned about their eligibility and freedom to marry" (*Clandestine* xiv). Ann Jennalie Cook explains how the church supported parental consent in mate selection by making it a requirement to secure a license:

> As early as 1559, the Articles of Inquiry sought to discover weddings performed without parents' approval, and subsequent articles in 1584, 1597, and 1604 prescribed suspension for any minister violating these rules. The requirements were especially strict for a license allowing a marriage to be solemnized more rapidly than usual. In these circumstances, for everyone save widows or widowers, regardless of age, *expresso concensu Parentum* had to be established either in person or upon the sworn testimony of an individual of good character well known to the church official granting the license. (*Making* 75)

Such a need as well as the cost of securing a license may account for the limited references to them in the depositions. In a discussion focusing on marriage licenses in London, Jeremy Boulton points out that although "there was no standard fee charged in London at all," marriage "by licence cost more than that of marriage by banns, often double" ("Itching" 19). Similarly, in a study of the marriage allegations for the London diocese for 1583 to 1620, Vivien Brodsky Elliott, who notes as well that "it cost twice as much money to marr by licence," concludes that "marriage by licence connoted a higher social status than marriage by banns" ("Marriage" 286). We can understand the price of marrying by license better when we compar the price of a license to the wages of a London craftsman. As Boulton calculates, it would take "a skilled London building craftsman . . . less than seven days" labor to pay for the "10*s* marriage licence" ("Itching" 17). To marry by contract need not cost him even his daily wages. To compare these figures to the price of a marriage by license a deponent mentioned in a London Consistory Court deposition underscores the difference in cost further. In one case the deponent testified that "he thinncketh M*a*ster Allen had about xxvii[s] for the licence bond and for marrnge them" (DL/C/215/48[v]).

In the London Consistory Court depositions that include licenses, licenses also served as a further form of proof of intent. John Wood and Jane Browne brought Christopher Hales, then curate of Islington Church, "a licence from the Court of ffaculties dated the day before viz the 30th of August 1595 by vertue of which licence he sayethe he . . . married . . . togither the same John Wood and Jane Browne . . . betwene x and xii a Clock that day" (DL/C/215/89ᵛ). Unlike with banns, the church did not publicize the intent to marry by the party or parties securing a license on three separate occasions; a license allowed a couple privacy and flexibility. A license, however, was not a guarantee of marriage. Two cases mention a person pur-loining a license in hopes of preventing a couple from marrying. In one case, Elizabeth Mathewe described John Hurlbote's failed attempt to prevent a marriage between Alice Twissleton and Thomas Curtys by stealing the license Thomas had secured for his union with Alice. After Thomas "procured a Licence for marriadge . . . betwene hym" and Alice, Elizabeth explained that she "kepte it a greate while her selfe," because Alice and Thomas "were nott fullye agreed but many and often tymes of and one." John, who "had hiered a shopp" of Alice and bore her goodwill, perceived "the goodwill that Thomas Curtys did bare her." John "verye secretlye stole awaye the saide Lycence." Rather than preventing a marriage between Thomas and Alice, Elizabeth pointed to this theft as the cause of their union: it "was thonly cause that made the said Thomas Curtyes contracte matrimonye with Alice and appoynte the marriadge daye. . . . they were married in the tower withowt anye lycence" (DL/C/213/171). The testimony in a different case includes that Master Hurtly, the step-father of Elizabeth Brode alias Ibotson, pinched the license to "prevent" her marriage to Leonard Ibotson (DL/C/215/25ʳ).

TWO SHAKESPEAREAN COMEDIES

It is no news that Shakespearean comedy tends rather relentlessly toward marriage. Despite this Shakespearean marriage imperative, many of the comedies do not specify the exact form of the marital contract or marriage ceremony that occurs onstage or offstage during the course of the play or will occur—as the close of the play suggests—in the immediate or distance future.[37] For example, do Claudio and Hero in *Much Ado About Nothing* participate in a *verba de praesenti* or *verba de futuro* contract in Act 2, scene 1? *Love's Labour's Lost* offers the promise of multiple marriages a year and a day after the play's ending. While this ending introduces a quasi-contractual note, it does not suggest what forms these marriages will take. A consideration of one of Shakespeare's earliest comedies—*The Two Gentlemen of Verona*—and a later comedy—*Twelfth Night*—highlights his exploitation of the fluidity of forms of marriage suggested by the London Consistory Court depositions and emphasizes that the basis of marriage is reciprocal, individual consent.

In *The Two Gentlemen of Verona*, some critics read the exchange of rings and a kiss between Julia and Proteus in Act 2, scene 2 as bordering on a *verba de praesenti* contract:

> *Julia.* Keep this remembrance for thy Julia's sake.
> *Proteus.* Why then we'll make exchange; here, take you this.
> *Julia.* And seal the bargain with a holy kiss.
> *Proteus.* Here is my hand, for my true constancy. (2.2.5–8)

Their verbal exchange lacks the specific language indicating consent. That is, while the giving and receiving of the rings and the kiss indicate their present intent, the words spoken here do not stress their mutual constancy, but instead threaten his inconstancy: "And when that hour o'erslips me in the day / Wherein I sigh not, Julia, for thy sake, / The next ensuing hour some foul mischance / Torment me for my love's forgetfulness" (2.2.9–12). As I noted in chapter 3, Julia supplies her intent in her gift of the ring when she delivers the ring she gave Proteus to Silvia: "This ring I gave him, when he parted from me, / To bind him to remember my good will" (4.4.97–98).

Silvia and Valentine both mention a formal commitment between them; however, neither one indicates whether they married in a *verba de praesenti* contract or promised to marry in a *verba de futuro* contract.[38] Valentine's reference to the event in Act 2 sounds more like a promise to marry than a marriage itself: "we are betroth'd; nay more, our marriage hour, / With all the cunning manner of our flight, / Determin'd of: how I must climb her window, / The ladder made of cords, and all the means / Plotted, and 'greed on for my happiness" (2.4.175–79). But from this description, we cannot be sure of the exact form of the commitment. In Act 4, Silvia refers to a "betrothal" between her and Valentine when she tries to dissuade Proteus' courtship: "yet Valentine thy friend / Survives; to whom (thyself ar witness) / I am betroth'd" (4.2.105–07). The mention of Proteus serving as a witness suggests some kind of formal verbal exchange. From the references in the play, it is difficult to determine what exactly took place—either a promise to marry or a contract of present consent. Their references to this union indicate that their mutual consent is more important than the exact kind of union. Yet one could argue that the final lines of the play suggest an irony here. That is, the mutability of Valentine's affections when he offers Silvia to Proteus at the end of the play undermines the idea of individual consent as the basis of a union. Contrastingly, one could argue that this undermining can be seen to indicate that a union needs to be built on reciprocal consent.

While *The Two Gentlemen of Verona* offers only elliptical scenes that allude to a possible marriage, *Twelfth Night* provides a more specific definition of the basis of marriage. In Act 5, scene 1, we learn of the marriage of two couples—Sebastian and Olivia, and Toby and Maria—and of the promise of a third—Orsino and Viola—if they can "entreat [Malvolio] . . . to a peace" to release the Captain so Viola can retrieve her clothing (5.1.379). Before considering the forms of the unions for the couples who we learn in Act 5 have married, we need to look at the form of Orsino's marriage proposal to Viola that also occurs in this scene, since the issue of marital consent arises here as well. After Sebastian identifies himself as Olivia's husband, Orsino confirms that Viola loves him and then makes his offer: "Give me thy hand, / And let me see thee in thy woman's weeds" (5.1.270–71). His request for her hand is, of course, a metaphor for marriage, though, as the depositions suggest, offstage it cannot stand alone. Later, after Olivia offers to "crown th'alliance" at "[her] . . . house, and at [her] . . . proper cost" (5.1.317–18), Orsino "embrace[s]" her offer and proposes more fully to Viola: "Here is my hand; you shall from this time be / Your master's mistress" (5.1.319–20). Olivia, not Viola, responds to the proposal: "A sister! you are she" (5.1.325). The play closes with Orsino referring to their union, which will occur later: "Cesario, come; / For so you shall be while you are a man; / But when in other habits you are seen, / Orsino's mistress, and his fancy's queen" (5.1.384–87).[39]

While we are left hanging as to whether this marriage will occur, the issue of consent between the two married couples is not in dispute. Although in Act 5, scene 1 Fabian does not describe the specifics of the marriage of Maria and Toby but only reports that Toby "married" Maria (5.1.363), nor does the Priest claim to have married them or witnessed their marriage, the other dramatic figures do not question Fabian's report that they did marry.[40] The dramatic figures' acceptance of the marriage suggests that Toby and Maria's consent to marry is more important than the form of their marriage, including whether witnesses were present to note Maria or Toby's consent.[41]

Contrastingly, the play contains a much fuller account of the marital form of Olivia and Sebastian. Despite the difference in the amount of detail, the validity of this marriage also depends on the consent of the marrying individuals. Olivia's exchange with Sebastian in their second meeting in Act 4, scene 3 indicates their reciprocal individual consent to marry. After she requests Sebastian to accompany her and the "holy man" (4.3.24) to the "chantry" (4.3.25), Olivia asks Sebastian to "Plight me the full assurance of your faith" to which Sebastian promises "I'll follow this good man, and go with you, / And having sworn truth, ever will be true" (4.3.26, 32–33). Olivia's use of the verb "plight" and her insistence on "faith"—"Plight me the full assurance of your faith"—with Sebastian's reply of "truth"— "having sworn truth, ever will be true"—echo the verbal exchanges in a plethora of the *verba de praesenti* marriage contracts documented in the depositions.

In Act 5, scene 1, the Priest provides a detailed account of the behaviors of Olivia and Sebastian during their offstage marriage. The language in his account of their union echoes contemporary legal understanding of the basis of marriage and behaviors as documented in the London Consistory Court depositions. While Sebastian uses the words "contracted" and "betroth'd" (5.1.259, 261) interchangeably and without clarification, the Priest describes a contract of individual consent:

> A contract of eternal bond of love,
> Confirm'd by mutual joinder of your hands,
> Attested by the holy close of lips,
> Strengthen'd by interchangement of your rings,
> And all the ceremony of this compact
> Seal'd in my function, by my testimony.
> (5.1.154–59)[42]

We have seen Shakespeare before give a clergyman the final authoritative word on the certainty of a marriage. In the final scene of *Romeo and Juliet*, Friar Laurence does not employ such conventional legal terminology as "contract," "mutual joinder," or "compact," yet it is his voice that authoritatively establishes the marriage of Romeo and Juliet: "Romeo, there dead, was husband to that Juliet, / And she, there dead, that Romeo's faithful wife. / I married them" (5.3.230–32). Still, readers of *Twelfth Night* continue to debate what kind of commitment occurs between Olivia and Sebastian.[43] In light of the attitudes and behaviors in the London Consistory Cour depositions, they marry. As we have seen, the usual kinds of evidence deponents cited to confirm marital consent in addition to the vows included the taking or holding of hands, kissing, and exchanging gifts. The Priest in *Twelfth Night* recaps that all three actions—joining of hands, kissing, and gift exchange—occurred and served to "confirm," "attest," and "strengthen" the marriage (5.1.155, 157, 159). The Priest's legal terminology in describing his role at the marriage of Olivia and Sebastian (especially in contrast to Friar Laurence's description of his role at the marriage of Romeo and Juliet) underscores the contractual basis of marriage further, since he labels his account as "testimony" and his function at their marriage as "sealing" their compact (5.1.159).[44]

Even though a Priest witnessed one of the two marriages included in this play neither marriage as described in this scene adheres to the forms promoted by the Church of England or required by the Roman Catholic Church. As I noted earlier, the Church of England urged that marital contracts be solemnized or in-church marriages occur at specified times, dates, and locations after the reading of the banns on three successive Sundays. A couple could forgo the reading of the banns and change the legislated times, dates, and locations by purchasing a license. In contrast, in Roman Catholic doctrine, the Twenty-Fourth session of the Council of Trent (1563) stipulates that "whoever contracts marriage otherwise than in the presence of the pastor and of two or three witnesses, does so invalidly" (H. J. Schroeder 183). The two marriages that occur during the course of these two plays—Sebastian and Olivia, and Toby and Maria—do not conform to these requirements. In terms of the Church of England, to cite just one difference, neither couple has their banns read or purchases a license. In terms of the Roman Catholic Church, neither marriage occurs "in the presence of the pastor and of two or three witnesses." In these two plays then, Shakespeare's portrayal of marriage becomes more catholic when it is less Catholic.

That a discussion of individual consent does not occur after Olivia discovers the identity of her husband may seem surprising. Carol Thomas Neely notes the paradox of this union. On the one hand, Olivia and Sebastian's union is an "exquisitely formal and decorously conventional wedding," yet, on the other hand, "while perfectly completed, this is, perhaps, the most irregular nuptial of all, for Sebastian both 'is and is not' (V.i.216) the object of Olivia's desires" (37). For Lisa Hopkins, the mistaken identity of Olivia's husband undercuts the importance of her consent. Hopkins points out how the Priest's description of the union is simultaneously "proper" and "odd": this passage, "perhaps the most pointedly proper and complete marriage ceremony in the Shakespearean canon, sits oddly alongside the confusions and uncertainties surrounding the actual identities of the participants" (35). She argues that Olivia "makes a nonsense of the whole issue of consent, so crucial in sixteenth-century marriage theory, when she marries a man about whose identity she is mistaken" (34).

But the confusion over the groom's identity at the end of the play highlights the importance of Olivia's individual consent. As Alexander Leggatt observes, Olivia's silence regarding the identity of her husband suggests her consent: "Olivia's marriage to Sebastian, seen literally would be a clear case for immediate annulment. We are not, however encouraged to take it this way. Olivia never speaks to Sebastian after she has learned the truth, and her only reference to her marriage is addressed to Orsino, stressing its formal aspect" (250). Even with the mistaken identity, Sebastian is what Olivia wants all along. Laurie E. Osborne points out how the structure of the play itself indicates the suitability of Olivia and Sebastian: "In the Folio, no sooner does Olivia express her desire for the unattainable Cesario than Viola's eminently suitable twin appears. The play seems to provide a substitute here, much as Orsino's desire for the unattainable Olivia in the play's opening is followed immediately by the arrival of another eligible young woman, also in mourning for *her* brother" ("Texts" 50).

The differences in the kinds of marriage arrangements that the plays under discussion exemplify suggest we cannot make any definitive statements regarding Shakespeare's portrayal of marital forms, apart from acknowledging the emphasis that seems to be placed on the reciprocal consent of individuals as the basis of marriage. As such, these comedies appear to reaffirm both the tenets of canon law and the recorded experiences of many individuals making a marriage as depicted in the depositions of the Consistory Court in early modern London. Consequently the emphasis on personal consent—regardless of an individual's gender or class—was the key element in the foundation of marriage.

POSTSCRIPT: ASSESSING PUBLIC FAME AND MAPPING THE MATRIMONIAL MAZE

William Sadler "did in the monethes and yeare libellated, to some of his frend*es* and acquayntannce, withein the pa*ri*she of Waldon and Awdley reporte tell affirme and confesse that . . . Debora Woodhall and hym-selfe were (as in very dedd they were) betroathed and suer togeth[er] in marriadge."

(DL/C/213/762–63)

And all the ceremony of this compact
Seal'd in my function, by my testimony.

(*Twelfth Night* 5.1.158–59)

In addition to the evidence that deponents offered regarding whether two people were married discussed in chapter 4, deponents from several matrimonial enforcement suits pointed to public fame, literally public rumor, as a final piece of evidence. Michael M. Sheehan's comments on the role of *publica vox et fama* in a four-teenth-century Ely register apply to the role of public fame in the late sixteenth- and early seventeenth-century London Consistory Cour depositions: "Couples used this common opinion about them as an argument for the existence and the validity of the contract they sought to defend" ("Formation" 249). To cite a typical example from these London records, William Lanam testified that "the publiq*ue* speche and fame in Cliff was and is that Henry Jackson and Jane Brown wear and are Contracted togither Lawfully" (DL/C/215/11ᵛ). As this quotation indicates, this category of evidence points to a more wide-spread knowledge of a union beyond the participating parties or wit-nesses and further suggests that individual consent was the basis of marriage. In addition, the use of this term in these records can be seen to be suggestive of our own behaviors and practices of examining early modern English marriage.

Of course, the participants themselves and witnesses served as sources of public fame. In terms of the participants themselves, as the epigraph to this postscript suggests, the eagerness of William Sadler to spread the knowledge of his contract with Deborah Woodhall is striking. In another case, Elizabeth Mathewe stressed the common understanding of the union of Thomas Curtys and Alice Twissleton by mentioning their telling of their marriage at various times and in front of various people: Alice and Thomas "did often and sondrye tymes in presence of dyvers persons openlye confesse themselves to be lawfull man and wyffe and soe were amonge the neighbours ther commonly reputed and taken to be" (DL/C/213/170).[1] In terms of the witnesses, Sheehan points to the importance of the witnesses at the contracts as sources for public fame: "the witnesses were the route whereby knowledge of the union of the couple passed to relatives and neighbours so that their circle considered them to be man and wife" ("Formation" 249). To cite a representative example from the depositions, Matthew Lips testified that "by reason of the former Contracte . . . John Payne and Susan Atkinson be reputed as man and wiffe amongst the nighbors who hard the said woordes within the parishe of St Margaretes at Westminster wher the woordes and contracte was made" (DL/C/213/331).

This category of evidence suggests that marriage in the diocese of early modern London was not defined by a specific, obligatory act. Deponents in these London records most often cited the living arrangements of a couple as the basis of public fame. While living together while not married might evoke social scandal, public fame of a marriage indicates that the couple either believed themselves to have contracted a lawful marriage and/or were willing that that end be the case. Two examples include: "Tompson and Butt dwelt togither in one howse as man and wife and wear comonlee reputed and held to be man and wife and married togither" (DL/C/214/139), and "William Armested and Katherin Garnett . . . have ever synce lyved and dwelt togither in St Sepulchrs parishe in a howse of his . . . as Lawfull man and wief And so have bynn Comonly reputed and taken" (DL/C/216/415ʳ-415ᵛ). One defendant even cited his knowledge of a couple's living together as his reason for calling a couple "man and wife" over the general reports of a marriage: "he knoweth not whether . . . Evan Griffith and Dorothy Bate have contracted marriage or be married . . . but onely by reporte of others but they lived in one howse togither as man and wiffe abowt a twelvemoneth within the parishe . . . and so wer reputed within the . . . sayd parishe . . . as man and wiffe" (DL/C/213/341). Pointing to the knowledge of others to determine the existence of a marriage does not undercut individual consent as the basis of marriage. For when deponents pointed to public fame, they almost always named the individuals separately, mentioning their distinct identities, rather than referring to them as a couple. In addition, the fact that a person lived with another for weeks, months, or years further suggests that she or he consented to the union.

Part of assessing public fame included the question of who knew of a marriage. Rather than witnesses and litigants in these matrimonial enforcement suits measuring public fame by the specific identity or number of individuals who considered a couple married, deponents most often identified how far the awareness of a union had spread. They most frequently referred to a parish, which cuts across boundaries of gender, class, occupation, ideologies, moralities, ethics, and the like, as the lines by which to define the geographical area in which public fame occurred.[2] Two quotations represent this pattern. In a deposition repeated on 27 January 1590/01, Daniel Ryngrose deposed that "he hathe heard it com*m*only reported in St Sepulchers pa*r*ish that . . . Henry Procter and Alice Deacon are man and wife" (DL/C/213/764). In a deposition repeated on 6 August 1591 from a different suit, Helen Johnson testified that "it was comonly reported in the ar*ticu*late pa*r*ishe that . . .[William Taylor] and she were man and wyffe togithers and married togithers as dyvers thoughte" (DL/C/214/59). One could argue that the identification of a parish is to be expected—since these deponents were testifying in an ecclesiastical court case, they would obviously define locations by parish. The number of deponents that cited a parish as their place of residence in the brief biographies at the beginning of the depositions would provide further evidence for such an argument. However, the deponents had narrative agency. In their testimonies, varying locations within which public fame occurred appear. Even in the brief biographies not all witnesses cited a parish; some named a city, town, or county even if they were from London. In addition, a parish could have more than ecclesiastical associations for the deponents, since it could have civic associations as well.

As in the depositions, in *Twelfth Night* sources of public fame for the two marriages are the marrying parties and a witness. In the union of Olivia and Sebastian, the bride and groom confirm their willing participation in the marriage, and they have a witness in the "holy man" (4.3.23) whose "testimony" "seals" their union (5.1.159). In the other marriage in this play—between Maria and Toby—Fabian reports their union without specifying whether he witnessed the marriage or was told about it. Such a comparison with the depositions highlights the difference in the way this play measures public fame. Here, this play focuses more on the making of the marriages, specifically on when dramatic figures act on their intentions or plan to act on their intentions, rather than how far the rumor of the union has spread. Such a focus could be a result of the limitations of dramatic representation or even of the genre of comedy, since Shakespearean comedies often conclude directly before or after a marriage.

Finally, the fact that many deponents measured the range of public fame in terms of a geographical area in which an awareness of a marriage existed may call attention to the need to be aware of the geographical areas that we examine regarding courting and marrying behaviors in this period. To understand courtship and marriage in late sixteenth- and early seventeenth-century England, we must be aware of regionalism as we explore the complex relationship among the letter of the law, literary texts, and actual attitudes and behaviors of people from a variety of social standings. Richard Adair points to the need for such awareness: "little attention has been paid to the possibility of differentials in marriage behaviour within a single country in the early modern period" (4). I have focused on the Consistory Court depositions from one diocese, and I have noted similarities and differences between the courting and marrying behaviors identified in the London Consistory Court depositions with those in studies by social historians of Consistory Court depositions from different localities, such as Canterbury, Chester, Durham, Ely, Norfolk, Norwich, Salisbury, Wiltshire, Winchester, and York. Yet courting and marrying behaviors require further exploration in contemporary depositions both within and without the diocese of London in order that we may understand better the experiences of men and women from a variety of social standings and geographical areas. More research on regional variations would aid in contextualizing patterns and in enabling scholars to map early modern England's matrimonial maze.

NOTES

INTRODUCTION CONSENTING ADULTS: "IN THE WAY OF MARRIAGE"

1. For information on ecclesiastical courts and marriage law, see Richard Adair, J. H. Baker, E. R. C. Brinkworth, Richard Burn, Eric Josef Carlson, Colin R. Chapman, Frederick J. Furnivall, Edmund Gibson, Loreen L. Giese, John R. Gillis, John Godolphin, Laura Gowing, Paul Hair R. H. Helmholz, William Holdsworth, Ralph Houlbrooke, Martin Ingram, Ronald A. Marchant, A. Percival Moore, Diana O'Hara, R. B. Outhwaite, James Raine, Peter Rushton, B. J. Sokol and Mary Sokol, Henry Swinburne, and Richard M. Wunderli.

   Discussions of ecclesiastical jurisdiction include Helmholz (*Roman* 28–54), Holdsworth (1: 614–32), Houlbrooke (*Church* 7–20 and "The Decline of Ecclesiastical Jurisdiction"), Dorothy Owen ("Ecclesiastical Jurisdiction in England"), and Susan Brigden (129–71). Contemporary discussions on the legitimacy of ecclesiastical jurisdiction include the unpublished, "Notes and Remembrances" (Bodleian Library, Tanner MS 176, 261^v–265^v), and "A Distinction Betweene the Ecclesiasticall Law and the Common Law" (British Library, Lansdowne MS 253, 138^r–178^v), and published works by John Bridges, Richard Cosin, and Thomas Ridley.

2. Reprints of the canons include those by J. V. Bullard and H. Chalmer Bell, Edward Cardwell (*Synodalia*), and H. J. Schroeder. Discussions of canon law include Cardwell (*Reformation*), Charles Donahue, Jr., Helmholz (*Roman*), Eric Waldram Kemp, Frederic William Maitland, E. Garth Moore, R. C. Mortimer, and Michael M. Sheehan.

3. Chapman (*Ecclesiastical Courts*), Francis Clarke, H[enry] C[onset], Henr Coote, Gibson, Helmholz (*Marriage* 6–24 and 123–40), Houlbrooke (*Church* 21–54), Thomas Oughton, Owen (*Records*), and J. S. Purvis discuss ecclesiastical court practices. For a discussion of the notaries, see C. W. Brooks, R. H. Hemholz [*sic*], and P. G. Stein.

4. In his study of the customs of spousals in early modern England, Adair comments, "It seems that in St Botolph Aldgate, at least, the custom of spousal was not yet dead in the late sixteenth century. It is hard to tell whether this finding is merely parochial or local, or applicable to London as a whole" (221). The cases in the London Consistory Court indicate that spousals were "not yet dead" for many other parishes as well.

5. Cook comments on how age and the kinds and terms of service affect courtship patterns: "As adolescents, young adults, or sometimes even as children, large numbers of both sexes left their homes to go into service in other households. Researchers estimate that perhaps 40 percent or more of the population were under twenty and that, among the 10 percent or so of all ages who were servants, the vast majority were between fifteen and twenty-four years old, with the proportion dropping sharply as people got older. Not only were household servants young, but they were rarely married, frequently orphaned, and usually cut off from direct supervision by their parents. The terms of employment varied in length, with a year the minimum, thus allowing a mobility that further intensified the problems of control over such persons. Against the practical values of learning skills and saving money before entering marriage stood the temptations to irregular courtship inherent in the relative freedom enjoyed by individuals at this age and social level" (*Making* 77–78).

6. Almost all cases concentrate on the courtships and marriages of the litigants. A few cases contain comments regarding how many other people also took a fancy to someone. For example, in a deposition repeated on 16 October 1599, Robert Crumwell deposed that James Harrison told him "that he . . . had done [Elizabeth Willson] . . . some wronge in that he had hindred her of divers marriages she might have had" (DL/C/215/350ᵛ). In a deposition from a different case repeated on 19 June 1610, Mary Awsten identified just how many people Roger Norris courted: "she knoweth of ii or iii . . . women yt the sayd Roger Norris was a suter unto for marriage at severall tymes and lykely to spede and to have had good matches and they refused to marrie with him by reason of the sayd Joice ffosters reportes for this deponent was a mediator to one widowe for him the sayd Roger and she sayd she would not have him because he was intangled to the sayd Joice ffoster" (DL/C/219/183ᵛ).

7. See Giese, *London Consistory Court Depositions* vii–xxvii.

8. For more information on Shakespeare's involvement in the case, see Katherine Duncan-Jones (206–08 and 241–44), Stephen Greenblatt (*Will in the World* 405–06), S. Schoenbaum (209–13), and Charles William Wallace.

9. For example, Lisa Hopkins points out that "Shakespeare insistently anglicises the social customs of even the most alien of his communities" (109). In terms of settings, Susan Baker comments on the resemblance between the settings in Shakespeare's plays to Shakespeare's England (304–05), and Keir Elam notes this connection between *Twelfth Night* and rural England in particular (31). M. St. Clare Byrne makes a more direct comparison between Olivia's household and contemporary ones in writing that "Olivia's household is one of the most accurately Elizabethan pictures of a noble household that Shakespeare has drawn" (209).

10. While important discussions concerning the status and significance of boy actors continue, I have not included them here since it is secondary

to my immediate purpose, which is to examine courting and marrying behaviors in the play texts. In these plays, I read the cross-dressed figures as women playing men. As Jean E. Howard points out, "at some level boy actors playing women must simply have been accepted in performance as a convention. Otherwise, audience involvement with dramatic narratives premised on heterosexual love and masculine/feminine difference would have been minimal" (37).

11. For a discussion of the development of courtship on the stage, see Cook, who argues that in the 1580s "wooing moves from literary fantasy to something sometimes approximating actuality. Here playwrights increasingly conflate familiar customs with dramatic situations. Here stage courtship is transformed" ("Transformation" 175).

12. See, for example, DL/C/214/165–67 and DL/C/219/21^r–22^v.

13. Two examples include Sara Mendelson and Patricia Crawford, who argue that the "betrothal ritual" was "an integral part of female culture which could serve as an instrument for female agency in the courtship process" (118–19), and Gillis, who writes that "betrothal could obliterate differences in rank and alter the relationship between the sexes. It gave females a measure of choice and a degree of power more equal to that of men. For a brief moment they were the center of attention. Having been courted and fought over, they were in a position to make demands that were not possible for mere spinsters or wives" (52).

14. All references to Shakespeare's plays are from Arden editions.

15. Rather than the much-praised Viola, it is Olivia who breaks out of the stereotypical sexual behavior by having and creating a definition of woman that differs from the monolithic one in the play. Critics of *Twelfth Night* have generally given little or no attention to Olivia, often leaving her to "what you will." In a 1938 article on Olivia, John W. Draper rightly observed that "critics have neglected her in favour of Viola" ("Wooing" 44); he himself, however, devoted most of his discussion to Olivia's suitors. Recently, in 1987, Douglas H. Parker came to Olivia's "defence," arguing she is a twin to Viola and seeing her "in the more positive image of the admirable Viola" (24). Yet he too practiced 'Viola worship' by calling Olivia an "Illyrian Viola" (24): Viola is the standard by which Olivia is to be measured. My point here is much in line with that of Howard, who also identifies Olivia as the figure who poses the threat: "the political threat of female insurgency enters the text not through Viola, the cross-dressed woman, but through Olivia, a figure whose sexual and economic independence is ironically reined in *by means* of the cross-dressed Viola" (32). She maintains that "the play records the traditional comic disciplining of a woman who lacks such a properly gendered subjectivity" (33). I argue, however, that Olivia is not ultimately "disciplined" but redefines a more enabling and autonomous position for women.

16. When making this statement, I exclude Cleopatra since she is royalty and has a historical reputation to uphold.

1 CHOOSING A SPOUSE

1. John T. Noonan, Jr. explains the legal debates surrounding choice in the middle ages. For a more general discussion of choice in England, see Macfarlane (*Marriage* 119–47). Discussions focusing more on early modern England include Carlson ("Courtship" 27–29), Houlbrooke (*English* 68–73), Ingram (*Church* 138–40 and 202–03), and Wrightson (*English* 66–88).

2. Other historians point to the practices of individuals choosing for themselves in early modern England: for example, Carlson states, "So successfully did young people monopolize the courtship process that parents often did not know it was going on and when they casually suggested possible suitors to their children, were surprised to hear that the children were already committed to others" (*Marriage* 109); Gowing also comments: "In practice, parental influence on marriages seems to have been low at social levels below the elite: parents approved, rather than enforced, their children's choices" (156); and Macfarlane notes: "The initiative in locating a likely marriage partner could be taken by a number of people: by the couple themselves, by parents, by relatives, by friends. It was the young couple themselves who often made the first choice, based on mutual attraction" (124). John R. Gillis suggests that consulting parents was more a matter of courtesy than necessity: "as the majority of the population fell into that category who, either because of class or birth order, could never expect to inherit, only a minority of young persons would have had reasons other than the sentimental to seek parental consent" (21). Houlbrooke points to the attitudes of the individuals in regard to individual consent: "There was a widespread belief among would-be marriage partners that freedom of choice was their right" (*English* 71).

   Susan Dwyer Amussen, Ann Jennalie Cook, Diana O'Hara, and Peter Rushton offer different views on the autonomy of individuals regarding choice of partner. In his study of the Durham Consistory cases for 1560 to 1630, Rushton concludes that what his study "demonstrates is that the moment of liberation had not yet occurred by the early seventeenth century. Recent tendentious accounts hailing the period (on the basis of this kind of material) as one of uncontrolled marriage and personal affection in the face of continually futile ecclesiastical attempts at social control ignore the evidence to the contrary: marriage and all personal affairs were still too important to others to be left entirely to the individual couple" ("Property" 216). Based on an examination of records from five Norfolk parishes, Amussen writes: "Marriage was too important to be left to the contracting parties. Parents, 'friends' and neighbours acted both to further and to prevent matches" (108). In her study of archival records from Kent, O'Hara concludes that couples experienced "constraining factors" that affected an individual's choice of partner, "from the internalised expectations of courting couples to the external pressures exercised by family, kin and community" (*Courtship* 30). Similarly, Cook states that "except in rare cases, parental consent was required" for marriages occurring "in Shakespeare's day" ("Mode" 126).

3. Houlbrooke and Wrightson also comment on the extent to which these factors affected the amount of choice an individual had. Houlbrooke writes: "The degree of freedom allowed the individual depended among other things upon his or her sex, prospects of inheritance and social rank" (*English* 69). Wrightson points out: "Adolescents of both sexes enjoyed considerably more freedom from parental tutelage than was usual even in the most generous of gentry families by virtue of the simple fact that they usually left home to enter service in their early teens. Moreover, if, as was common enough, they had already lost one or both parents, they were very rarely subject to the constraints of wardship. . . . Such inhibitions as they experienced in the matter were the outcome not of their parents' marital strategies but of their common recognition of the desirability of gaining consent to, or at least approval of, their matches from a variety of interested parties. Even so, the significance of such endorsement varied a good deal between social groups, and between the sexes" (*English* 74–75).

4. In terms of the letter of the law and consent, Macfarlane notes the uniqueness of the English system: "Here we come to one of the central features of the English marriage system, which sets it apart for centuries from most other societies—namely, the lack of the need for parental consent" (*Marriage* 124). Michael M. Sheehan points to the autonomy surrounding choice this law allowed: "It meant that medieval society had developed a theory of matrimony that enabled the individual to escape the control of family, feudal lord and even the king in a choice of marriage partner" ("Formation" 229).

5. For other canons that include the need for parental consent in marriage, see canons 62, 101–04. For a discussion of the issues surrounding marriage discussed in Parliament, see J. E. Neale (356–58). For an account of the progress of the bill regarding the "taking away of Women against their wills unlawfully" in Parliament, see Simonds D'Ewes (527–28, 529, 552, and 557).

6. Like Ingram, Wrightson sees the influence of friends as having some importance: "In matches between individuals for whom lack of property rendered the question of settling dowries and portions irrelevant, the advice of personal friends among their peers may also have been of some importance, the more so if they were servants living at some distance from their parishes of origin" (*English* 77). Gillis offers a different perspective by identifying the peer group as the most influential: "Under these conditions, the family delegated much of its authority to other institutions, not only to the heads of other households, who were endowed by law with surrogate patriarchal authority, but to kin, neighbors, and especially to the peer group, which, in conjunction with communal norms, took the most direct and active role in regulating the heterosexuality of young people throughout this period. Peers, not parents, were the strongest influence

not only for servants and apprentices, but also for those living at home in still relatively homogeneous rural or urban communities" (22).

7. In some cases, women acknowledged that their choices were contingent on their parents—"Anne [Harrison] wold have byn willinge as she her selfe sayde both to have contracted and solemnized matrimonye with this respondent upon her parents likinge and not otherwise" (DL/C/213/308).

8. For discussions of the roles mothers played in the selection of spouses, see Gowing (154–57) and Mendelson and Crawford (112–13).

9. Hole argues: "A Tudor or Stuart marriage was a matter of family policy rather than romance. The modern belief in freedom of choice and the necessity of romantic love as a basis of married happiness would have been quite incomprehensible to the parents of that age, and even the young people seem to have had some doubts upon the matter" (55).

10. See Stone (*Family* and "Marriage" 204–05). The reactions to and revisions of Stone have been many. Ingram, for instance, comments on the incongruency of Stone's argument: "Stone's analysis of the processes involved in matchmaking is in some points congruent with reality; but overall he exaggerates the strength of parental influence, underestimates the role of romantic love and gives inadequate attention to the middling groups who played such an important part in parish society" (*Church* 138). Likewise, Wrightson underscores the bias in Stone's work to the upper classes: "Professor Stone's interpretation of change may well be sound for the highest social groups, with which he is primarily concerned and of which his knowledge is unrivalled. But neither his characterization of conventional practice, nor his account of change seem adequate as descriptions of the experience of the greater part of the English people. There was no single 'English' norm in this matter, but rather a persisting variety of coexisting practices, a range of experiences broad enough to call into question the validity of any single evolutionary schema" (*English* 79). Also, see Wrightson (*English* 70–88), Macfarlane (Review of Stone 103–26), and J. A. Sharpe (57–62).

11. For further discussion of forced unions among the laboring classes, see Mendelson and Crawford (114–16).

12. Henry "Eyre's" will, dated 9 January 1598/99, details the custodial responsibilities of Elizabeth for Sara (PROB 11/94/198[r]). For a discussion of the amount of Sara's legacy, see the records from the Court of Orphans (CLA/002/01/1/107[v] and 125[r]).

13. Mendelson and Crawford identify variables which could affect attitudes to sexual intercourse before a church marriage: "There was in fact a wide spectrum of opinion on the question of sexual relations between espoused couples; we can chart substantial variations not only by age and social rank, but also by geographical region. Parents, the elite, women, and inhabitants of lowland regions generally insisted that sexual relations were taboo before marriage. But their complementary counterparts—young men, the lower ranks, and those who lived in the highland regions

of England—were considerably more tolerant of pre-marital intercourse, and tended to assume that pregnancy would serve as a cue for a church marriage" (120). For discussions of the attitudes towards couples who had intercourse before soleminzation, see Adair, Ingram (*Church* 219–37 and "Reform" 146–60), David Levine and Wrightson, and Wrightson, "Nadir."

14. For a different view, see Linda Bamber, who maintains "in the comedies, the women tend to avoid making choices" (114).

15. For a discussion of parental authority in more than the two plays under discussion, see Cook (*Making* 69–103).

16. For a discussion of the psychological ramifications and ritual structures of fathers giving away their daughters in marriage in Shakespeare's plays, see Lynda E. Boose ("The Father").

17. Frey discusses "the perversity of fathers' claims to direct their daughters' destinies in marriage" in Shakespeare's plays: "We hear throughout the plays of proprietary acts and attitudes taken by fathers in regard to or rather disregard of their daughters. . . . To the father's combined claims of legal and emotional interest in the daughter's marriage choice, the Elizabethans were, obviously, well attuned. So intense, moreover, is the emotional investment of Shakespeare's fathers in their daughters' love that the thwarting of the fathers' expectations often brings forth imprecations and diatribes of surpassing bitterness" (64–65).

18. In terms of the date of performance, Leslie Hotson maintains: "We now know that the year of the production is 1600; it will not be 1601 until Lady Day, March 25. What says the almanac to that? It announces that 1600 is leap-year, the year of ladies' law—'What, 'tis women's year! Dian doth rule, and you must domineer.' Leap-year, when the woman chooses, when the woman woos. God forbid that it should be otherwise. And great luck for Shakespeare, whose Dian-Elizabeth-Olivia must rule, must choose for herself" (129).

19. Stephen Ratcliffe sees some influence of Viola's father on her choice in her ambiguous reference to "he" in Act 1, scene 2, line 29. He writes, "the grammatical bonding of the father with Orsino provides a foundation upon which the patriarch's choice of a suitable husband for his daughter can take place" (208).

20. Porter Williams, Jr. also argues that Olivia loving Viola is preparation for loving Sebastian: "we see Olivia fall in love with Viola and then Sebastian at first sight, while at the same time we can also say that the mistake of loving Viola has really prepared Olivia for giving herself generously to Sebastian. In this sense, she loves Sebastian before seeing him because she has learned to love him through Viola" (39). Similarly, Helene Moglen writes that "In admitting that 'Ourselves we do not owe (I, v, 311),' Olivia "acknowledges herself to be part of a developmental process which she cannot control. It is the odd logic of this process which defines her actions, attracting her to Viola, attaching her to Cesario and leading her to accept quite readily the eventual substitution of Sebastian" (16).

21. Cristina Malcolmson presents a different view of the patterns of personal choice on and off the stage: "*Twelfth Night* considers advancement in terms of a marriage market which in the play is much more open to personal choice and status exogamy than it is in traditional society, and which also firmly closes down at particular moments" (31). While she does not specifically define "traditional society" in this usage, my comparison of behaviors are of those in these two Shakespeare comedies with those in the London Consistory Court depositions.

2   DETERMINING MARITAL SUITABILITY

1. The selection criteria litigants and witnesses detailed differed from the criteria of English canon law. The English Church assessed consent and suitability in terms of consanguinity, affinity, existence of a pre-contract, religion, abduction, duress, insanity, mistake, impotency, and sexual frigidity. The consideration from this list that appears most often in the depositions is marital status, for many individuals sued one another to enforce a contract she or he had made with someone who was previously married, who remarried another, or who contested a marriage. For a discussion of the impediments according to the letter of the law, see J. H. Baker (560–62), Eric Josef Carlson (*Marriage* 21–22), Cressy (*Birth* 311–15), F. R. H. du Boulay (84–86), R. H. Helmholz (*Marriage* 76–100), and B. J. Sokol and Mary Sokol (140–42). For a discussion of the application of these impediments in sixteenth-century England, see Carlson (*Marriage* 136–38).
2. For further discussions of criteria in the period, please see Carlson ("Courtship" 26), Cressy (*Birth* 255–63), Gowing (167–77), Houlbrooke (*Church* 62–64 and *English* 73–78), Ingram (*Church* 125–42), Alan Macfarlane (*Marriage* 174–208 and 245–90), Diana O'Hara (*Courtship* 30–56), and Wrightson (*English* 79–86). For discussions of how regional boundaries influenced selection for the aristocracy, see Lawrence Stone ("Marriage"). For a discussion of the financial arrangements of marriage, see Ann Jennalie Cook (*Making* 120–50).
3. In a rare reference to household goods, in *Alice Stondon v. George Adams*, George Stondon referred to George Adams' concern that he and Alice "might have suche howshould stull" as he "then had in his howse which belonged" to Alice (DL/C/215/222ᵛ). Another reference to "howsehould stuff" is in DL/C/213/170. In his study, *The English Family, 1450–1700*, Houlbrooke notes: "In practice estimates of personal worth were often based on practical considerations of skill and competence, whether within house and kitchen or in running farm or business" (76). Similarly, for the "propertyless," of which "we know much less," Wrightson says that "a girl might favor a man who looked likely to be a good provider, while men would look for girls who could run a careful household and contribute to family income" (*English* 83–84).

4. Discussions regarding women, property, and marriage portions include those by Maria L. Cioni, Amy Louise Erickson, and Pearl Hogrefe. In terms of the link between marriage contracts and a woman's concern for control of her property, Erickson writes: "How many women took advantage of irregular forms of marriage in the belief that doing so preserved their personal property rights remains unknown. In all probability, the number was negligible, particularly in light of the evidence presented here that women at all social levels did establish some kind of 'separate estate', but in the form of simple bonds rather than equitable trusts" (147).

5. Stone comments that while lower orders clearly had more freedom of choice, love and personal attraction did not play a key role in the criteria in choosing a partner even at this level (*Family* 180–94). Likewise, Christina Hole argues that "Love as a serious consideration in match-making did not come into fashion until the end of the eighteenth century, or a little later Before then it was a matter for the poets; marriage, on the other hand, was the concern of the parents, and love between those most intimately affected was looked for after, not before the wedding" (55).

6. For canons specifying at what age parental consent is required, see canons 62 and 100–04 (Cardwell, *Synodalia* 282, 304–06). For discussions of age at marriage for a variety of socioeconomic groups in England, see Wrightson (*English* 67–70) and Houlbrooke (*English* 63–68), who argues that in Elizabethan and Stuart England analysis of parish registers "points to a mean age of marriage for women of about 26, for men one varying between 27 and 29" (63). For discussions of the ages of brides and grooms in London based on marriage allegations, see Vivien Brodsky Elliott ("Mobility" and "Single"), who argues that "Migration was far mor important a factor in determining marriage age than status in early seventeenth-century London" ("Single" 86). Also see M. Drake, Peter Laslett (21), David Levine, Roger Schofield, Henry Swinburne (18–54), Keith Thomas (specifically 225–27), and E. A. Wrigley. For a discussion of the age at marriage for the peerage, see Stone ("Marriage"198). For an in-depth discussion of age and marriage on and off the stage, see Cook (*Making* 17–38 and "Mode"). Bruce W. Young discusses marriage age in *Romeo and Juliet* in light of contemporary patterns.

7. Discussions of such considerations by either widows or their suitors include those by Charles Carlton, Elizabeth Foyster, Amy M. Froide, Sara Mendelson and Patricia Crawford, and Todd, while Margaret Pelling discusses the considerations of widowers. For a discussion of the economic factors that influenced a widow to remarry, please see Erickson (particularly 153–55 and 193–95). For a discussion of the influence of age and status of widows on their choice of partner, see Elliott ("Mobility" and "Single"). Margaret Lael Mikesell considers the widow in light of religious perspectives, while Tim Stretton examines the experiences of widows in relation to English law.

8. Another example of the variety of criteria mentioned in regard to suitability occurs when the Duke describes his "competitor" to the lady of Verona,

since he describes him in terms of his status, worth, and age in referring to him as a "youthful gentleman of worth" (3.1.107).

9. For a discussion of "a ritualized catechetical comparison of men as potential lovers and/or husbands," see Lori Schroeder Haslem, who argues that "Throughout Shakespeare's plays women frequently enact versions of the ritual when they discuss and debate the relative worth of specific men" (124).

10. Edward Cahill identifies Malvolio's role differently than as a suitor to Olivia, since he argues that Olivia chooses Malvolio as "a kind of temporary, substitute husband" (80) based on his role as "keeper of the house": "So long as Olivia has 'abjured the sight and company of men' (1.2.40–41), Malvolio, as her keeper of the house, retains a special significance. He is, in fact, the most important *man* in her life, which she admits when, noting his 'distract' behavior, she declares, 'I would not have him miscarry for the half of my dowry' (3.4.62–63)" (68–69).

11. For a reading which argues that Maria feels "disgust" at the behavior of Toby and Andrew in Act 1, scene 3, see Jessica Tvordi (123–24).

12. In Act 2, scene 4, Valentine refers to the worth of Silvia: "To her whose worth makes other worthies nothing" (161). In his edition of the play, Clifford Leech glosses worth in terms of her "excellences" (42).

13. For a discussion of social status in other Shakespearean dramas in addition to the two under discussion, see Cook (*Making* 39–68).

14. In assessing Orsino as a suitor to Olivia, Rene Girard argues that "Orsino feels that his prestige as a handsome young man and as a duke makes him superior to all potential suitors" (" 'Tis Not' " 131). I do not see any passages in the play where he assesses his suitability for her.

15. I read Olivia's choice of partner based on Toby's list differently than Tvordi, who argues that Olivia's "seven-year plan is clever in that it gives her ample time to master her skills as a mistress, and may, as she ages, take her out of the marriage market altogether. More significant, it will also allow her to continue to share both her authority and her bed exclusively with Maria, who would indeed seem to be the perfect 'match,' because she is not above her mistress in degree or estate" (126).

16. For a different reading of Olivia's autonomy at the end of the play, see Ann Rosalind Jones, who argues, "the symmetrical coupling with which the comedy ends places all of its heroines under male jurisdiction" (28).

17. Leggatt notes that their union is structural only: "Her pairing with Sebastian is part of a formal design, and we are encouraged to think of it in those terms alone" (250). For critics who see that loving Viola has prepared Olivia easily to love Sebastian, see footnote 20 in chapter 1, and Karen Newman's discussion of the marriage cited later in this chapter.

18. For an examination of the role affection played in Shakespeare's dramas, see Cook (*Making* 69–103).

19. Similar to Malcolmson, Cook argues that dramatic figures in this play consider personal qualities more carefully than social status: "In the topsy-turvy holiday world of *Twelfth Night*, not only do servants marry

masters—Maria's and Sir Toby's nuptials the comic counterpart of the other two matches—but, paradoxically, order is thereby restored. They may not have titles, but Maria is assuredly a good-natured curb on Sir Toby's riotous indulgences, Viola the very pattern of restraint for a self-indulgent Orsino, and Sebastian the forceful male needed to manage Olivia's chaotic household. Moreover, while some of lesser status do wed their social betters, not one of them actively pursues such advancement. Inferior birth here brilliantly balances superior personal qualities. The lack of these qualities, together with their own absurdly ambitious hopes, dooms the aspirations of Malvolio and Sir Andrew" (*Making* 62).

In terms of Malvolio, many critics note his primary interest in status. Levin writes of Malvolio's desire to manage Olivia's household: "What captures his imagination is not possession of Olivia's love but rather management of her household" (139). Other readers identify social status in particular as his primary interest over love or sex. John Astington comments that "the fantasy of high social rank runs slightly ahead of dreams of sexual indulgence" (24), and Malcolmson maintains: "Malvolio does not pursue Olivia with the poetic abandon of the other lovers in the play; he sees her as his ticket to a higher social position" (44). In addition, Cahill notes Malvolio's specific interest is in social position and authority: "Malvolio's identification with rank and authority, with real power as he most directly experiences it through Olivia, is stronger than his identification with his masculinity and even heterosexual desire" (72).

For a different view than that held by Malcolmson, see Woong-jae Shin, who maintains, "Shakespeare, firm in the medieval and Renaissance tradition of viewing blood quality in terms of social hierarchy, always sees that blood quality determines what his characters are and how they behave" (733).

20. Other views of the basis of the unions in *Twelfth Night* include those of J. Dennis Huston, who maintains, for instance, "In a world so marked by constriction, marriage may also appear as another form of imprisonment, particularly when it is entered upon in such haste and for such foolish reasons. Olivia does not even know the name of her husband, Sir Toby has married Maria to repay her for gulling Malvolio, and Orsino is betrothed to Viola because he liked her when she was a boy" (288).

Some critics note a generosity of spirit as making one partner suitable for another. Porter Williams, Jr., for example, writes: "A willingness to love and, something more, perhaps the gift to recognize a kindred spirit and to risk all, are the touchstones to Shakespeare's serious world of romantic comedy. Olivia's words, 'Love sought is good . . . but given unsought is better' (III.i.158), seem to be the dominant note for those who win happiness in terms of love and friendship, but such giving and receiving must be done without counting the cost or measuring the risk" (34). In terms of the union of Olivia and Sebastian, Newman notes that Sebastian's "faith and generosity . . . prove him a worthy partner in marriage" (*Shakespeare's Rhetoric* 105), while Draper comments on

Sebastian's faith and silence as making him an appropriate match for Olivia: "in the last hundred and fifty lines, Sebastian sinks into a politic silence, an earnest perhaps of future years; and, if his faithfulness to Antonio expresses his true character, he made Olivia just the sort of husband that she craved. So perhaps the end of the marriage justified its dubious dramatic means" (*Twelfth Night* 156–57). Taft assesses the suitability of Sebastian for Olivia in terms of his virtues and masculinity: "our knowledge of Sebastian's masculinity, his many virtues, and his free, open nature convinces us that this couple will be not only good lovers, but good friends" (413). Nevo sees the femininity and masculinity of Viola as determining her suitability for Orsino and Olivia, respectively. In terms of the former, Nevo writes: "We begin to understand Orsino's self-delusion. Olivia represents to him the sonneteer's lady he believes himself in love with, while what his nature truly needs and responds to is the youthful, dependent, and devoted femininity of Viola which is scarcely veiled by the page disguise" (209). In terms of the latter, Nevo points to the willow cabin speech as indicating Viola's masculinity: "The touch of reckless forthrightness, the spirit, the candour, the imaginative panache with which the willow cabin fantasy is described and courtly compliment revivified in the loyal cantons of condemned love in which Cesario would 'Hallow your name to the reverberate hills,/And make the babbling gossip of the air/Cry out 'Olivia'!' (I. V. 272–74)—these are surely precisely the self-assertive, masculine qualities which have been lacking in Orsino and which promptly bring out the womanly Olivia, a 'bringing out' in which discretion becomes impetuosity and composure disintegrates in distracted doting upon the Duke's peevish messenger" (207). A. B. Taylor also focuses on the willow cabin speech as determining Viola's suitability for Olivia, but he reads this suitability differently than Nevo by noting Olivia's perception of herself "as an object of real desire" rather than noting her perception of Viola's masculinity: "The speech proves the turning point of the interview. Brief and hypothetical though it is, it has apparently offered Olivia the novel prospect of herself as an object of real desire; and this does more for her than any amount of reasoning has been able to do for suddenly, all opposition forgotten, she falls in love. The irony, of course, is that the feelings expressed in the speech have nothing to do with her; they are no more than an *echo* of Viola's passionate but frustrated love for Orsino" (86). Cahill also considers Olivia's perceptions as determining the suitability of Viola, but he reads these perceptions as "narcissism": "Olivia's visual fixations, indicative of her own narcissism, initially cause her to fall in love with Viola/Cesario (and later enable her to switch to Sebastian in Act 5 without a second thought)" (75). Newman assesses Viola's suitability for Olivia differently: "Viola's beauty, sincerity, and particularly her description of how she would woo (I, v, 254 ff.), win Olivia's love" (*Shakespeare's Rhetoric* 102).

For Viola and Maria, Malcolmson points to their "skillful intelligence" as a criterion for their matchings: "The skilful intelligence of Viola and Maria wins for them marriages which will improve their social estate: clearly for Maria, whose role as a gentlewoman-in-waiting places her beneath Sir Toby, kinsman to Olivia; and mostly likely for Viola, whose father's noble position is never precisely identified, and is probably beneath the rank of Duke Orsino" (34). In regard to the union of Viola and Orsino, Huston comments that "we might wonder just how we are supposed to feel about the betrothal of this vain, self-serving Duke to such an energetic and interesting heroine" (276). Barry B. Adams assesses their suitability differently: "For an Orsino who is capable of reflecting critically on his own addiction to the self-indulgent language of conventional romanticizing cannot be as shallow as most modern critics have painted him and may come to deserve a heroine as sensible and clear-sighted as Viola" (59).

21. I have not included the passage in which the Duke notes how Viola's appearance and voice will help persuade Olivia to listen to his suit as evidence that Orsino finds Viola's physical appearance suitable for a wife, since he points to her specific features as appropriate for her role as a go-between: "Diana's lip / Is not more smooth and rubious: thy small pipe / Is as the maiden's organ, shrill and sound, / And all is semblative a woman's part. / I know thy constellation is right apt / For this affair" (1.4.31–36). Although Viola acknowledges that "If she be so abandon'd to her sorrow / As it is spoke, she never will admit me," Orsino identifies Viola's physical appearance as a power to overcome her sorrow (1.4). Nevo comments on how this passage demonstrates Orsino's opinions regarding wooing: "The speech tells us much: of the way Orsino conceives of the role of suitor; of what he imagines the wishes of the lady he is wooing to be; and of those features of his new page which have caught his eye and noticeably advanced the page in his affections" (203).

22. Girard argues that Proteus' assessment of Silvia's suitability is due to his "mimetic desire": "Mimetic desire can strike with the speed of lightning because it does not really depend upon the visual impact made by the object; it only seems to. Proteus desires Silvia not because their brief encounter made a decisive impression on him but because he is predisposed in favor of whatever Valentine desires" ("Love" 232).

23. Richard J. Jaarsma maintains that the Duke in *The Two Gentlemen of Verona* finds the widow suitable for sexual reasons: "The widow becomes for him the sexual alternative for Sylvia while he punishes his daughter by stripping her of her dowry and consequently her ability to enjoy the sexual attentions of anyone else beside her father" (201).

24. In the Arden edition of the play, as J. M. Lothian and T. W. Craik note, "complexion" can mean "temperament" or "disposition," here the "parallel passages" indicate that it means "colouring" (64).

25. Levin identifies the criteria on which Toby makes his choice differently: Toby "marries Maria, it would seem, not out of gratitude or love, but because he relies on her wit to protect his interests" (151).

26. Another possible criterion, which is very different from playing a trick and assessing domestic skills, can be seen to derive from the structure of

Twelfth Night itself. As I discuss in chapter 4, Osborne comments on how the structure of the play suggests the suitability of the main two couples. F. H. Mares also notes the role the structure of the drama plays in determining suitability: "It is worth noting how cunningly the first appearance of Sebastian is timed. He appears in the interval while Malvolio is following Viola with the ring from Olivia: directly after Olivia has declared her love for 'Cesario', and directly before Viola admits her love for Orsino. Before the complications really begin we are assured that the solution is at hand" (107–08).

3   COURTING BEHAVIORS: TALKING, TOKENS, AND TOUCHING

1. For further discussions of courting behaviors and courtship practices in early modern England, see Eric Josef Carlson, David Cressy (*Birth*), John R. Gillis, Laura Gowing, Ralph Houlbrooke, Martin Ingram, and Diana O'Hara.

2. While deponents sometimes included where and how the couple became acquainted, they very rarely pointed to a couple's initial meeting. The case of Henry Caplin against Margery Cuthauck contains such information: "betwene Easter and whitsontide last past she . . . beinge invited one daye to diner to one Hurle [. . .] howse her neighbo*ur* did then and ther dyne in Companye w*i*th . . . Henry Caplyn w*i*th whom she had no acquayntance before that time" (DL/C/214/651).

3. Many critics compare the courting behaviors in the plays to other literary conventions. In his book on *Courtship in Shakespeare*, William G. Meader identifies what he sees as the "map" for courtship practices in Shakespeare's canon: "Shakespeare's heroes and heroines follow the same paths mapped by Andreas and followed by the romances" (164).

   In regard to *The Two Gentlemen of Verona*, many critics examine the relationship of courtly love to the play. To cite one example, Harold F. Brooks writes that

   > The love is courtly. Julia, seeming at first full of "daunger", soon reveals her "pité", and later sets out as Love's pilgrim. Valentine, like Troilus in Chaucer, begins as the Love-heretic, but quickly becomes the penitent votary. Proteus, from Love-idolator falls to Love-traitor, until reclaimed and redeemed from his treachery both to love and friendship by the sacrificial fidelity of his lover and the sacrificial magnanimity of his friend. Thurio is Love's Philistine, and the clowns, in this pattern, are Love's plebeians. (93)

   For a discussion of the wooing in terms of courtly service, see M. C. Bradbrook. H. B. Charlton connects the conventions of romantic love in this play to Petrarchan and neo-Platonic conventions. Inga-Stina Ewbank, however, reads the conventions differently: "The echoes here of themes and images from several sonnets may help us to see that, as in the sonnets, Shakespeare is working *through* the convention. At least one of the finest moments in the play is arrived at—much like Sonnet 130, 'My mistress' eyes are nothing like the sun'—through a kind of anti-sonnet technique" (46).

In regard to *Twelfth Night*, while some critics examine the courtly love traditions in the play, many more critics discuss its Petrarchan conventions. In terms of the former, while Thad Jenkins Logan writes, "It is the characteristic situation of courtly love; the roles Olivia and Orsino choose to play are familiar ones" (230), Elizabeth Freund notes, "The 'character' Viola/Cesario is no more than a text echoing Orsino's (and Shakespeare's) intertextual relations with the literary genre of courtly poetry" (485). In terms of the latter, Barbara Everett comments on the centrality of Petrarchan conventions to this play: "The comedy holds at its heart the question of the value and meaning of the high-Petrarchan romantic love most at home in a Court" (192). Much of the criticism in regard to the Petrarchanism in this play focuses on Orsino. For instance, Orsino, according to Ruth Nevo, "is conducting his amorous affairs in the style of woeful and love-lorn Petrarchanism which had been the target of the satirical mockery of Speed, Moth and Ganymede himself" (203).

4. Deponents seldom mentioned the length of time in which women and men "moved" each other to marry. The case of Richard Warren and Margaret Perry alias More is a rare instance of a quick courtship. Two witnesses testified that Richard and Margaret contracted themselves during their first meeting. One of these witnesses, Elizabeth Lane, deposed that Richard and Margaret never "were in company togither or spake one to thother before that night in w*hi*ch they contracted them selfes togither in marriage" (DL/C/219/87ʳ). Most references to the length of a courtship were, however, for longer periods: from "halfe a yeare togith*er* and above" (DL/C/213/762) to "above a twelve mone[th]" (DL/C/215/29ʳ) to "a yeare an an halfe" (DL/C/215/399ᵛ) to "abowtt two yeares" (DL/C/214/11) to the unspecified for a "longe time" (DL/C/213/159) and "a greate while before and many tymes of and on" (DL/C/213/170).

5. For further discussions of gift giving, see Carlson ("Courtship" 24–25 and *Marriage* 111–12), Cressy (*Birth*), Gillis (31–34), Gowing, Houlbrooke (*Church* 60–62 and "Making of Marriage" 344), Ingram (*Church* and "Spousals" 46–47), Alan Macfarlane (*Marriage* 300–03), Marcel Mauss, O'Hara (*Courtship* and "Language of Tokens"), and Peter Rushton. See Henry Swinburne for an account of the legal implications of kissing and recovering courtship gifts (229–31).

6. For a general discussion of how the context of exchanging tokens influences their meaning, see Gillis (31–34). Cressy also comments on the fluidity of their meaning, noting that "it was no easy matter to determine whether the proffering and acceptance of a gift was in jest or in earnest, whether it should be understood as a token of goodwill or as a sign of matrimonial consent" (*Birth* 263–64).

For a differing view, see Carlson (*Marriage* 127 and 136). Similarly, Meader argues that rings and gloves had specific meanings. In terms of the former, he maintains, "the gifts themselves carried degrees of implications in their value and their form. A ring was the most obvious of all, and when it was given the recipient seems to have been justified in regarding it as a declaration of an intention of marriage" (138). In regard to the latter, "The gift of gloves, perhaps more often than any other single object, serves as a simple declaration of affection. The request for close relationship is nevertheless there, as in any gift" (143).

7. For more information on the making and wearing of stockings, see Carlo Marco Belfanti, S. D. Chapman, Pauline Croft, Arthur Wilfred Eley, F. W. Fairholt, Jeremy Farrell, Milton Grass and Anna Grass, James Robinson Planche, Richard Rutt, Kay Staniland, Joan Thirsk, F. A. Wells, C. Willett and Phillis Cunnington, and David L. Wykes.

   For more information on apparel and dress accessories, see, for example, Janet Arnold, Iris Brooke, Geoff Egan and Hazel Forsyth, Fairholt, F. M. Kelly, M. Channing Linthicum, Planche, Max Von Boehn, and Willett and Cunnington.

8. For more information on gloves, see S. William Beck and Valerie Cumming.

9. For information on early modern purses, see Vanda Foster (chapter 1) and Egan and Forsyth (233). Foster comments on the different purposes of a purse: "The seventeenth-century purse had a variety of functions and the finest examples may well have been novelties, souvenirs, and elaborate packaging for a gift of perfume or money" (13). For an example of the latter, see Figure 3.1.

10. For more information on shoes, see June Swann, R. Turner Wilcox (83–116), and Eunice Wilson (114–35). For a discussion of the female and male genital symbols in early modern footwear, see William A. Rossi (222–23).

11. See C. E. Challis (199–247).

12. *Ibid.* (150–98).

13. For more information on jewelry of the period, see Joan Evans (*English Jewellery* 68–138 and *History* 81–148), and Diana Scarisbrick.

   For information on finger rings, see O. M. Dalton, Egan and Forsyth (229–30), Evans, Charlotte Gere, William Jones, Charles Oman, and Scarisbrick. For information on finger ring collections in England, see Gerald Taylor's catalog of those in the Ashmolean Museum, Oman's catalog of those in the Victoria and Albert Museum, and Dalton's catalog of those in the British Museum. For more information on the different behaviors of wearing rings, see Evans (*English Jewellery* 104), Oman (*Catalogue* 6–8), and Scarisbrick (*Tudor* 90–92 and 93–95). I refer to sources on the particular kinds of rings that were mentioned in the depositions. I have not directly referred to discussions of love and marriage rings in all cases since the rings used here were for love and marriage. The categories often break down since signet rings and memento mori rings were used as courtship gifts as well as at marriages. For information on these types of rings, please see endnotes 27 and 28 in chapter 4.

14. For further discussions of the role of affection in determining the suitability of a partner in the depositions and the dramas, please see chapter 2.

15. For more information on the case of *John Newton v. Joan Waters*, see Loreen L. Giese ("Theatrical Citings and Bitings").

16. The depositions and *Twelfth Night* are more specific regarding courting locations than is *The Two Gentlemen of Verona*. While the courtship of Silvia, which occurs mainly in her father's house, is in keeping with many instances cited in the depositions, courtship in this play is mainly carried out through written texts. Thus, location does not play such an important role. The courtship locations in *Twelfth Night* are in keeping with the patterns in the depositions in that the locations are at places of employment and at the house of the woman being courted.

17. Although we do not see Olivia sharing a drink with any of her suitors "in the way of marriage" like parties in the depositions, Toby includes Maria in his drinking sessions with Andrew by calling her to fetch the wine: "Marian, I say! a stoup of wine!" (2.3.14). The dramatic figures in the play refer to drinking more in the context of assessing Toby's suitability to remain in Olivia's house—"That quaffing and drinking will undo you: I heard my lady talk of it yesterday" (1.3.14–15)—or as a husband for Maria—"if Sir Toby would leave drinking, thou wert as witty a piece of Eve's flesh as any in Illyria" (1.5.26–27)—rather than as an occasion during which courtship directly occurs between two parties.

18. Some critics point out that Valentine's name points to written texts. William C. Carroll, for instance, argues that "Valentine's very name was understood as synonymous with 'a lover' (*OED* s.v., 2) and perhaps love-token (*Lance*: 'There's not a hair on's head but 'tis a Valentine', 3.1.191–92), and Saint Valentine was the patron saint of lovers" (58). Jonathan Goldberg identifies Valentine's name as indicating two forms of written texts: "Not merely the swain of pastoral romance, Valentine's name means lover. Appearing *in* a letter, a valentine, one must recall, *is* letter, a folded slip of paper on which the name of a lover is inscribed. A valentine is also a legal instrument, a sealed letter from the Crown for the apprehension of persons offending against the law. In the forest, Valentine, the outlawed lover, embodies both of these letters that name him" (71–72). Goldberg argues this point further in terms of Silvia as well since he notes the appropriateness of the letter between Silvia and Valentine in light of their names: "If Silvia and Valentine are these literal figures, characters, that is, who voice the letters in which they are written, it can come as no surprise that their first scene together is played around a letter" (72). He sees the connection of a dramatic figure with the contents of the letter as being so close that the figures "are" the letters: "The being of characters is their textuality. Literally figures, they are placed within an image repertoire in which they seem as exchangeable as the

letters they convey . . . . For they *are* those letters, and similitude is their being" (77).

19. Alexander Leggatt comments on the role of language in wooing in this play: "Major declarations are made by letter, and the men especially display their love by displaying their verbal wit: Valentine and Thurio fight for Silvia, not with sword or lance, but with (to quote Silvia herself) 'a fine volley of words' (II.iv.30); in applauding the skill of the players, she underlines the artificial, set-piece quality of their dialogue" (29). Ewbank also points to how in the play speeches do not seem to generate from the figures themselves: "love as courtship, and love and friendship as social forces, are handled through language alone—to the point where we feel that characters are used as an excuse for speeches and the plot as a device to bring about situations where characters can make speeches or engage in duologues. In this respect the play is still close to the descriptive-contemplative mode of non-dramatic poetry" (40).

20. Since this project focuses on gifts given in courtship by courting partners, I have not included Valentine's offer of Silvia to Proteus at the end of the play, an offer which attracts much critical discussion. On the amount of criticism this scene receives, Stanley Wells comments: "Of the entire play, no scene has given rise to more unfavourable comment than the last; it has been emended, rewritten, reviled and rejected" (164). To cite just one of many possible examples, Ewbank writes that "Not only is the love convention, in attitudes and speech, tested and found absurd but, in a microcosm of the play's whole pattern, it is seen to explode in violence" (48). For a discussion of the technical and organic qualities of this scene, see Wells (164–70). For a discussion of the "dream-situation" of the final act, see William E. Stephenson (167–68). For a discussion of some preformative representations of this scene, see Michael D. Friedman.

The gift patterns in the depositions can also inform our reading of gifts in other plays such as the rings in *The Merchant of Venice* and the handerkerchief in *Othello*. Discussions of the rings in *The Merchant of Venice* include those by S.P. Cerasano, Lisa Jardine ("Cultural"), and Karen Newman ("Portia's Ring"), and of the handkerchief in *Othello* include those by Lynda E. Boose ("Othello's Handkerchief") and Paul Yachnin.

21. One could argue that Proteus' lines, "Silvia is too fair, too true, too holy, / To be corrupted with my worthless gifts" (4.2.5–6), quantify the worth of his gifts. However, his very general reference differs from the very specific calculations seen in the depositions.

22. In the depositions as well as in these two dramas, some go-betweens had more involved roles in the courtship process than simply delivering a gift as seen in the case of *Thomas Wye v. Agnes Bushey*. In some cases, a go-between wooed one person for another. For instance, John Newton sent a friend to "earnestly move and sollicite the said [Joan] Waters to take liking in the way of marriage to the said Newton" (DL/C/219/418ʳ). However, unlike in the dramas, in the depositions

deponents did not note that the go-betweens were either cross-dressed or became the objects of affection of the person they were sent to woo.

23. I disagree with Woong-jae Shin, who maintains that Launce's "sufferings for the sake of the dog" are "primarily comic in nature, and Launce's decision to give Crab to Silvia as a substitute for the lost dog makes us doubt the sincerity of his feeling for Crab" (725).

24. Brooks' reading of this specific gift also points to its meaning as intrinsic rather than contextual. In "hinting a comparison of Proteus with Crab," Brooks argues, "as a present for Silvia, Crab resembles the love that Proteus proffers her. He is a sorry changeling for the true love gift Proteus meant to bestow. He is unfit for Silvia (persecuting her with most objectionable attentions!), and offensive where true courtliness should rule. Like Proteus, he gets his friend into trouble" (99). For a discussion of how the relationship of Launce and Crab relates to the "main plot and theme, a theme of false friendship and love" (18), see Ralph M. Tutt. For other discussions of Crab's faithfulness in relation to that of the wooers in the play, see Louise Schleiner.

25. This reading differs from that of Carroll who argues that the confusion over "the ring" in the final scene suggests that the meaning of the item is inherent in itself: "The circle of transactions concerning Silvia is paralleled, in this final scene, by the exchanges, circulation, and restoration of the rings which Julia carries, when she confuses her own 'ring' with Silvia's. What is at stake in all these transactions is male possession and gifting of the woman's 'ring'—her sexuality; 'ring' was of course a slang term for the female genitalia" (61).

26. To cite just two examples, J. Dennis Huston (286) and D. J. Palmer (74) both comment on Orsino being more in love with the image of the beloved rather than the beloved.

27. Leslie Hotson argues that the actor says these lines to the queen not to Olivia: "For when it becomes evident that such rapturous lines as *Now heaven walks on earth* put into Orsino's mouth are *not* dramatic, but transparent lyric worship of the listening Queen—shooting the shuttle of attention from the playing-floor to the throne—these extreme sentiments take their proper place as excellent passages of Elizabethan poetic tribute, of 'writing the Queen anew' " (124–25).

28. Porter Williams, Jr. comments on the "free flow" of money in this play: "Seldom in a play does money flow so freely or so readily to symbolize generous love and friendship. Olivia specializes in sending rings and pearls to those she loves, though not quite so spontaneously as to be unaware that 'youth is bought more oft than begged or borrowed' (III.iv.3); and even the irritable Orsino sends to inform his 'sovereign cruelty' that neither her 'quantity of dirty lands' nor her fortune interests him" (34–35). Yet money does not exchange hands as a courtship gift as much as in the depositions. For more information on coins in Shakespeare's plays, see J. Eric Engstrom.

29. As I noted in chapter 1, Hotson attributes the female initiative in the play to its date: "Because the time is leap-year, Shakespeare gracefully gives the ladies control: they all must woo and win, and Maria must rule as Sovereign of the Sports" (223).

30. Strong notes the role miniatures played in early modern courtship: "After 1570 the taste for them [portrait miniatures] spread to include the nobility and gentry and eventually even the wives of the worthy citizens of London. The portrait miniature responded to and assimilated the cult of emblems and *imprese*, and extended its social significance by being adopted into the patterns of contemporary courtship" (*English* 9). Yet, in the courtship patterns documented in the depositions of some gentry and "worthy citizens of London," they seldom appear. The instance I cited in chapter 2 in which John Griffith showed Ann Hyde a "pickture" of Alexander Hollinworth is a rare example of miniatures being mentioned in the depositions, and in this rare instance John does not give it to Ann. For more information on miniatures, see Strong and Carl Winter.

31. In terms of interpreting the content of Maria's letter to Malvolio, Barbara Freedman (192–235) and Laurie E. Osborne ("Letters") offer Lacian readings. In regard to the meaning of M.O.A.I. in particular, Paul N. Siegel writes, "The riddle . . . is not meant to have an answer: it has been contrived by Maria with the knowledge that Malvolio will force an interpretation of the line to suit his wish" (222). Many critics have discussed the ambiguity or offered answers of their own. For interpretations of the meaning of "M.O.A.I.," see, for example, Matthias Bauer, John Russell Brown, Edward Cahill, Robert F. Fleissner, Alastair Fowler, Theodore C. Hoepfner, Hotson, Inge Leimberg, Vincent F. Petronella, J. L. Simmons ("A Source"), Peter J. Smith, and J. J. M. Tobin.

32. Terry Box reads the giving of the letter to Malvolio differently: "The exchange of love letters becomes a part of the courtly love tradition, so Shakespeare, with the fake letter, is possibly satirizing this aspect of the tradition" (51).

33. What words she uses when she gives Sebastian the pearl before Act 4, scene 3 we shall never know. He reads the gift as proof that he is not dreaming: "This is the air, that is the glorious sun, / This pearl she gave me, I do feel't, and see't, / And though 'tis wonder that enwraps me thus, / Yet 'tis not madness" (4.3.1–4).

34. For a discussion of Viola's line "She took the ring of me," please see John V. Robinson. I read this line as he does, maintaining that the actor and reader should speak or read this line "in a questioning tone of voice rather than as a statement of fact" (6).

35. Critics disagree on the extent to which Viola controls the gift and the context of the exchange or the gift and the context of the exchange control her. In terms of the former, Charlton argues, "She seizes a situation on the instant; and even when the outcome is not clearly to be forseen, she acts in a manner which will save unnecessary suffering to others: 'she took the ring of me,' is her lie to Malvolio, guessing at once

how the distraught Olivia had tried to hide her device from her steward and messenger" (287). In terms of the latter, Osborne believes, "Cesario/Viola may refuse the ring, but she is still controlled by its power as a sign addressed to her and cannot refuse the position of 'beloved' which it establishes" ("Letters" 71).

36. In addition to the main three categories of courting behaviors, *Twelfth Night* also contains other kinds of evidence to determine emotional commitment and intent. For example, Fabian turns Olivia's wooing of Cesario into proof of her affection for Andrew in telling him that it is only to make him jealous, thus showing her real interest in him (3.2.16–38). Strangely, another sign of goodwill in the play is to agree to be killed. After Orsino threatens to "sacrifice the lamb that I do love" (5.1.128), Viola heartily consents to the sacrifice: "I most jocund, apt, and willingly, / To do you rest, a thousand deaths would die" (5.1.130–31). As Olivia questions her apparent husband on why he follows Orsino, Viola's willingness demonstrates her love for Orsino: "After him I love / More than I love these eyes, more than my life, / More, by all mores, than e'er I shall love wife. / If I do feign, you witnesses above / Punish my life, for tainting of my love" (5.1.132–36). Such dramatic rhetoric about the extreme difficulties one would suffer for a beloved may sound similar to suitors in chapter 1.

4   CONTRACTING COUPLES: VOWS, HAND HOLDING, AND GIFT GIVING

1. For a discussion of the relationship between the theoretical formation of canon law and its acceptance into practice in medieval England, see Charles Donahue, Jr., R. H. Helmholz, George Elliott Howard (1: 287–363), Michael M. Sheehan, and John Witte, Jr. For a discussion of the impact of the conciliar and synodial legislation of marriage on the family, see Sheehan ("Marriage and Family").

2. The conclusions of this study differ from those of Chilton Latham Powell in terms of the importance of gift exchange in relation to other kinds of evidence to confirm contracts in off-stage unions. Powell argues that "Next to the vows, the exchange of gifts, principally from the man to the woman, was the most important feature of spousals" (19).

3. In terms of gift giving, I include in this chapter gifts that deponents claimed parties gave and received during or after a marriage and those that deponents denied confirmed a marriage. I include a gift in this chapter rather than in chapter 3 when at least one deponent claimed it was a token to confirm a marriage.

4. Discussions of marriage contracts in early modern England include Richard Adair, Eric Josef Carlson, David Cressy (*Birth*), John R. Gillis, Laura Gowing, Ralph Houlbrooke, Howard, Martin Ingram, Diana O'Hara, B. J. Sokol and Mary Sokol, and Henry Swinburne. Discussions

of marriage contracts in Shakespeare's dramas include Ann Jennalie Cook, Lisa Hopkins, Lorna Hutson, Kathryn Jacobs, Carol Thomas Neely, Alan W. Powers, and Margaret Loftus Ranald. Most discussions of contracts in Shakespeare's plays have, of course, centered on *Measure for Measure*. See, for instance, J. Birje-Patil, Alberto Cacicedo, Davis P. Harding, Harriett Hawkins, Victoria Hayne, S. Nagarajan, A. D. Nuttall, Ernest Schanzer, Margaret Scott, and Karl P. Wentersdorf.

5. For further discussions of consent, see F. R. H. du Boulay (82–83) and Sheehan ("Marriage and Family" 212–14).

6. For further discussions of the church's requirements, see chapter 2.

7. For more information on prohibitions or forbidden times, see Cressy (*Birth* 298–305 and "Seasonality"). For a discussion of wedding days in this period for church weddings, see Jeremy Boulton ("Economy").

8. For examinations of pre-solemnization pregnancy, see Adair, Susan Dwyer Amussen, Hayne, Ingram, Peter Laslett, and David Levine and Keith Wrightson. Act 4, scene 1 of *Much Ado About Nothing* offers a contemporary literary discussion of this topic.

9. In regard to clandestine marriage, Outhwaite points out that "Clandestine marriage may have meant different things to different people at different times" (*Clandestine* 20). This point could be made of people now as well as in early modern England. Outhwaite differentiates seven types of clandestiny (*Clandestine* 21–37).

10. Six other examples of contracts occurring in the afternoon and evening are DL/C/213/149–50, DL/C/214/266–67, DL/C/215/96ᵛ, DL/C/216/279ᵛ, DL/C/219/22ᵛ, and DL/C/219/85ʳ. For another church marriage occurring at non-canonical hours, see DL/C/215/21ʳ.

11. Some witnesses simply testified that the contract occurred in a house or tavern—DL/C/213/762, DL/C/215/181ᵛ, DL/C/217/48, DL/C/218/322—or in a "room" or "chamber" within the tavern or house—DL/C/213/348 and DL/C/214/138.

12. For more references to halls see DL/C/215/201ʳ and DL/C/219/82ᵛ and to kitchens see DL/C/215/120ᵛ and DL/C/219/87ʳ. For references to upper chambers see DL/C/215/13ʳ, DL/C/216/292ᵛ, and DL/C/219/420ʳ. For more references to a room's location regarding the front or back of a house see DL/C/213/335 and DL/C/219/420ʳ and to stairs see DL/C/215/96ᵛ, DL/C/217/22, and DL/C/219/82ᵛ.

13. References to a couple being near a window include DL/C/218/549 and DL/C/219/82ᵛ and to a couple being near a chimney or fire include DL/C/215/201ʳ, DL/C/216/328ʳ, and DL/C/219/22ᵛ.

14. While deponents most often cited people as witnesses for marriages occurring in and away from church, deponents pointed to register books in a few of the marriages which took place in church as partial evidence: DL/C/214/631 and DL/C/218/6. Some deponents in these few cases apparently shared the opinion of the appropriately named John Clerke, the parish clerk of St. Botolphes, who testified that "their

Register booke is faithfully kept and commonly accompted for a record of credite" (DL/C/219/34ᵛ).

15. For discussions of migration and mobility, see Amussen, Peter Clark and David Souden, and Vivien Brodsky Elliott ("Mobility").

16. An example of a *verba de futuro* contract is in DL/C/216/281ᵛ–282 and of a conditional contract is in DL/C/216/292ᵛ–293ʳ.

17. Houlbrooke makes a similar point about deponents: "Depositions of witnesses in matrimonial causes often suggest that parties were not fully aware of the difference between the two types of contract" (*Church* 57). Margaret Scott reaches a similar conclusion about Shakespeare's audience (796–97).

18. Some other cases that include these legal terms are DL/C/213/489, DL/C/213/815, DL/C/214/171, and DL/C/218/362.

19. Carlson reaches a similar conclusion for cause papers in Ely and York: "what these examples of care with words and witnesses are intended to suggest is that knowledge of what was necessary to enforce a matrimonial agreement was widespread" (*Marriage* 127).

20. To a few deponents, the expression "giving faith and troth" alone without the "taking" was the primary proof of consent. Daniel Ryngrose, a witness in the case of *Henry Procktor v. Alice Deacon*, suggested that an exchange of "faith and trothe" was the basis of a marriage: "he is a married man, and he thinkethe to geve faith and troth one to another is a contracte" (DL/C/213/778). Some other forms that emphasize present consent ar "I am your husband" (DL/C/218/531) and "I am your wife" (DL/C/219/83ᵛ). Few variations occur on the adjectives modifiying wife or husband, such as "wedded" (DL/C/213/185, DL/C/215/9ᵛ DL/C/215/106ᵛ, DL/C/216/281ᵛ–282ʳ, DL/C/219/81ᵛ, and DL/C/219/409ᵛ), and a couple of cases say "lawfull" husband or wife (DL/C/213/159–60 and DL/C/218/532). Variations that occur in the vows usually include the use of "forsake" and "till death do us part," indicators of time, and clauses of exclusivity. Women and men, according to the witnesses, pledged never to forsake each other, especially while they lived or until God or death did part them (DL/C/214/170, DL/C/218/542, DL/C/219/23ᵛ), and to "forsake all others" (DL/C/214/266, DL/C/215/12ʳ, DL/C/218/531). Richard Houghton and Frances Edmondes were more generous in their individual contracts in what they were willing to forsake for their respective spouses. Houghton promised to "for sake all the worlde" for Katharine Hawes alias Mone (DL/C/214/550). Although John Stubbes offered only to "for sake all other women" for Francis Edmondes, she "would for sake ffather and mother and all the world and betake her selfe only to him" (DL/C/216/312ʳ). Some couples added until "death us depart" (DL/C/219/410ʳ) to their vows; some of these instances are, of course, those vows deponents cited from the Book of Common Prayer. Along with death, some couples added other markers of time to their contracts such as

"from this day forward" (DL/C/214/59), "duringe my lyffe" (DL/C/213/160), "for ev*er*" (DL/C/217/13, DL/C/214/170), "so long as I lyve" (DL/C/218/531, DL/C/215/12^r), "so longe as thow lyvest" (DL/C/219/86^v), and "so longe as we bothe shall live" (DL/C/215/37^v). Some witnesses reported that couples included their exclusivity in their vows as well. A representative example is "beetake my self onlie unto the" (DL/C/214/266).

21. Some other nonchurch ceremonies that referred to this similarity are DL/C/213/178, DL/C/219/362^v, and DL/C/219/419^r. In his study of depositions from matrimonial cases from the Durham Consistory Court for 1560 to 1630, Rushton notes that "Oddly enough, when a cleric presided or was present as a witness, the words tended to be less official, possibly because of fear of prosecution for clandestine marriage (outside a church or with no banns)" ("Testament" 28). Such a study would be difficult for the matrimonial cases in the London Consistory Court depositions for 1586 to 1611 because many deponents who cited a cleric officiating at a marriage simply referred to the wording as being that from the Book of Common Prayer without supplying the specific language used. Such usage actually suggests the opposite for London from what Rushton found in Durham.

22. In *Antony and Cleopatra*, Cleopatra also comments on a low voice. Part of her questions to the Messenger about Octavia includes "didst hear her speak? is she shrill-tongu'd or low?" The Messenger's information— "Madam, I heard her speak; she is low-voic'd"—causes Cleopatra to conclude: "That's not so good: he cannot like her long" (3.3.12–14).

23. Three depositions which specify a hand are DL/C/214/59, DL/C/216/278^r, and DL/C/216/292^v.

24. For other witnesses who label the item a "toothpicker" rather than an ear picker, see DL/C/213/331–37. For more information on tooth-picks and ear-picks, see Joan Evans (*English Jewellery* 81) and Diana Scarisbrick (*Tudor* 98).

25. Discussions of the use of the ring during the church ceremony include Carlson (*Marriage* 46–47), Cressy (*Birth* 342–47), Gillis (62), and Charles Oman (*British Rings* 36). For a discussion of the "sexual and material symbolism" of the wedding ring, see Lynda E. Boose ("The Father" 343).

26. As Gerald Taylor defines it, "The gimmel (from Latin *jumellus*, twin) appears to be one ring but in fact is made up of two interlaced hoops, with an engraved inscription round the interfaces of each and a separate bezel, which can be snugly joined together" (76). Charlotte Gere comments that the idea of splitting the ring into two was not solely a myth: "The two hoops were supposed to be given separately at the betrothal and joined together after the marriage. The surviving examples of these conjoined gimmals do not show evidence of this practice being followed, and it might be assumed to be merely a charming myth, were it not for the existence of one of a pair, bearing only half of the usual inscription" (98).

Others, however, question the extent to which couples divided the ring. O. M. Dalton writes: "It does not appear that the gimmel was always, or even often, actually divided, each lover wearing a half, though such would be its natural destination. In the case of most rings described under this title the two hoops work into each other, but can only be divided by being cut; moreover, the sharpness of the edges would make the sundered halves very uncomfortable to wear" (xlvii–xlviii). Likewise, Oman argues: "It seems doubtful whether this troublesome ritual was often performed in actual practice, for the more common variety of gimmel consisted of two interlacing hoops which could only be parted and rejoined by a jeweller, and it is rare to find any trace of this having happened on an extant example. This objection does not, of course, apply to the variety with pivoted hoops, but in either case the sharp edges of the divided ring must have been a constant and unpleasant reminder of the plighted troth!" (*Catalogue* 19–20). For more information on gimmal rings, see Dalton (xlvii–xlviii), William Jones (313–22), Oman (*British Rings* 38 and *Catalogue* 19–20), Scarisbrick (*Rings* 51, 62–63, 83–84, 106–07, 112), and Taylor (76). For other examples of gimmal rings in the Ashmolean, see Taylor (75–76); for those in the Victoria and Albert, see Oman (*Catalogue* 105–08 and plate xxviii); and for those in the British Museum, see Dalton (153–74 and plates xvi–xvii); here, the gimmal rings are interspersed in a section on Love and Marriage Rings.

27. Edward Elmhirst defines the kinds of rings used as mourning rings in early modern England: "Before the middle of the 17th century it was not infrequent for mention to be made in wills of rings that were to be bequeathed to friends in memory of the deceased. Such jewellery, however, was seldom distinctive and usually bore no inscription or reference to the donor. Frequently they were merely rings that had once been in the possession of the individuals that had died; often they were simply emblematic of mortality" (2059). In keeping with this diversity, historians place memento mori rings in different categories. Some historians separate them into their own category, while others such as Oman include them with religious and magical rings for the early modern period. As he explains, "the use of these rings as a warning to the wearer of his own approaching end seems to have become confused with the idea of them as memorials of the dead. At first, doubtless, the two ideas were combined, but by the close of the 17th century the presence of complete obituary inscriptions and a general uniformity of design prove that these last Memento Mori rings were no more and no less than mourning rings, as which they are here catalogued" (*Catalogue* 24) and "Although some of the 'memento mori' rings of this period bear names and initials, there is usually nothing about them, such as the age and date of death, which makes it possible definitely to distinguish them from rings worn with a purely religious motive" (*Catalogue* 38–39).

For more information on memento mori and memorial rings, see Dalton (xlix–liii), Evans (*English Jewellery* 126–30), Jones (355–89),

Oman (*British Rings* 71–77, plates 85–93 and 123–28, and *Catalogue* 38–41), and Scarisbrick (*Rings* 52–53, 68–69, 84–86, 102–03, and 109 and *Tudor* 51). For the memento mori rings in the Ashmolean, see Taylor (76); for those in the Victoria and Albert, see Oman (*Catalogue* plate xxxi and 112–13 and from later periods 120–29 and plates xxxiv and xxxv); and for those in the British Museum, see Dalton (195–239 and plates xix–xxii).

28. For more information about signet rings, see Dalton (xxix–xxxii), Oman (*British Rings* 29–34, plates 36–52 and 101–09, and *Catalogue* 8–16), Scarisbrick (*Rings* 47–49, 58, 80–81, and 104–05, and *Tudor* 92–93), and Taylor (29). For examples in the Ashmolean, see Taylor (68–71 and 78–79); for those in the Victoria and Albert, see Oman (*Catalogue* 85–101 and plates xx–xxvi); and for those in the British Museum, see Dalton (37–103 and plates iii–x and, for the period from 1450 to 1650, see 50–98).

29. For more information on posie rings, see Dalton (xlvii and 174–89), Evans (*English Posies*), and Jones (390–418).

30. I am grateful to John Keyworth, Curator, Bank of England Museum, for his generous assistance with the value of gold and silver and to Hazel Forsyth, Curator of Post Medieval, Early Department, Museum of London, for calling this act to my attention.

31. In discussing this behavior as found in the Durham Consistory Court depositions, Rushton finds that "the equal division of a single object" took place in "only one in seven of the cases mentioning tokens" and concludes, which "perhaps indicates that the custom was seen as an optional rather than an obligatory form of establishing a bond" ("Testament" 26).

32. Other items to confirm a contract include "a greate broade broche of gould" (DL/C/213/747), a—as mentioned earlier—"bracelett of pearle and bugle" (DL/C/215/114ᵛ), a "Jewell called an Aggat" (DL/C/215/121ᵛ), and "holland in a trunck" (DL/C/216/327ᵛ).

33. For a further discussion of the role alcohol played in the case of *John Newton v. Joan Waters*, see Loreen L. Giese ("Theatrical Citings and Bitings").

34. Cook offers a different view of the time between a contract and its solemnization: "Since it took a minimum of two weeks for three Sundays to elapse, betrothals usually lasted about a month or so. However, the time could be greatly shortened by the purchase of a special license from the consistory court, which required not only a substantial bond but also oaths from reliable witnesses that no legal or religious barriers existed" (*Making* 158).

35. For a discussion of the procedures and function of the reading of banns, see Carlson (*Marriage* 128–30), Cressy (*Birth* 305–09), and Gillis (52–54). For a discussion of the rules and their enforcement, see Helmholz (*Marriage* 107–08) and Houlbrooke (*Church* 59).

36. Discussions of licenses include Cressy (*Birth* 309–10), Gillis (90–92), and E. Garth Moore (87–88). Boulton ("Itching" 26–29), Macfarlane

(*Marriage* 311), and Outhwaite ("Age" 66–69) all consider the reasons why licenses might be preferable to banns. For the concerns in the latter sixteenth century over licenses see Boulton, Carlson (*Marriage* 85–86), and Cressy (*Birth* 310–11). For information regarding the drawing up of a "Bill for the reformation of the abuses by Licences for Marriages without Banes," see Simonds D'Ewes (555, 556, 558, 560, and 561–62). For a discussion of how regionalism affected marrying by license, see Boulton ("Itching" 17). Boulton ("Itching") and Elliott ("Single") offer the most thorough discussions of marriage licenses in the capital.

37. Shakespeare may have left church marriages offstage because of his religion. If Shakespeare were a Catholic, he may not have dramatized marriage, because marriage was considered a sacrament within the doctrine of Catholicism. In addition, Shakespeare's lack of specificity of whether a marriage occurred according to the forms promoted by the Church of England or required by the Roman Catholic Church can be seen to appeal to a wider audience. Regardless of the reason, the lack of specificity places the emphasis on the consent of the two individuals rather than on the form of the marriage itself.

38. While William G. Meader labels this exchange specifically a "spousal *de futuro*" (101), Cook calls it "a secret spousal" (*Making* 204).

39. Lisa Jardine reads these lines differently: "the 'discovery' of Viola's concealed sex prompts a betrothal—a mutual exchange of passionate vows and a hand-fasting" (*Reading* 74).

40. Since the dramatic figures do not question the marriage of Maria and Toby, I accept Fabian's account as accurate. William B. Bache, however does not: "since Fabian is lying in the rest of his speech, we may conclude that no marriage has really taken place at all" (58).

41. In referring to Ben Jonson's *New Inn*, Leslie Hotson comments on the form of Maria and Toby's marriage: "The contract of marriage is her made without a priest, by a simple declaration before witnesses, which no doubt was Toby's and Maria's method too" (159–60).

42. This form of marriage would solve a problem that J. Dennis Huston raises in regard to the mistaken identity of the groom: "Olivia could hardly marry Sebastian while confused about his identity, because the error would be exposed during the exchange of vows. Even in his euphoric state of wonder, Sebastian would have to recognize that he was not 'Cesario' " (275–76). With a *verba de praesenti* contract, such a discovery need not be possible during the marriage.

43. Critics continue to debate the kind of contract that Olivia and Sebastian perform and whether they marry. While Harding labels their union as a "*de praesenti* contract" (143), Cook thinks that "the text indicates only that it is a spousal" (*Making* 175). Timothy G. A. Nelson (207) and Marianne Novy (36) label it a "betrothal," and Boose ("The Father" 342), Jardine (*Reading* 76), Robert Ornstein (159), and Porter Williams, Jr. (36) identify it as a marriage. Cristina Malcolmson offers an alternative view calling it a "marriage betrothal" (49). Anne Barton reads

these lines differently than some: "He evinces the same kind of scrupulosity in *Twelfth Night* when distinguishing Olivia's 'contract of eternal bond of love' (v.i.156), complete with clergyman and exchange of rings, in a private chapel, from her actual marriage (and that of Viola and Orsino) at the end" (11). David Bevington notes that the contract in Act 5, scene 1 "has been highly unusual, lacking witnesses or anyone to give away the bride" (143). The behaviors included in the depositions suggest that such a union was not "highly unusual" for many in the diocese of early modern London.

44. Dennis R. Preston reads the Priest's line differently in arguing that "into this excellent comedy of romance Shakespeare chooses to insert a fatuous Priest, whose lines could not have been taken seriously" (171).

POSTSCRIPT: ASSESSING PUBLIC FAME AND MAPPING THE MATRIMONIAL MAZE

1. The term "neighbor," which would identify the relationship of one individual to another by a location in which they both heard the public fame, does not appear much in the London Consistory Court depositions when assessing the public fame of a union. The infrequent use of this term in relation to public fame is all the more surprising in light of Laura Gowing's conclusion about the importance of reputation in her study of defamation: "Reputation in the neighbourhood was understood to be a reliable measure of credit not just socially, but in the courts, where compurgation by neighbours could prove innocence or guilt" (132). If the reputation of a deponent weighed so heavily in determining the judgment of a suit, one might expect individual neighbors to be specifically identified in the records in terms of their knowledge of a union.

2. For more information on the importance of the parish, see Ian W. Archer, Michael Berlin, Jeremy Boulton (*Neighbourhood*), Gowing, and Keith Wrightson (*English* and "Politics").

Works Cited

Primary Sources

Bodleian Library
  Tanner MS 176
British Library
  Harley MS 6910
  Lansdowne MS 131
  Lansdowne MS 253
London Metropolitan Archives
  CLA/002/01/1
  DL/C/213 6 December 1586–17 June 1591
  DL/C/214 7 June 1591–13 November 1594
  DL/C/215 8 October 1597–9 June 1600
  DL/C/216 10 June 1600–7 June 1603
  DL/C/217 3 February 1606/07–22 June 1607
  DL/C/218 11 May 1608–23 November 1609
  DL/C/219 28 November 1609–10 June 1611
The National Archives
  PROB 11/94

Secondary Sources

Adair, Richard. *Courtship, Illegitimacy and Marriage in Early Modern England*. Manchester: Manchester University Press, 1996.

Adams, Barry B. "Orsino and the Spirit of Love: Text, Syntax, and Sense in *Twelfth Night*, I.i.1–15." *Shakespeare Quarterly* 29 (1978): 52–59.

Amussen, Susan Dwyer. *An Ordered Society: Gender and Class in Early Modern England*. New York: Columbia University Press, 1988.

Archer, Ian W. *The Pursuit of Stability: Social Relations in Elizabethan London*. Cambridge: Cambridge University Press, 1991.

Arnold, Janet. *Patterns of Fashion: The Cut and Construction of Clothes for Men and Women, c. 1560–1620*. London: Macmillan, 1985.

Astington, John. "Malvolio and the Eunuchs: Texts and Revels in *Twelfth Night*." *Shakespeare Survey* 46 (1993): 23–34.

Bache, William B. "Levels of Perception in *Twelfth Night*." *Forum* 5 (1964): 56–58.

Baker, J. H. *An Introduction to English Legal History*. 3rd ed. London: Butterworths, 1994.

Baker, Susan. "Personating Persons: Rethinking Shakespearean Disguises." *Shakespeare Quarterly* 43 (1992): 303–16.

Bamber, Linda. *Comic Women, Tragic Men: A Study of Gender and Genre in Shakespeare*. Stanford, CA: Stanford University Press, 1982.

Barber, C. L. *Shakespeare's Festive Comedy: A Study of Dramatic Form and Its Relation to Social Custom*. 1959. Cleveland, OH: Meridian, 1966.

Barton, Anne. *Essays, Mainly Shakespearean*. Cambridge: Cambridge University Press, 1994.

Bauer, Matthias. "Count Malvolio, Machevill and Vice." *Connotations* 1 (1991): 224–43.

Beck, S. William. *Gloves, Their Annals and Associations: A Chapter of Trade and Social History*. 1883. Detroit, MI: Detroit Singing Tree Press, 1969.

Belfanti, Carlo Marco. "Fashion and Innovation: The Origins of the Italian Hosiery Industry in the Sixteenth and Seventeenth Centuries." *Textile History* 27 (1996): 132–47.

Berlin, Michael. "Reordering Rituals: Ceremony and the Parish, 1520–1640." *Londinopolis: Essays in the Cultural and Social History of Early Modern London*. Ed. Paul Griffiths and Mark S. R. Jenner. Manchester: Manchester University Press, 2000. 47–66.

Berry, Ralph. *Shakespeare and Social Class*. Atlantic Heights: Humanities Press International, 1988.

Bevington, David. *Action Is Eloquence: Shakespeare's Language of Gesture*. Cambridge: Harvard University Press, 1984.

Birje-Patil, J. "Marriage Contracts in *Measure for Measure*." *Shakespeare Studies* 5 (1969): 106–11.

Boose, Lynda E. "The Father and the Bride in Shakespeare." *PMLA* 97 (1978): 325–47.

———. "Othello's Handkerchief: 'The Recognizance and Pledge of Love.'" *ELR* 5 (1975): 360–74.

Boulton, Jeremy. "Economy of Time? Wedding Days and the Working Week in the Past." *LPS* 43 (1989): 28–46.

———. "Itching after Private Marryings? Marriage Customs in Seventeenth-Century London." *The London Journal* 16 (1991): 15–34.

———. *Neighbourhood and Society: a London Suburb in the Seventeenth Century*. Cambridge: Cambridge University Press, 1987.

Box, Terry. "Shakespeare's *Twelfth Night*: 'The Miller's Tale' Revisited." *CLA* 37:1 (1993): 42–54.

Bradbrook, M. C. "Courtier and Courtesy: Castiglione, Lyly and Shakespeare's *Two Gentlemen of Verona*." *Theatre of the English and Italian Renaissance*. Ed. J. R. Mulryne and Margaret Shewring. London: Macmillian, 1991. 161–78.

Bridges, John. *A Defence of the Gouernment Established in the Churche of Englande for Ecclesiasticall Matters*. London, 1587.

Brigden, Susan. *London and the Reformation*. Oxford: Clarendon Press, 1989.

Brinkworth, E. R. C. *Shakespeare and the Bawdy Court of Stratford*. London: Phillimore, 1972.

Brooke, George C. *English Coins: From the Seventh Century to the Present Day* 1932. London: Methuen, 1966.

Brooke, Iris. *English Costume in the Age of Elizabeth: The Sixteenth Century* 1933. London: Adam and Charles Black, 1950.

———. *English Costume of the Seventeenth Century*. 1934. New York: Barnes and Noble, 1964.

Brooks, C. W., R. H. Hemholz [*sic.*], and P. G. Stein. *Notaries Public in England Since The Reformation*. Norwich: The Society of Public Notaries of London, 1991.

Brooks, Harold F. "Two Clowns in a Comedy (to say nothing of the Dog): Speed, Launce (and Crab) in 'Two Gentlemen of Verona.'" *Essays and Studies* 16 (1963): 91–100.

Brown, John Russell. "More About Laughing at 'M.O.A.I.' (A Response to Inge Leimberg)." *Connotations* 1 (1991): 187–90.

Bullard, J. V. and H. Chalmer Bell, eds. *Lyndwood's Provinciale: The Text of the Canons Therein Contained, Reprinted from the Translation Made in 1534.* London: The Faith Press, 1929.

Burn, Richard. *Ecclesiastical Law*. 2 Vols. London, 1763/1765.

Byrne, M. St. Clare. "The Social Background." *A Companion to Shakespear Studies*. Ed. Harley Granville-Barker and G. B. Harrison. New York: Macmillan, 1934. 187–218.

Cacicedo, Alberto. " 'She is fast my wife': Sex, Marriage, and Ducal Authority in *Measure for Measure*." *Shakespeare Studies* 23 (1995): 187–209.

Cahill, Edward. "The Problem of Malvolio." *College Literature* 23:2 (1996): 62–82.

Cardwell, Edward, ed. *The Reformation of the Ecclesiastical Laws as Attempted in the Reigns of King Henry VIII, King Edward VI, and Queen Elizabeth* Oxford: Oxford University Press, 1850.

———. *Synodalia: A Collection of Articles of Religion, Canons, and Proceedings of Convocations in the Province of Canterbury, from the Year 1547 to the Year 1717*. Oxford: Oxford University Press, 1842.

Carlson, Eric Josef. "Courtship in Tudor England." *History Today* 43 (1993): 23–29.

———. *Marriage and the English Reformation*. Oxford: Blackwell, 1994.

Carlton, Charles. "The Widow's Tale: Male Myths and Female Reality in 16th and 17th Century England." *Albion* 10 (1978): 118–29.

Carroll, William C. " 'And love you 'gainst the nature of love': Ovid, Rape, and *The Two Gentlemen of Verona*." *Shakespeare's Ovid: The Metamorphoses in the Plays and Poems*. Ed. A. B. Taylor. Cambridge: Cambridge University Press, 2000. 49–65.

Cerasano, S. P., ed. *A Routledge Literary Sourcebook on William Shakespeare's* The Merchant of Venice. New York: Routledge, 2004.

Challis, C. E. *The Tudor Coinage*. Manchester: Manchester University Press, 1978.

Chapman, Colin R. *Ecclesiastical Courts, Their Officials and Their Records.* Dursley, England: Lochin, 1992.

———. *Marriage Laws, Rites, Records and Customs.* Dursley, England: Lochin, 1996.

Chapman, S. D. "The Genesis of the British Hosiery Industry, 1600–1750." *Textile History* 3 (1972): 7–50.

Charlton, H. B. *Shakespearian Comedy.* 1938. London: Methuen, 1955.

Cioni, Maria L. *Women and Law in Elizabethan England with Particular Reference to the Court of Chancery.* New York: Garland, 1985.

Clark, Peter and David Souden, eds. *Migration and Society in Early Modern England.* Totowa, NJ: Barnes and Noble, 1988.

Clarke, Francis. *Praxis in Curijs Ecclesiasticis.* Dublin, 1666.

C[onset], H[enry]. *The Practice of the Spiritual or Ecclesiastical Courts.* 3rd ed. London, 1708.

Cook, Ann Jennalie. *Making a Match: Courtship in Shakespeare and His Society.* Princeton: Princeton University Press, 1991.

———. "The Mode of Marriage in Shakespeare's England." *Southern Humanities Review* 11 (1977): 126–32.

———. "The Transformation of Stage Courtship." *The Elizabethan Theatre XI.* Ed. A. L. Magnusson and C. E. McGee. Ontario: P. D. Menay, 1990. 155–75.

———. "Wooing and Wedding: Shakespeare's Dramatic Distortion of the Customs of His Time." *Proceedings Comparative Literature Symposium Texas Tech University Volume 12: Shakespeare's Art from a Comparative Perspective.* Ed. Wendell M. Aycock. Lubbock: Texas Tech Press, 1981. 83–100.

Coote, Henry. *The Practice of the Ecclesiastical Courts.* London: H. Butterworth, 1847.

Cosin, Richard. *An Apologie for Sundrie Proceedings by Iurisdiction Ecclesiasticall.* London, 1591.

Craig, John. *The Mint: A History of the London Mint from A.D. 287 to 1948.* Cambridge: Cambridge University Press, 1953.

Cressy, David. *Birth, Marriage, and Death: Ritual, Religion, and the Life-Cycle in Tudor and Stuart England.* 1997. Oxford: Oxford University Press, 1999.

———. "The Seasonality of Marriage in Old and New England." *Journal of Interdisciplinary History* 16 (1985): 1–21.

Croft, Pauline. "The Rise of the English Stocking Export Trade." *Textile History* 18 (1987): 3–16.

Cumming, Valerie. *Gloves.* London: B. T. Batsford, 1982.

Dalton, O. M. *Franks Bequest: Catalogue of the Finger Rings.* London: British Museum, 1912.

Davis, Natalie Zemon. *The Gift in Sixteenth-Century France.* Madison: University of Wisconsin Press, 2000.

D'Ewes, Simonds. *A Compleat Journal of the Votes, Speeches and Debates, Both of the House of Lords and House of Commons Throughout the Whole Reign of*

Queen Elizabeth, of Glorious Memory. 1693. Wilmington, DE: Scholarly Resources, n.d.

Dolan, Frances E. *Dangerous Familiars: Representations of Domestic Crime in England, 1550–1700.* Ithaca, NY: Cornell University Press, 1994.

Donahue, Charles, Jr. "The Canon Law on the Formation of Marriage and Social Practice in the Later Middle Ages." *Journal of Family History* 8 (1983): 144–58.

———. *Why the History of Canon Law is Not Written.* London: Selden Society, 1986.

Drake, M. "Age at Marriage in the Pre-Industrial West." *Population Growth and the Brain Drain.* Ed. F. Bechhofer. Edinburgh: Edinburgh University Press, 1967. 196–208.

Draper, John W. *The* Twelfth Night *of Shakespeare's Audience.* Stanford, CA: Stanford University Press, 1950.

———. "The Wooing of Olivia." *Neophilologus* 23 (1938): 37–46.

du Boulay, F. R. H. *An Age of Ambition: English Society in the Late Middle Ages.* London: Thomas Nelson, 1970.

Duncan-Jones, Katherine. *Ungentle Shakespeare: Scenes from His Life.* London: Arden Shakespeare, 2001.

Dusinberre, Juliet. *Shakespeare and the Nature of Women.* 1975. London: Macmillan Press, 1985.

Egan, Geoff and Hazel Forsyth. "Wound Wire and Silver Gilt: Changing Fashions in Dress Accessories c.1400–c.1600." *The Age of Transition: the Archaeology of English Culture, 1400–1600.* Ed. David Gaimster and Paul Stamper. Oxford: Oxbow Books, 1997. 215–38.

Elam, Keir. "The Fertile Eunuch: *Twelfth Night*, Early Modern Intercourse, and the Fruits of Castration." *Shakespeare Quarterly* 47 (1996): 1–36.

Eley, Arthur Wilfred. *Stockings: Silk, Cotton, Rayon, Nylon.* Leicester: Hosier Trade Journal, 1953.

Elliott, Vivien Brodsky. "Marriage Licences and the Local Historian." *Local Historian* 10 (1973): 282–90.

———. "Mobility and Marriage in Pre-Industrial England." Diss. Cambridge University, 1978.

———. "Single Women in the London Marriage Market: Age, Status and Mobility, 1598–1619." *Marriage and Society: Studies in the Social History of Marriage.* Ed. R. B. Outhwaite. New York: St. Martin's Press, 1982. 81–100.

Elmhirst, Edward. "Mourning Rings." *Country Life* 25 June 1953: 2059.

Engstrom, J. Eric. *Coins in Shakespeare: A Numismatic Guide.* Hanover: Dartmouth College Museum Publications, 1964.

Erickson, Amy Louise. *Women and Property in Early Modern England.* London: Routledge, 1993.

Evans, Joan. *English Jewellery from the Fifth Century A.D. to 1800.* New York: E. P. Dutton and Co., n.d.

———. *English Posies and Posy Rings.* London: Oxford University Press, 1931.

———. *A History of Jewellery, 1100–1870.* 1953. Boston, MA: Boston Book and Art, 1970.

Everett, Barbara. "Two Damned Cruces: *Othello* and *Twelfth Night.*" *RES ns* 37 (1986): 184–97.

Ewbank, Inga-Stina. " 'Were man but constant, he were perfect': Constancy and Consistency in 'The Two Gentlemen of Verona.' " *Shakespearian Comedy.* Ed. Malcolm Bradbury and David Palmer. New York: Crane, Russak, and Co., 1972. 31–57.

Fairholt, F. W. *Costume in England: A History of Dress to the End of the Eighteenth Century.* 1885. 2 Vols. Detroit: Singing Tree Press, 1968.

Farrell, Jeremy. *Socks and Stockings.* London: B. T. Batsford, 1992.

Fleissner, Robert F. "Malvolio's Manipulated Name." *Names* 39 (1991): 95–102.

Forsyth, Hazel and Geoff Egan. "Wound Wire and Silver Gilt: Changing Fashions in Dress Accessories *c.*1400–*c.*1600." *The Age of Transition: the Archaeology of English Culture, 1400–1600.* Ed. David Gaimster and Paul Stamper. Oxford: Oxbow Books, 1997. 215–38.

Foster, Vanda. *Bags and Purses.* London: B.T. Batsford, 1982.

Foucault, Michel. *The History of Sexuality.* Trans. Robert Hurley. New York: Vintage, 1980.

Fowler, Alastair. "Maria's Riddle." *Connotations* 2 (1992): 269–70.

Foyster, Elizabeth. "Marrying the Experienced Widow in Early Modern England: The Male Perspective." *Widowhood in Medieval and Early Modern Europe.* Ed. Sandra Cavallo and Lyndan Warner. Singapore: Longman, 1999. 108–24.

Freedman, Barbara. *Staging the Gaze: Postmodernism, Psychoanalysis, and Shakespearean Comedy.* Ithaca, NY: Cornell University Press, 1991.

Freund, Elizabeth. "*Twelfth Night* and the Tyranny of Interpretation." *ELH* 53 (1986): 471–89.

Frey, Charles H. *Experiencing Shakespeare: Essays on Text, Classroom, and Performance.* Columbia: University of Missouri Press, 1988.

Friedman, Michael D. " 'To be slow in words is a woman's only virtue': Silence and Satire in *The Two Gentlemen of Verona.*" *Selected Papers from the West Virginia Shakespeare and Renaissance Association.* Ed. Edmund M. Taft. Huntington: West Virginia Shakespeare and Renaissance Association, 1994. 1–9.

Froide, Amy M. "Marital Status as a Category of Difference: Singlewomen and Widows in Early Modern England." *Singlewomen in the European Past, 1250–1800.* Ed. Judith M. Bennett and Froide. Philadelphia: University of Pennsylvania Press, 1999. 236–69.

Furnivall, Frederick J., ed. *Child Marriages, Divorces, and Ratifications, & c. in the Diocese of Chester, A. D. 1561–1566.* London: K. Paul, Trench, Trubner, & Co., 1897.

Gere, Charlotte. "Rings from 1500 to 1900." *The Ring from Antiquity to the Twentieth Century.* Ed. Anne Ward, John Cherry, Gere, and Barbara Cartledge. London: Thames and Hudson, 1981. 87–133.

Gibson, Edmund. *Codex Juris Ecclesiastici Anglicani.* 2nd ed. 2 Volumes. Oxford, 1761.

Giese, Loreen L., ed. *London Consistory Court Depositions, 1586–1611: List and Indexes.* London: London Record Society, 1997 for 1995.

———. "Theatrical Citings and Bitings: Some References to Playhouses and Players in London Consistory Court Depositions, 1586–1611." *Early Theatre* 1 (1998): 113–28.

Gillis, John R. *For Better, For Worse: British Marriages, 1600 to the Present* 1985. New York: Oxford University Press, 1988.

Girard, Rene. "Love Delights in Praises: A Reading of *The Two Gentlemen of Verona.*" *Philosophy and Literature* 13 (1989): 231–47.

———. " 'Tis Not So Sweet As It Was Before': Orsino and Olivia in *Twelfth Night.*" *Stanford Literature Review* 7 (1990): 123–32.

Godolphin, John. *Repertorium Canonicum, or an Abridgement of the Ecclesiastical Laws.* London: 1678.

Goldberg, Jonathan. *Voice Terminal Echo: Postmodernism and English Renaissance Texts.* New York: Methuen, 1986.

Gossett, Suzanne. " 'I'll Look to Like': Arranged Marriages in Shakespeare's Plays." *Sexuality and Politics in Renaissance Drama.* Ed. Carole Levin and Karen Robertson. Lewiston, New York: Mellen, 1991. 57–72.

Gowing, Laura. *Domestic Dangers: Women, Words, and Sex in Early Modern London.* Oxford: Clarendon Press, 1996.

Grass, Milton and Anna Grass. *Stockings for a Queen: The Life of the Rev William Lee, the Elizabethan Inventor.* 1967. South Brunswick: A. S. Barnes, 1969.

Greenblatt, Stephen. *Shakespearean Negotiations: The Circulation of Social Energy in Renaissance England.* Berkeley: University of California Press, 1988.

———. *Will in the World: How Shakespeare Became Shakespeare.* New York: W. W. Norton, 2004.

Hair, Paul, ed. *Before the Bawdy Court: Selections from church court and other records relating to the correction of moral offences in England, Scotland and New England, 1300–1800.* London: Elek, 1972.

Harding, Davis P. "Elizabethan Betrothals and 'Measure for Measure.' *JEGP* 49 (1950): 139–58.

Hartman, Geoffrey H. "Shakespeare's Poetical Character in *Twelfth Night. Shakespeare and the Question of Theory.* Ed. Patricia Parker and Hartman. New York: Methuen, 1985. 37–53.

Haslem, Lori Schroeder. " 'O Me, the Word Choose!': Female Voice and Catechetical Ritual in *The Two Gentlemen of Verona* and *The Merchant of Venice.*" *Shakespeare Studies* 22 (1994): 122–40.

Hawkins, Harriett. "What Kind of Pre-contract Had Angelo? A Note on Some Non-problems in Elizabethan Drama." *College English* 36 (1974): 173–79.

Hayne, Victoria. "Performing Social Practice: The Example of *Measure for Measure.*" *Shakespeare Quarterly* 44 (1993): 1–29.

Helmholz, R. H. *Canon Law and English Common Law.* London: Selden Society, 1983.

———. *Marriage Litigation in Medieval England.* Cambridge: Cambridge University Press, 1974.

———. *Roman Canon Law in Reformation England.* 1990. Cambridge: Cambridge University Press, 1994.

Hoepfner, Theodore C. "M.O.A.I.—'Twelfth Night.' " *Notes and Queries* ns 5 (1958): 193.

Hogrefe, Pearl. "Legal Rights of Tudor Women and the Circumvention by Men and Women." *Sixteenth-Century Journal* 3 (1972): 97–105.

Holdsworth, William. *A History of English Law.* 7ᵗʰ ed. 14 vols. London: Methuen, 1956.

Hole, Christina. *English Home-Life, 1500–1800.* 1947. London: B. T. Batsford, 1949.

Hopkins, Lisa. *The Shakespearean Marriage: Merry Wives and Heavy Husbands.* London: Macmillan, 1998.

Hotson, Leslie. *The First Night of* Twelfth Night. New York: Macmillan, 1954.

Houlbrooke, Ralph. *Church Courts and the People during the English Reformation, 1520–1570.* Oxford: Oxford University Press, 1979.

———. "The Decline of Ecclesiastical Jurisdiction under the Tudors." *Continuity and Change: Personnel and Administration of the Church in England, 1500–1642.* Ed. Rosemary O'Day and Felicity Heal. Leicester: Leicester University Press, 1976. 239–57.

———. *The English Family, 1450–1700.* London: Longman, 1984.

———. "The Making of Marriage in Mid-Tudor England: Evidence from the Records of Matrimonial Contract Litigation." *Journal of Family History* 10 (1985): 339–52.

Howard, George Elliott. *A History of Matrimonial Institutions.* 1904. Volume 1. New York: Humanities Press, 1964.

Howard, Jean E. "Cross-Dressing, the Theatre, and Gender Struggle in Early Modern England." *Crossing the Stage: Controversies on Cross-Dressing.* Ed. Lesley Ferris. London: Routledge, 1993. 20–46.

Huston, J. Dennis. " 'When I Came to Man's Estate' *Twelfth Night* and Problems of Identity." *MLQ* 33 (1972): 274–88.

Hutson, Lorna. *The Usurer's Daughter: Male Friendship and Fictions of Women in Sixteenth-Century England.* London: Routledge, 1994.

Ingram, Martin. *Church Courts, Sex and Marriage in England, 1570–1640.* 1987. Cambridge: Cambridge University Press, 1990.

———. "The Reform of Popular Culture? Sex and Marriage in Early Modern England." *Popular Culture in Seventeenth-Century England.* Ed. Barry Reay. New York: St. Martin's Press, 1985. 129–65.

———. "Spousals Litigation in the English Ecclesiastical Courts *c.* 1350–*c.*1640." *Marriage and Society: Studies in the Social History of Marriage.* Ed. R. B. Outhwaite. New York: St. Martin's Press, 1982. 35–57.

Jaarsma, Richard J. "The 'Lear Complex' in *The Two Gentlemen of Verona*. *Literature and Psychology* 22 (1972): 199–202.

Jacobs, Kathryn. *Marriage Contracts from Chaucer to the Renaissance Stage* Gainesville: University Press of Florida, 2001.

Jardine, Lisa. "Cultural Confusion and Shakespeare's Learned Heroines: 'These are old paradoxes.' " *Shakespeare Quarterly* 37 (1987): 1–18.

———. *Reading Shakespeare Historically*. London: Routledge, 1996.

Jenkins, Harold. "Shakespeare's *Twelfth Night*." *Shakespeare the Comedies: A Collection of Critical Essays*. Ed. Kenneth Muir. Englewood Cliffs, NJ: Prentice Hall, 1965. 72–87.

Jones, Ann Rosalind. "Revenge Comedy: Writing, Law, and the Punishing Heroine in *Twelfth Night, The Merry Wives of Windsor*, and *Swetnam the Woman-Hater*." *Shakespearean Power and Punishment*. Ed. Gillian Murray Kendall. Madison, WI: Fairleigh Dickinson University Press, 1998. 23–38.

Jones, William. *Finger-Ring Lore: Historical, Legendary, Anecdotal*. London: Chatto and Windus, 1877.

Jorgensen, L. Caitlin. " 'A Madman's epistles are no gospels': Alienation in *Twelfth Night* and Anti-Martinist Discourse." *Renaissance Papers 1999* Ed. T. H. Howard-Hill and Philip Robinson. New York: Camden House, 1999. 67–78.

Kelly, F. M. *Shakespearian Costume for Stage and Screen*. Boston, MA: Walter H. Baker, 1938.

Kemp, Eric Waldram. *An Introduction to Canon Law in the Church of England*. London: Hodder and Stoughton, 1957.

Kermode, Jennifer and Garthine Walker. "Introduction." *Women, Crime and the Courts in Early Modern England*. Ed. Kermode and Walker. Chapel Hill: University of North Carolina Press, 1994. 1–25.

Kerrigan, John. "Secrecy and Gossip in *Twelfth Night*." *Shakespeare Survey* 50 (1997): 65–80.

Kiefer, Frederick. "Love Letters in *The Two Gentlemen of Verona*." *Shakespear Studies* 18 (1990): 65–85.

Laslett, Peter. "The Bastardy Prone Sub-Society." *Bastardy and Its Comparative History*. Ed. Laslett, Karla Oosterveen, and Richard M. Smith. Cambridge: Harvard University Press, 1980. 217–40.

Leggatt, Alexander. *Shakespeare's Comedy of Love*. 1974. London: Methuen, 1983.

Leimberg, Inge. "Maria's Theology and Other Questions (An Answer to John Russell Brown)." *Connotations* 1 (1991): 191–96.

Levin, Richard A. *Love and Society in Shakespearean Comedy: A Study of Dramatic Form and Content*. Newark: University of Delware Press, 1985.

Levine, David. " 'For Their Own Reasons': Individual Marriage Decisions and Family Life." *Journal of Family History* 7 (1982): 255–64.

Levine, David and Keith Wrightson. "The Social Context of Illegitimacy in Early Modern England." *Bastardy and Its Comparative History*. Ed. Peter Laslett, Karla Oosterveen, and Richard M. Smith. Cambridge: Harvard University Press, 1980. 158–75.

Linthicum, M. Channing. *Costume in the Drama of Shakespeare and His Contemporaries*. Oxford: Clarendon Press, 1936.

Logan, Thad Jenkins. "*Twelfth Night*: The Limits of Festivity." *SEL* 22 (1982): 223–38.

Macfarlane, Alan. "Illegitimacy and Illegitimates in English History." *Bastardy and Its Comparative History*. Ed. Peter Laslett, Karla Oosterveen, and Richard M. Smith. Cambridge: Harvard University Press, 1980. 71–85.

———. *Marriage and Love in England: Modes of Reproduction, 1300–1840*. 1986. Oxford: Blackwell, 1993.

———. Rev. of *The Family, Sex and Marriage in England, 1500–1800*, by Lawrence Stone. *History and Theory* 18 (1979): 103–26.

Maitland, Frederic William. *Roman Canon Law in the Church of England*. London: Methuen, 1898.

Malcolmson, Cristina. " 'What You Will': Social Mobility and Gender in *Twelfth Night*." *The Matter of Difference: Materialist Feminist Criticism of Shakespeare*. Ed. Valerie Wayne. New York: Harvester, 1991. 29–57.

Marchant, Ronald A. *The Church under the Law: Justice, Administration and Discipline in the Diocese of York, 1560–1640*. Cambridge: Cambridge University Press, 1969.

Mares, F. H. "Viola and Other Transvestist Heroines in Shakespeare's Comedies." *Stratford Papers, 1965–67*. Ed. B. A. W. Jackson. Montreal, Ontario: McMaster University Library Press, 1969. 96–109.

Mauss, Marcel. *The Gift: Forms and Functions of Exchange in Archaic Societies*. Trans. Ian Cunnison. London: Cohen and West, 1954.

Meader, William G. *Courtship in Shakespeare: Its Relation to the Tradition of Courtly Love*. New York: King's Crown Press, 1954.

Mendelson, Sara and Patricia Crawford. *Women in Early Modern England, 1550–1720*. Oxford: Clarendon Press, 1998.

Mikesell, Margaret Lael. "Catholic and Protestant Widows in *The Duchess of Malfi*." *Renaissance and Reformation* ns 7 (1983): 265–79.

Moglen, Helene. "Disguise and Development: The Self and Society in *Twelfth Night*." *Literature and Psychology* 23 (1973): 13–20.

Moore, A. Percival. "Marriage Contracts or Espousals in the Reign of Queen Elizabeth." *Reports and Papers Read at the Meetings of the Architectural Societies of the County of Lincoln . . . And County of Leicester During the Year MDCCCCIX*. Vol. 30. Lincoln: W. K. Morton, 1909. 261–98.

Moore, E. Garth. *An Introduction to English Canon Law*. Oxford: Clarendon Press, 1967.

Mortimer, R. C. *Western Canon Law*. London: Adam and Charles Black, 1953.

Nagarajan, S. "*Measure for Measure* and Elizabethan Betrothals." *Shakespeare Quarterly* 14 (1963): 115–19.

Neale, J. E. *Elizabeth I and Her Parliaments, 1584–1601*. London: Jonathan Cape, 1957.

Neely, Carol Thomas. *Broken Nuptials in Shakespeare's Plays*. New Haven, CT: Yale University Press, 1985.

Nelson, Timothy G. A. "The Rotten Orange: Fears of Marriage in Comedy from Shakespeare to Congreve." *Southern Review* 8 (1975): 205–26.

Nevo, Ruth. *Comic Transformations in Shakespeare*. London: Methuen, 1980.

Newman, Karen. "Portia's Ring: Unruly Women and Structures of Exchange in *The Merchant of Venice*." *Shakespeare Quarterly* 37 (1987): 19–33.

———. *Shakespeare's Rhetoric of Comic Character: Dramatic Convention in Classical and Renaissance Comedy*. New York: Methuen, 1985.

Noonan, John T., Jr. "Power to Choose." *Viator* 4 (1973): 419–34.

Novy, Marianne. *Love's Argument: Gender Relations in Shakespeare*. Chapel Hill: University of North Carolina Press, 1984.

Nuttall, A. D. " 'Measure for Measure': The Bed Trick." *Shakespeare Survey* 28 (1975): 51–56.

O'Hara, Diana. *Courtship and Constraint: Rethinking the Making of Marriage in Tudor England*. Manchester: Manchester University Press, 2000.

———. "The Language of Tokens and the Making of Marriage." *Rural History* 3 (1992): 1–40.

———. " 'Ruled by my friends': Aspects of Marriage in the Diocese of Canterbury, *c*. 1540–1570." *Continuity and Change* 6.1 (1991): 9–41.

Oman, Charles. *British Rings, 800–1914*. Totowa, NJ: Rowman and Littlefield, 1974.

———. *Catalogue of Rings*. London: Victoria and Albert Museum, 1930.

Ornstein, Robert. *Shakespeare's Comedies: From Roman Farce to Romantic Mystery*. Newark: University of Delware Press, 1986.

Osborne, Laurie E. "Letters, Lovers, Lacan: Or Malvolio's Not-So-Purlioned Letter." *Assays: Critical Approaches to Medieval and Renaissance Drama* 5 (1989): 63–89.

———. "The Texts of *Twelfth Night*." *ELH* 57 (1990): 37–60.

Oughton, Thomas. *Ordo Judiciorum*. 2 Vols. London, 1738.

Outhwaite, R. B. "Age at Marriage in England from the Late Seventeenth to the Nineteenth Century." *Transactions of the Royal Historical Society*. Fifth Series. Vol. 23. London: Offices of the Royal Historical Society, 1973. 55–70.

———. *Clandestine Marriage in England, 1500–1850*. London: Hambledon Press, 1995.

Owen, Dorothy. "Ecclesiastical Jurisdiction in England, 1300–1550: The Records and Their Interpretation." *The Materials Sources and Methods of Ecclesiastical History*. Ed. Derek Baker. New York: Barnes and Noble, 1975. 199–221.

———. *Records of the Established Church*. London: British Records Association, 1970.

Palmer, D. J. " 'Twelfth Night' and the Myth of Echo and Narcissus." *Shakespeare Survey* 32 (1979): 73–78.

Panek, Jennifer. *Widows and Suitors in Early Modern English Comedy* Cambridge: Cambridge University Press, 2004.

Parker, Douglas H. "Shakespeare's Female Twins in *Twelfth Night*: In Defence of Olivia." *ESC* 13 (1987): 23–34.

Pelling, Margaret. "Finding Widowers: Men without Women in English Towns before 1700." *Widowhood in Medieval and Early Modern Europe.* Ed. Sandra Cavallo and Lyndan Warner. Singapore: Longman, 1999. 37–54.

Petronella, Vincent F. "Anamorphic Naming in Shakespeare's *Twelfth Night*." *Names* 35 (1987): 139–46.

Planche, James Robinson. *A Cyclopedia of Costume or Dictionary of Dress.* 2 Vols. London: Chatto and Windus, 1876–79.

Powell, Chilton Latham. *English Domestic Relations, 1487–1653.* New York: Columbia University Press, 1917.

Powers, Alan W. " 'Meaner Parties': Spousal Conventions and Oral Culture in *Measure for Measure* and *All's Well That Ends Well*." *The Upstart Crow* 8 (1988): 28–41.

Preston, Dennis R. "The Minor Characters in *Twelfth Night*." *Shakespeare Quarterly* 21 (1970): 167–76.

Prouty, Charles Tyler. "*Twelfth Night*." *Stratford Papers, 1965–1967.* Ed. B. A. W. Jackson. Hamilton, Ontario: McMaster University Press, 1969. 110–28.

Purvis, J. S. *An Introduction to Ecclesiastical Records.* London: St. Anthony's Press, 1953.

Raine, James, ed. *Depositions and Other Ecclesiastical Proceedings from the Courts of Durham, Extending from 1311 to the Reign of Elizabeth.* London: J. B. Nichols, 1845.

Ranald, Margaret Loftus. " 'As Marriage Binds, and Blood Breaks': English Marriage and Shakespeare." *Shakespeare Quarterly* 30 (1979): 68–81.

Ratcliffe, Stephen. " 'Conceal Me What I Am': Reading The Second Scene of *Twelfth Night*." *University of Mississippi Studies in English* ns 11–12 (1993–95): 195–225.

Ridley, Thomas. *A View of the Civile and Ecclesiastical Law.* London: 1607.

Rixon, Penny. "Twelfth Night." *Shakespeare: Texts and Contexts.* Ed. Kiernan Ryan. Basingstoke: Macmillan, 2000. 189–211.

Robinson, John V. "A Ring of Truth: Another Look at a Crux in *Twelfth Night*." *ELN* 34.2 (1996): 1–6.

Roell, Michaela. " 'Three'-floating Sexuality: Viola's Identity in Shakespeare's *Twelfth Night*." *The Upstart Crow* (18) 1998: 39–55.

Rossi, William A. *The Sex Life of the Foot and Shoe.* New York: E. P. Dutton, 1976.

Rushton, Peter. "Property, Power and Family Networks: The Problem of Disputed Marriage in Early Modern England." *Journal of Family History* 11 (1986): 205–19.

———. "The Testament of Gifts: Marriage Tokens and Disputed Contracts in North-East England, 1560–1630." *Folk Life* 24 (1985–1986): 25–31.

Rutt, Richard. *A History of Hand Knitting*. Loveland, Colorado: Interweave Press, 1987.

Scarisbrick, Diana. *Jewellery in Britain, 1066–1837*. Norwich: Michael Russell, 1994.

———. *Rings: Symbols of Wealth, Power and Affection*. New York: Harry N. Abrams, 1993.

———. *Tudor and Jacobean Jewellery*. London: Tate Publishing, 1995.

Schanzer, Ernest. "The Marriage-Contracts in *Measure for Measure*. *Shakespeare Survey* 13 (1960): 81–89.

Schleiner, Louise. "Voice, Ideology, and Gendered Subjects: The Case of *As You Like It* and *Two Gentlemen*." *Shakespeare Quarterly* 50 (1999): 285–309.

Schoenbaum, S. *William Shakespeare: A Documentary Life*. New York: Oxford University Press, 1975.

Schofield, Roger. "English Marriage Patterns Revisited." *Journal of Family History* 10:1 (1985): 2–20.

Schroeder, H. J. *Canons and Decrees of the Council of Trent*. 1941. St. Louis: B. Herder Book Co., 1960.

Scott, Margaret. " 'Our City's Institutions': Some Further Reflections on the Marriage Contracts in *Measure for Measure*." *ELH* 49 (1982): 790–804.

Shakespeare, William. *Antony and Cleopatra*. Ed. John Wilders. Arden Edition. London: Methuen, 1995.

———. *King Lear*. Ed. Kenneth Muir. Arden Edition. 1972. London: Methuen, 1982.

———. *King Richard III*. Ed. Antony Hammond. Arden Edition. London: Methuen, 1981.

———. *Measure for Measure*. Ed. J. W. Lever. Arden Edition. 1965. London: Methuen, 1984.

———. *The Merchant of Venice*. Ed. John Russell Brown. Arden Edition. 1955. London: Methuen, 1984.

———. *A Midsummer Night's Dream*. Ed. Harold F. Brooks. Arden Edition. 1979. London: Methuen, 1984.

———. *Much Ado About Nothing*. Ed. A. R. Humphreys. Arden Edition. 1981. London: Methuen, 1984.

———. *Romeo and Juliet*. Ed. Brian Gibbons. Arden Edition. London: Methuen, 1980.

———. *Twelfth Night*. Ed. J. M. Lothian and T. W. Craik. Arden Edition. 1975. London: Methuen, 1994.

———. *The Two Gentlemen of Verona*. Ed. Clifford Leech. Arden Edition. 1969. London: Methuen, 1984.

———. *The Winter's Tale*. Ed. J. H. P. Pafford. Arden Edition. 1963. London: Methuen, 1984.

Shapiro, Michael. *Gender in Play on the Shakespearean Stage: Boy Heroines and Female Pages*. Ann Arbor: University of Michigan Press, 1994.

Sharpe, J. A. *Early Modern England: A Social History, 1550–1760*. London: Edward Arnold, 1987.

Sheehan, Michael M. "The Formation and Stability of Marriage in Fourteenth-Century England: Evidence of an Ely Register." *Medieval Studies* 33 (1971): 228–63.

———. "Marriage and Family in English Conciliar and Synodal Legislation." *Essays in Honour of Anton Charles Pegis.* Ed. J. Reginald O'Donnell. Toronto, Ontario: Pontifical Institute of Medieval Studies, 1974. 205–14.

———. "Marriage Theory and Practice in the Conciliar Legislation and Diocesan Statutes of Medieval England." *Medieval Studies* XL (1978): 408–60.

Shin, Woong-jae. "*Two Gentlemen of Verona* and *Diana Enamorada*: Shakespeare's Class-Oriented Modifications of His Sources." *English Language and Literature* 35 (1989): 717–33.

Siegel, Paul N. "Malvolio: Comic Puritan Automaton." *New York Literary Forum* 5–6 (1980): 217–30.

Simmons, J. L. "Coming Out in Shakespeare's *The Two Gentlemen of Verona.*" *ELH* 60 (1993): 857–77.

———. "A Source for Shakespeare's Malvolio: The Elizabethan Controversy with the Puritans." *Huntington Library Quarterly* 36 (1972–73): 181–201.

Smith, Peter J. "M.O.A.I. 'What should that alphabetical position portend?' An Answer to the Metamorphic Malvolio." *Renaissance Quarterly* 51 (1988): 1199–224.

Sokol, B. J. and Mary Sokol. *Shakespeare, Law, and Marriage.* Cambridge: Cambridge University Press, 2003.

Staniland, Kay. "Getting These, Got It: Archaeological Textiles and Tailoring in London, 1330–1580." *The Age of Transition: the Archaeology of English Culture, 1400–1600.* Ed. David Gaimster and Paul Stamper. Oxford: Oxbow Books, 1997. 239–49.

Stephenson, William E. "The Adolescent Dream-World of *The Two Gentlemen of Verona.*" *Shakespeare Quarterly* 17 (1966): 165–68.

Stone, Lawrence. *The Family, Sex and Marriage in England, 1500–1800.* New York: Harper and Row, 1977.

———. "Marriage among the English Nobility in the 16th and 17th Centuries." *Comparative Studies in Society and History* 3 (1961): 182–215.

Stretton, Tim. *Women Waging Law in Elizabethan England.* Cambridge: Cambridge University Press, 1998.

Strong, Roy. *Artists of the Tudor Court: The Portrait Miniature Rediscovered, 1520–1620.* London: Victoria and Albert Museum, 1983.

———. *The English Renaissance Miniature.* New York: Thames and Hudson, 1983.

Summers, Joseph H. "The Masks of *Twelfth Night.*" *Shakespeare Modern Essays in Criticism.* 1957. Ed. Leonard F. Dean. London: Oxford University Press, 1967. 134–43.

Swann, June. *Shoes.* 1982. London: B. T. Batsford, 1984.

Swinburne, Henry. *A Treatise of Spousals, or Matrimonial Contracts: Wherein All the Questions Relating to that Subject are ingeniously Debated and Resolved.* 1686. New York: Garland, 1978.

Taft, Edmund M. "Love and Death in *Twelfth Night.*" *Iowa State Journal of Research* 60 (1986): 407–16.

Taylor, A. B. "Shakespeare Rewriting Ovid: Olivia's Interview with Viola and the Narcissus Myth." *Shakespeare Survey* 50 (1997): 81–89.

Taylor, Gerald. *Finger Rings from Ancient Egypt to the Present Day.* London: Lund Humphries, 1978.

Thirsk, Joan. *Economic Policy and Projects: The Development of a Consumer Society in Early Modern England.* Oxford: Clarendon Press, 1978.

———. "The Fantastical Folly of Fashion: the English Stocking Knitting Industry, 1500–1700." *Textile History and Economic History. Essays in Honour of Miss Julia de Lacy Mann.* Ed. N. B. Harte and K. G. Ponting. Manchester: Manchester University Press, 1973. 50–73.

Thomas, Keith. "Age and Authority in Early Modern England." *Proceedings of the British Academy* 62 (1976): 205–48.

Tobin, J. J. M. "Malvolio and His Capitals." *AN & Q* 23.5/6 (1985): 69–71.

———. "A Response to Matthias Bauer, 'Count Malvolio, Machevill and Vice.'" *Connotations* 2.1 (1992): 76–81.

Todd, Barbara J. "The Remarrying Widow: A Stereotype Reconsidered." *Women in English Society, 1500–1800.* Ed. Mary Prior. London: Methuen, 1985. 54–92.

———. "The Virtuous Widow in Protestant England." *Widowhood in Medieval and Early Modern Europe.* Ed. Sandra Cavallo and Lyndan Warner. Singapore: Longman, 1999. 66–83.

Tutt, Ralph M. "Dog Imagery in *The Two Gentlemen of Verona, King Lear* and *Timon of Athens.*" *The Serif* 1.2 (1964): 15–22.

Tvordi, Jessica. "Female Alliance and the Construction of Homoeroticism in *As You Like It* and *Twelfth Night.*" *Maids and Mistresses, Cousins and Queens: Women's Alliances in Early Modern England.* Ed. Susan Frye and Karen Robertson. New York: Oxford University Press, 1999. 114–30.

Von Boehn, Max. *Modes and Manners: The Seventeenth Century.* Vol. 3. Trans. Joan Joshua. London: George G. Harrap and Co., 1935.

———. *Modes and Manners: The Sixteenth Century.* Vol. 2. Trans. Joan Joshua. London: George G. Harrap and Co., 1932.

Wallace, Charles William. "Shakespeare and His London Associates as Revealed in Recently Discovered Documents." *University Studies of the University of Nebraska* X (1910): 261–360.

Wells, F. A. *The British Hosiery and Knitwear Industry: Its History and Organisation.* New York: Barnes and Noble, 1972.

Wells, Stanley. "The Failure of *The Two Gentlemen of Verona.*" *Shakespear Jahrbuch* 99 (1963): 161–73.

Wentersdorf, Karl P. "The Marriage Contracts in 'Measure for Measure': A Reconsideration." *Shakespeare Survey* 32 (1979): 129–44.

Wilcox, R. Turner. *The Mode in Footwear.* New York: Charles Scribner's Sons, 1948.

Willett, C. and Phillis Cunnington. *Handbook of English Costume in the Seventeenth Century.* 1955. London: Faber and Faber, 1963.

———. *Handbook of English Costume in the Sixteenth Century.* London: Faber and Faber, 1954.

Williams, Porter, Jr. "Mistakes in *Twelfth Night* and Their Resolution: A Study in Some Relationships of Plot and Theme." *Twentieth-Century Interpretations of Twelfth Night.* Ed. Walter N. King. Englewood Cliffs, NJ: Prentice-Hall, 1968. 31–44.

Williamson, Marilyn L. *The Patriarchy of Shakespeare's Comedies.* Detroit, MI: Wayne State University Press, 1986.

Wilson, Eunice. *A History of Shoe Fashions.* London: Sir Isaac Pitman and Sons, 1969.

Winter, Carl. *Elizabethan Miniatures.* London: Penguin Books, 1943.

Witte, John, Jr. *From Sacrament to Contract: Marriage, Religion, and Law in the Western Tradition.* Louisville, KY: Westminster John Knox Press, 1997.

Wrightson, Keith. *English Society, 1580–1680.* 1982. New Brunswick: Rutgers University Press, 1990.

———. "The Nadir of English Illegitimacy in the Seventeenth Century." *Bastardy and Its Comparative History.* Ed. Peter Laslett, Karla Oosterveen, and Richard M. Smith. Cambridge: Harvard University Press, 1980. 176–91.

———. "The Politics of the Parish in Early Modern England." *The Experience of Authority in Early Modern England.* Ed. Paul Griffiths, Adam Fox, and Steve Hindle. New York: St. Martin's Press, 1996. 10–46.

Wrigley, E. A. "Family Limitation in Pre-Industrial England." *The Economic History Review* 19 (1966): 82–109.

Wunderli, Richard M. *London Church Courts and Society on the Eve of the Reformation.* Cambridge: Medieval Academy of America, 1981.

Wykes, David L. "The Origins and Development of the Leicestershire Hosiery Trade." *Textile History* 23 (1992): 23–54.

Yachnin, Paul. "Wonder-effects: Othello's handkerchief." *Staged Properties in Early Modern English Drama.* Ed. Jonathan Gil Harris and Natasha Korda. Cambridge: Cambridge University Press, 2002. 316–34.

Young, Bruce W. "Haste, Consent, and Age at Marriage: Some Implications of Social History for *Romeo and Juliet.*" *Iowa State Journal of Research* 62 (1988): 459–74.

INDEX